GLENCOE

African American Literature

Glencoe McGraw-Hill

New York, New York   Columbus, Ohio   Woodland Hills, California   Peoria, Illinois

Program Advisors

Janice Brown
Houston ISD
Houston, Texas

Kay Licona
Franklin High School
El Paso, Texas

Beverly Ann Chin
University of Montana
Missoula, Montana

William Ray
Lincoln-Sudbury Regional High School
Sudbury, Massachusetts

Rosa Fonseca
Franklin High School
El Paso, Texas

Jacqueline Jones Royster
Ohio State University
Columbus, Ohio

Acknowledgments

"Follow the Drinking Gourd," adapted by John L. Haag, from *All American Folk, Volume 1*. Copyright © 1982 and 1986 Creative Concepts Publishing Corp. Used by permission.

Excerpt from "Episode 4: Hey, Hey, Ho, Ho, Segregation's Got to Go" of *Will the Circle Be Unbroken: A Personal History of the Civil Rights Movement in Five Southern Communities*. Copyright © Southern Regional Council. Reprinted by permission. All rights reserved.

❖ *cont. on page 383*

Glencoe/McGraw-Hill

A Division of The **McGraw-Hill** Companies

Send all inquiries to:
Glencoe/McGraw-Hill
8787 Orion Place
Columbus, Ohio 43240-4027

ISBN 0-07-822925-1

Printed in the United States of America

1 2 3 4 5 6 7 8 9 10   071   05 04 03 02 01 00

Contents

❖

Theme One: Talking Roots

James Weldon Johnson	The Creation	POEM	**3**

❖ Connecting to West Africa

Birago Diop	Forefathers	POEM	**8**
❖ Focus on	The Oral Tradition		**10**
Frances E. W. Harper	Bury Me in a Free Land	POEM	**13**
Traditional	Follow the Drinking Gourd	SONG	**17**
Robert Hayden	Runagate Runagate	POEM	**20**
❖ Media Connection	The Precious Lord Story and Gospel Songs		**24**
Thomas A. Dorsey	Take My Hand, Precious Lord	SONG	**27**
Langston Hughes	The Negro Speaks of Rivers	POEM	**30**
Olaudah Equiano	*from* The Life of Olaudah Equiano	NONFICTION	**33**
Countee Cullen	Leaves	POEM	**40**

Theme Two: Smoldering Embers

Frederick Douglass	*from* My Bondage and My Freedom	NONFICTION	**45**
Booker T. Washington	An Address Delivered at the Opening of the Cotton States' Exposition in Atlanta, Georgia, September, 1895	NONFICTION	**54**
W. E. B. DuBois	Of Mr. Booker T. Washington and Others	NONFICTION	**60**
Gwendolyn Brooks	A Bronzeville Mother Loiters in Mississippi. Meanwhile, a Mississippi Mother Burns Bacon./Last Quatrain	POEM	**72**

❖ Connecting to West Africa

Aimé Césaire	State of the Union	POEM	**80**
❖ Focus on	The Struggle for Civil Rights		**84**
Traditional	Keep Your Hand on the Plow	SONG	**87**
Traditional	Keep Your Eyes on the Prize	SONG	**88**
Martin Luther King Jr.	*from* Stride Toward Freedom	NONFICTION	**92**
❖ Media Connection	Connecting to the Civil Rights Movement		**96**
Sheyann Webb	*from* Freedom's Children	NONFICTION	**99**
Sam Cornish	Death of Dr. King	POEM	**108**

Theme Three: Scattered Branches

Sterling A. Brown	Southern Road	POEM	113
Zora Neale Hurston	Isis	FICTION	117
❖ **Media Connection**	Hemenway Sets Author's Story Straight		124
Jean Toomer	November Cotton Flower	POEM	127
Kevin Young	The Preserving	POEM	130
Toni Cade Bambara	Blues Ain't No Mockin Bird	FICTION	133
Raymond Patterson	I've Got a Home in That Rock	POEM	140
Malcolm X	*from* The Autobiography of Malcolm X	NONFICTION	143
Maya Angelou	*from* I Know Why the Caged Bird Sings	NONFICTION	160
❖ **Focus on**	The Great Migration		166
Stevie Wonder	Living for the City	SONG	169
Richard Wright	*from* The Man Who Lived Underground	FICTION	172
Nikki Giovanni	Nikki-Roasa	POEM	178
Dorothy West	Jack in the Pot	FICTION	181
Toi Derricotte	The Weakness	POEM	195
Quraysh Ali Lansana	aunt rubie goes to market	POEM	199
Edwidge Danticat	New York Day Women	FICTION	202
Jamaica Kincaid	A Walk to the Jetty	NONFICTION	208
Rohan B. Preston	Letter from Foreign	POEM	216
Paule Marshall	To Da-duh, in Memoriam	NONFICTION	220
Yusef Komunyakaa	April Fools' Day	POEM	230
❖ **Connecting to Peru**			
César Vallejo	Black Stone Lying on a White Stone	POEM	234

Theme Four: We Wear the Mask

Phillis Wheatley	On Being Brought from Africa to America	POEM	239
Jacqueline Johnson	A Knowing	POEM	242
Paul Laurence Dunbar	We Wear the Mask	POEM	245
❖ **Connecting to Central Africa**			
Wole Soyinka	Telephone Conversation	POEM	248
Alice Childress	Florence	PLAY	251
Michael Warr	Back to Baton Rouge	POEM	267

Margaret Walker	Lineage	POEM	271
Sojourner Truth	And Ain't I a Woman?	NONFICTION	274
Toni Morrison	*from* The Bluest Eye	FICTION	277
Naomi Long Madgett	Purchase	POEM	282
Lucille Clifton	fury	POEM	285
Irma McClaurin	The Power of Names	POEM	288
❖ **Focus on**	The Black Arts Movement		290
Haki R. Madhubuti	Poet: What Ever Happened to Luther?	POEM	293
❖ **Media Connection**	Conversation with Haki Madhubuti		296
Amiri Baraka	Preface to a Twenty Volume Suicide Note	POEM	299
James Baldwin	My Dungeon Shook	NONFICTION	302
Glenis Redmond	Lament for Brothers	POEM	308
Sonia Sanchez	This Is Not a Small Voice	POEM	311
Ishmael Reed	What's American About America?	NONFICTION	314

Theme Five: Tree of Life

Robert Johnson	Preaching Blues	BLUES SONG	321
Al Young	The Blues Don't Change	POEM	325
Langston Hughes	Juke Box Love Song	POEM	328
❖ **Focus on**	The Harlem Renaissance		330
Helene Johnson	Sonnet to a Negro in Harlem	POEM	333
Cornelius Eady	My Mother, If She Had Won Free Dance Lessons	POEM	336
Jackie Torrence	*from* The Importance of Pot Liquor	NONFICTION	340
Bob Kaufman	Battle Report	POEM	350
Quincy Troupe	A Poem for "Magic"	POEM	353
Thomas Sayers Ellis	Being There	POEM	357
Samuel Allen	To Satch	POEM	360
❖ **Media Connection**	Negro League Baseball: The People's Game		362
Alice Walker	We Alone	POEM	365
Rita Dove	Geometry	POEM	368
Jewelle L. Gomez	A Swimming Lesson	NONFICTION	371
❖ **Connecting to Jamaica**			
Bob Marley	Redemption Song	SONG	375
Ruth Forman	If You Lose Your Pen	POEM	378

The Migration of the Negro, Panel #57, c. 1940. Jacob Lawrence. Casein tempera on hardboard, 18 x 12 in. The Phillips Collection, Washington DC.

Talking Roots

*The one who lives between
the mountains and the sky,
whose slave is he?*

— *Swahili proverb*

Before You Read

The Creation

James Weldon Johnson
1871–1938

"The world does not know that a people is great until that people produces great literature and art."

About Johnson

To say that James Weldon Johnson was a man of many talents is an understatement. Throughout his life, Johnson wore multiple hats—high school principal, lawyer, lyricist, diplomat, novelist, poet, and officer in the National Association for the Advancement of Colored People. Through his songs and his writing, Johnson celebrated and preserved the African American culture of his time. His poem "The Creation" is a verse sermon written in the speech patterns of the black folk preacher. Johnson's life story is told in his autobiography, *Along This Way* (1933).

Johnson's Folk Sermons and Spirituals

"The Creation" was published in *God's Trombones,* Johnson's first collection of folk sermons, in 1927, but he had been composing in this style since 1917. He presented the rhythms and metaphors of the black folk preacher and included lines from well-known hymns and spirituals of the day. Johnson argued that the music and language of spirituals evolved from African chants and rhythms.

The Creation

— *James Weldon Johnson*

And God stepped out on space,
And He looked around and said,
"I'm lonely
I'll make me a world."

5   And as far as the eye of God could see
Darkness covered everything,
Blacker than a hundred midnights
Down in a cypress swamp.

Then God smiled,
10   And the light broke,
And the darkness rolled up on one side,
And the light stood shining on the other,
And God said, *"That's good!"*

Then God reached out and took the light in His hands,
15   And God rolled the light around in his hands
Until He made the sun;
And He set that sun a-blazing in the heavens.
And the light that was left from making the sun
God gathered it up in a shining ball
20   And flung it against the darkness,
Spangling the night with the moon and stars.
Then down between
The darkness and the light
He hurled the world;
25   And God said, *"That's good."*

The Creation

Then God Himself stepped down—
And the sun was on His right hand
And the moon was on His left;
The stars were clustered about His head,
30   And the earth was under His feet.
And God walked, and where He trod
His footsteps hollowed the valleys out
And bulged the mountains up.

Then He stopped and looked, and saw
35   That the earth was hot and barren.
So God stepped over to the edge of the world
And He spat out the seven seas;
He batted His eyes, and the lightnings flashed;
He clapped His hands, and the thunders rolled;
40   And the waters above the earth came down,
The cooling waters came down.

Then the green grass sprouted,
And the little red flowers blossomed,
The pine tree pointed his finger to the sky,
45   And the oak spread out his arms,
And the lakes cuddled down in the hollows of the ground,
And the rivers ran to the sea;
And God smiled again,
And the rainbow appeared,
50   And curled itself around His shoulder.

Then God raised His arm and He waved His hand,
Over the sea and over the land,
And He said, *"Bring forth. Bring forth."*
And quicker than God could drop His hand
55   Fishes and fowls
And beasts and birds
Swam the rivers and the seas,
Roamed the forests and the woods,
And split the air with their wings.
60   And God said, *"That's good."*

The Creation

Then God walked around,
And God looked around
On all that He had made.
He looked at His sun,
65 And He looked at His moon,
And He looked at His little stars;
He looked on His world,
With all its living things,
And God said, *"I'm lonely still."*

70 Then God sat down
On the side of a hill where He could think;
By a deep, wide river He sat down;
With His head in His hands,
God thought and thought,
75 Till He thought, *"I'll make me a man."*

Up from the bed of a river
God scooped the clay;
And by the bank of the river
He kneeled Him down;
80 And there the great God Almighty
Who lit the sun and fixed it in the sky,
Who flung the stars to the most far corner of the night,
Who rounded the earth in the middle of His hand;
This Great God,
85 Like a mammy bending over her baby,
Kneeled down in the dust
Toiling over a lump of clay
Till He shaped it in His own image;

Then into it He blew the breath of life,
90 And man became a living soul.
Amen. Amen.

Responding to the Selection

Questions for Discussion

1. What motivates God to create the universe?

2. How would you describe the speech of the speaker in Johnson's poem? Which words and phrases in the poem reflect this voice?

3. The King James version of the Bible describes the creation of the sun, moon, and stars this way:

   And God made two great lights; the greater light to rule the day, and the lesser light to rule the night: He made the stars also. And God set them in the firmament of the heaven to give light upon the earth.

   How is this passage similar to and different from the fourth stanza of Johnson's poem?

Activities

Writing an Essay

1. Investigate creation stories from other cultures—the Lakota Sioux or ancient Maya, for example. Then write an **expository essay** in which you discuss another culture's creation story, explaining how it is similar to and different from the story told in Johnson's poem.

Researching a Black National Anthem

2. One of Johnson's best-loved poems is "Lift Every Voice and Sing," which he later set to music. Use the Internet to find out more about this song. What makes it special to many African Americans? What do the words say to you?

Before You Read

Forefathers

Birago Diop
1906–1989

> "Diop unites in his contes
> [stories] an individual aware-
> ness and a feeling for the
> symbolic connotations of the
> natural world."
>
> — Abiola Irele

About Diop

In 1933, fresh from the University of Toulouse where he had studied veterinary surgery, Birago Diop looked forward to a career caring for animals in his native Senegal, a French colony. And so he did for many years. However, as he traveled throughout what was then known as French West Africa, Diop realized that French colonialism was steadily overwhelming the culture of his people, the Wolof. While in France, Diop had met writers who founded a movement called

Négritude, which stressed a return to traditional African values. Appreciating the importance of Négritude, he decided to add his voice to the movement.

To help preserve the Wolof culture, Diop began translating their folklore into French. He published four award-winning volumes of stories: *The Tales of Amadou Koumba* (1947), *The New Tales of Amadou Koumba* (1958), *Tales and Commentaries* (1963), and *Tales of Awa* (1978). The lyric poetry Diop wrote from 1925 through 1960 was published in a volume titled *Lures and Glimmerings*. Diop also served as independent Senegal's ambassador to Tunisia and as a member of the Senegalese cabinet.

The Négritude Movement

Négritude was a literary movement of the 1930s, '40s, and '50s begun by French-speaking African and Caribbean writers who had come by their language as a result of French colonialism. Négritude stressed the need for Africans throughout the world to rethink the significance of Western values in their lives and to revive and nurture the culture, traditions, and dignity of their ancestors.

Forefathers

— Birago Diop

      Listen more often to things rather than beings.
      Hear the fire's voice,
      Hear the voice of water.
      In the wind hear the sobbing of the trees,
5   It is our forefathers breathing.

      The dead are not gone forever.
      They are in the paling shadows
      And in the darkening shadows.
      The dead are not beneath the ground,
10   They are in the rustling tree,
      In the murmuring wood,
      In the still water,
      In the flowing water,
      In the lonely place, in the crowd;
15   The dead are not dead.

      Listen more often to things rather than beings.
      Hear the fire's voice.
      Hear the voice of water.
      In the wind hear the sobbing of the trees.
20   It is the breathing of our forefathers
      Who are not gone, not beneath the ground,
      Not dead.

      The dead are not gone forever.
      They are in a woman's breast,
25   A child's crying, a glowing ember.

The dead are not beneath the earth,
They are in the flickering fire,
In the weeping plant, the groaning rock,
The wooded place, the home.
30 The dead are not dead.

Listen more often to things rather than beings.
Hear the fire's voice,
Hear the voice of water.
In the wind hear the sobbing of the trees.
35 It is the breath of our forefathers.

Responding to the Selection

Questions for Discussion

1. What does the speaker suggest you will hear if you listen to "things rather than beings"?

2. The speaker says "The dead are not gone forever." How do the spirits of the dead remain in the world?

3. What is the central theme of the Négritude movement, and how does the poem echo that theme?

4. The literary technique of attributing human characteristics to nonhuman things ("the sobbing of the trees") is called **personification.** Find other examples in the poem. Why might Diop have chosen personification to impart meaning in his poem?

Activities

Writing a Memoir

1. How has the wisdom of your ancestors been passed on to you? How does it shape your values and behavior? Write a **memoir** about a moment when a conversation, a letter, or an object gave you insight into your family's history and values. Explain how that insight affected you.

Writing a Report

2. Explore the geography of West Africa and the impact of French colonialism in this region. Prepare a brief **report** describing what you discover. When did this period begin and how long did it last? What happened to the culture of the native peoples?

Focus on . . .
The Oral Tradition

For thousands of years, the continent of Africa has been home to many economically rich, socially advanced, and culturally varied civilizations. Because many of these civilizations had no tradition of written language, their histories and literature were handed down orally from one generation to the next. When Europeans began colonizing Africa, they mistook the continent's lack of a written language tradition as an indication that the people and their ways of life were primitive. Finding nothing to read, the colonists assumed Africa's people had nothing to say. What the colonists failed to do was listen.

Had the Europeans listened, they would have heard the history and literature of the African people told in the beautiful music of the continent's hundreds of languages and dialects. For millennia, the *djeli*, or storytellers, (griots) carefully memorized the genealogy of families and the epics and songs of civilizations, and they retold this rich cultural history so that the people could appreciate who they were, what they stood for, and where they came from. The *djeli*, however, were more than just storytellers. Throughout Africa's history, they served as advisors to rulers, diplomats, and translators. They officiated at such important ceremonies as namings,

initiations, marriages, and funerals. Highly respected, the *djeli*, known today by their French name *griots*, were and remain living libraries of Africa's glories.

The griots are the caretakers of an impressive cultural and historical repertoire. They can recite the genealogy of entire villages and spellbind their listeners with stories of epic heroism, often to the accompaniment of music. The griots use tales and fables to teach important lessons, especially to children, and myths and legends to relate sacred history. Proverbs and riddles transmit the wisdom of ancestors, and songs enliven important ceremonies and events.

The European nations that colonized Africa ignored the oral tradition, failing to understand its richness and importance. Many colonial powers encouraged Africans to adopt European languages and cultural traditions. Missionaries fanned out across the continent to convert African people to European Christianity. As a result, Africa's oral tradition came perilously close to being lost. During the 1930s, French-speaking African and Caribbean students in Paris formulated a literary and philosophical movement called Négritude. This movement stressed both a rejection of colonialism and Eurocentric culture and a return to Africa's social and cultural history and traditions. Today, Africa has a rich written literature; nevertheless, the oral tradition continues to function as a vital link to Africa's past.

Linking to . . .
- As you read the selections in this anthology, think about the effect the elements of oral tradition have had, and continue to have, on African American writing.

Before You Read

Bury Me in a Free Land

Frances E. W. Harper
1825–1911

"What matters it if they do forget the singer, so they don't forget the song."

About Harper

Frances E. W. Harper was born to free black parents in Maryland. She spent much of her life fighting for civil rights and educating Americans about racism, classism, and feminism.

Harper was the first woman to teach at the Union Seminary in Ohio. While teaching in Pennsylvania, she lived at an Underground Railroad station, where she saw firsthand the trials and terror of enslaved blacks attempting to find freedom in the North. In 1854 new slavery laws made it impossible for Harper to return to Maryland. She set off on a long lecture tour, reading her poetry and prose and challenging her audiences to join with her in the fight against oppression. Harper became a popular author whose poetry, fiction, and essays brought her recognition as a champion of freedom and dignity.

Abolitionist Movement

In the late-eighteenth century, the European abolitionist movement was responsible for ending the transatlantic slave trade and chattel slavery. In the United States, abolitionists fought to prohibit slavery in western territories that were being admitted to the Union as well as in the Southern states, where the economy and the way of life were dependent on the forced labor of slaves. The U.S. abolition movement drew its support from members of the clergy, educators, former slaves who were part of the free-black community, and writers such as Frances E. W. Harper. Their efforts were rewarded when President Lincoln signed the Emancipation Proclamation in 1863, freeing Southern slaves, and Congress approved the Thirteenth Amendment to the Constitution in 1865, freeing all slaves.

Bury Me in a Free Land

— *Frances E. W. Harper*

Make me a grave where'er you will,
In a lowly plain, or a lofty hill;
Make it among earth's humblest graves,
But not in a land where men are slaves.

5   I could not rest if around my grave
I heard the steps of a trembling slave;
His shadow above my silent tomb
Would make it a place of fearful gloom.

I could not rest if I heard the tread
10   Of a coffle gang to the shambles led,
And the mother's shriek of wild despair
Rise like a curse on the trembling air.

I could not sleep if I saw the lash
Drinking her blood at each fearful gash,
15   And I saw her babes torn from her breast,
Like trembling doves torn from their parent nest.

Bury Me in a Free Land

I'd shudder and start if I heard the bay
Of bloodhounds seizing their human prey,
And I heard the captive plead in vain
20   As they bound afresh his galling chain.

If I saw young girls from their mothers' arms
Bartered and sold for their youthful charms,
My eye would flash with a mournful flame,
My death-paled cheek grow red with shame.

25   I would sleep, dear friends, where bloated might
Can rob no man of his dearest right;
My rest shall be calm in any grave
Where none can call his brother a slave.

I ask no monument, proud and high,
30   To arrest the gaze of the passers-by;
All that my yearning spirit craves,
Is bury me not in a land of slaves.

Responding to the Selection

Questions for Discussion

1. Why is the speaker so insistent about being buried in a free land? Cite lines from the poem that support your explanation.

2. In your own words, describe how the speaker portrays the horrors of slavery.

3. What literary technique is at work in the first two lines of the fourth stanza? What technique does the poet employ in the last two lines of that stanza?

4. Reread the following lines from the seventh stanza:

   I would sleep, dear friends, where bloated might
   Can rob no man of his dearest right;

   What do the phrases "bloated might" and a man's "dearest right" mean to you?

Activities

Sharing Your Opinion

1. The slave trade and chattel slavery have been outlawed in the United States for over 150 years. Many people believe, however, that other forms of slavery still exist—economic, gender, and educational, for example. Imagine you are a contemporary abolitionist. Write either a **persuasive essay** or a **poem** that describes one of these other forms of slavery and what you think about it.

In Lincoln's Words

2. In the Emancipation Proclamation, President Lincoln spoke directly to the enslaved people he was freeing. Find a copy of the proclamation, either in a history textbook or on the Internet. What specific advice did Lincoln give to the newly freed blacks? What did he caution them about? Why?

Before You Read

Follow the Drinking Gourd

Anonymous

> *"Tonight we ride the*
> *underground train.*
> *It runs on tracks that are*
> *covered with pain.*
> *The whole of Humanity*
> *makes up the crew*
> *And Liberty's the engineer*
> *to carry us through."*
>
> — Charles L. Blockson

About "Follow the Drinking Gourd"

"Follow the Drinking Gourd" is a spiritual and has its roots in the pre–Civil War oral traditions of enslaved African Americans. Spirituals, or sorrow songs, were created anonymously and combine the tunes and texts of Christian hymns with the rhythms, finger snapping, clapping, and stamping of traditional African music. Many follow a call-and-response pattern in which a leader sings the verses and is answered by a choir.

Some spirituals written in the mid-nineteenth century were encoded with messages through which enslaved field-workers, forbidden to speak with one another, could communicate information about the time and location of "praise meetings," or plans for escape. Because some enslaved people likened their situation to that of the Jews in ancient Egypt, whom Moses led to freedom, typical code words and phrases included *Egypt,* referring to the South and a state of bondage, and the *Promised Land* or *Heaven,* referring to the North and freedom. In "Follow the Drinking Gourd," the drinking gourd is the Big Dipper, which points directly to the North Star, in the direction of freedom. This song was taught to those escaping enslavement by Peg Leg Joe, a one-legged sailor who served as a conductor on the Underground Railroad. He made marks—a "left foot" and a "peg foot"—for them to follow on their journey north. The three rivers mentioned in the song are the Tombigbee River in Alabama, the Tennessee River, and the Ohio River.

Follow the Drinking Gourd

— Anonymous

When the sun comes back and the first quail calls,
   Follow the drinking gourd,
For the old man is a-waiting for to carry you to freedom
   If you follow the drinking gourd.

5   Follow the drinking gourd,
   Follow the drinking gourd,
For the old man is a-waiting for to carry you to freedom
   If you follow the drinking gourd.

The river bank will make a very good road,
10   The dead trees show you the way,
Left foot, peg foot traveling on
   Follow the drinking gourd.

The river ends between two hills
   Follow the drinking gourd.
15   There's another river on the other side,
   Follow the drinking gourd.

Where the little river meets the great big river,
   Follow the drinking gourd.
The old man is a-waiting for to carry you to freedom,
20   If you follow the drinking gourd.

Responding to the Selection

Questions for Discussion

1. Why is following the drinking gourd so important? Why do you think this line is repeated so often in the song?

2. Why do you suppose a riverbank makes a good road?

3. Who is "the old man . . . a-waiting for to carry you to freedom"?

Activity

Summarizing a Narrative

Pay an online visit to the American Memory collection of the Library of Congress (www.loc.gov). Search using the key term "Underground Railroad." Among the items listed, you will find the complete text of William Still's *The Underground Railroad: A Record of Facts, Authentic Narratives, Letters,* published in 1879. Browse through the book and choose one letter, one illustration, or one authentic narrative that you find especially interesting. Print your selection and write two paragraphs summarizing the selection and your reactions to it.

Before You Read

Runagate Runagate

Robert Hayden
1913–1980

"[My poetry is] a way of coming to grips with reality . . . a way of discovery and definition. It is a way of solving for the unknowns."

About Hayden

Much of Robert Hayden's poetry focuses on African American heroes and history. Nevertheless, like Countee Cullen before him, Hayden did not want to be known as a "Negro poet." He believed such labels forced black writers into "a kind of literary ghetto, where the standards of other writers" did not apply and where black writers were restricted "to racial themes." During the Civil Rights movement in the United States, Hayden's beliefs drew protests from other African American writers who were intent on writing poetry that was as political as the movement itself.

Hayden's interest in African American history originated when he joined the Federal Writer's Project and began researching black folklore and the history of the Underground Railroad. Later, Hayden incorporated his research into formal, graceful poems about the Civil War, the experiences of enslaved African Americans, and such historical figures as Frederick Douglass, Harriet Tubman, Nat Turner, and Malcolm X.

Although Hayden's first book of poetry, *Heart-Shape in the Dust,* was published in 1940, he received little critical attention until 1966, when *A Ballad of Remembrance,* first published in 1962, was awarded a grand prize at the First World Festival of Negro Arts in Dakar, Senegal. In 1976 Hayden became the first African American to be appointed poetry consultant to the Library of Congress.

Runagate Runagate

— *Robert Hayden*

I.

Runs falls rises stumbles on from darkness into darkness
and the darkness thicketed with shapes of terror
and the hunters pursuing and the hounds pursuing
and the night cold and the night long and the river
5   to cross and the jack-muh-lanterns beckoning beckoning
and blackness ahead and when shall I reach that somewhere
morning and keep on going and never turn back and keep on going
              Runagate
                      Runagate
10   Runagate

Many thousands rise and go
many thousands crossing over

                      O mythic North
              O star-shaped yonder Bible city

15   Some go weeping and some rejoicing
some in coffins and some in carriages
some in silks and some in shackles

              Rise and go or fare you well

No more auction block for me
20   no more driver's lash for me

If you see my Pompey, 30 yrs of age,
new breeches, plain stockings, negro shoes;
if you see my Anna, likely young mulatto
branded E on the right cheek, R on the left,
25   catch them if you can and notify subscriber.
Catch them if you can, but it won't be easy.
They'll dart underground when you try to catch them,
plunge into quicksand, whirlpools, mazes,
turn into scorpions when you try to catch them.

30   And before I'll be a slave
I'll be buried in my grave

        North star and bonanza gold
        I'm bound for the freedom, freedom-bound
        and oh Susyanna don't you cry for me

35   Runagate

                  Runagate

        II.
Rises from their anguish and their power,

            Harriet Tubman,

            woman of earth, whipscarred,
40   a summoning, a shining

            Mean to be free

    And this was the way of it, brethren brethren,
way we journeyed from Can't to Can.
Moon so bright and no place to hide,
45   the cry up and the patterollers riding,
hound dogs belling in bladed air.
And fear starts a-murbling, Never make it,
we'll never make it. *Hush that now,*
and she's turned upon us, levelled pistol
50   glinting in moonlight:
*Dead folks can't jaybird-talk, she says;
you keep going now or die, she says.*

> Wanted Harriet Tubman alias The General
> alias Moses Stealer of Slaves

55   In league with Garrison Alcott Emerson
      Garrett Douglass Thoreau John Brown

Armed and known to be Dangerous

Wanted Reward Dead or Alive

          Tell me, Ezekiel, oh tell me do you see
60   mailed Jehovah coming to deliver me?

Hoot-owl calling in the ghosted air,
five times calling to the hants in the air.
Shadow of a face in the scary leaves,
shadow of a voice in the talking leaves:

65   Come ride-a my train

          Oh that train, ghost-story train
          through swamp and savanna movering movering,
          over trestles of dew, through caves of the wish,
          Midnight Special on a sabre track movering movering,
70   *first stop Mercy and the last Hallelujah.*

          Come ride-a my train

              Mean mean mean to be free.

Responding to the Selection

Questions for Discussion

1. Read the first stanza aloud, without pausing. How does the absence of any punctuation impart meaning to the poem?

2. When you say "Runagate / Runagate / Runagate" quickly, what word comes to mind? How does this word add meaning to the poem?

3. Why does the speaker describe the North as "mythic"? What do you think the "star-shaped yonder Bible city" represents?

4. Why does Harriet Tubman point a gun at frightened runaway slaves? What does "Dead folks can't jaybird-talk" mean?

5. Hayden uses the phrase "Mean to be free" twice in the second part of the poem. What does the phrase mean? Does it mean the same thing in both places? Discuss the possible differences.

Activities

Writing an Expository Paragraph

1. Research the history of the word *runagate*. Where did the word originate? How has its meaning changed over the centuries? Write an **expository paragraph** that details your findings.

Bringing Words to Life

2. Prepare a **dramatic reading** of the poem. Where will you pause, and where will your words tumble out, bunched together? Will your voice sound calm, out of breath, or a combination of the two? When will your voice rise? When will it fall? When will you shout, and when will you whisper? When you've perfected your reading, share it with others.

MEDIA connection

Web Page

Here, Dorsey writes about the early
stages of his musical life and shares
the story of how his most famous
song came to be.

The Precious Lord Story and Gospel Songs

— *by Thomas A. Dorsey*

In 1921 at the National Baptist
Convention in Chicago, I heard a
Professor Nix and saw him raise that
huge audience singing a religious song,
"I Do, Don't You." I was converted in
that meeting and said that is the type
of music I would like to do. At that
time I was a jazz musician playing
piano in wine rooms and buffet flats
up and down State Street.

There were no gospel songs then,
they were called evangelistic songs.
After writing three or four songs of
this kind, the National Baptist
Publishing Board published two of my
songs, one in the Gospel book and
the other in the Baptist Hymnal
which was circulated in a big way
nationally and is still being circulated
to this day.

In the early 1920's, I coined the
words "Gospel Songs" after listening
to a group of five people on Sunday
morning on the far south side of
Chicago. This was the first I heard of
Gospel Choir. After dedicating my all
writing Gospel Songs I took a position
playing at a little Baptist Church in
South Chicago, but I would still help
the "jazz boys" out now and then until
I got a firm footing in gospel songs.

I traveled over the country in a
1930 Ford Car. I didn't have any
money for train fare—that was out.
But later on tragedy struck. In August
of 1932 I had the greatest shock of my
young life just as things began to look
promising for a great future. I left
home for St. Louis, MO. I left my wife
who was soon to become a mother. I
got my clothing, got into my car with
E. C. Davis, another gospel song aspi-
rant and we started for St. Louis to
sing in a revival meeting. I turned and
went back to my home, went into the
room, my wife was asleep, I did not
want to awake her or
disturb her sleep. I
eased my music
case out and went
back to the car.
The man that was
going with me
changed his mind and
said, "I'm not going,
drop me out at the
corner." So I did and
went on alone. The
next night in St. Louis
while I was singing in
the meeting a boy
brought

me a telegram to the church. I opened it and read: "Your wife just died." I could not cry out in the meeting, but as soon as I could get out I called home in Chicago and all I could hear them say was "Nettie is dead, Nettie is dead."

After putting my wife and baby away in the same casket I began to feel that God had done me an injustice. I didn't want to serve him anymore or write any more gospel songs. I wanted to return back to the jazz world that I once knew so well before. Then a voice spoke to me and said: "You are not alone. I tried to speak to you before, it was you that should have gotten out of the car and not gone to St. Louis instead of the other man that got out and stayed at home." I said "Thank you Lord. I understand. I'll never make that same mistake again." Everyone was so kind to me in these sad hours. The next Saturday night Professor Theodore R. Frye and I went up to the Madam Malone's Poro College which had a beautiful and comfortable music room—well equipped and a good piano.

There in my solitude, I began to browse over the keys like a gentle herd pasturing on tender turf. Something happened to me there. I had a strange feeling inside. A sudden calm; a quiet stillness. As my fingers began to manipulate over the keys, words began to fall in place on the melody like drops of water falling from the crevice of a rock.

I wanted to change it to Blessed Lord, Take My Hand, but Professor Frye said, "No, call him Precious Lord." This is the greatest song I have written out of near four hundred, exceeding the new two hundred blues and jazz songs written in my sinful days.

Questions for Discussion

1. Before Dorsey "got a firm footing in gospel songs," he continued to play jazz and blues music. What do you think the jazz musicians thought about his musical change? How do you think the gospel musicians felt about his other life?

2. Read "Take My Hand, Precious Lord." How does knowing Dorsey's story affect your interpretation of the song?

Before You Read

Take My Hand, Precious Lord

Thomas A. Dorsey
1899–1993

> "I borrowed five dollars and sent out 500 copies of my song, 'If You See My Savior,' to churches throughout the country. . . . It was three years before I got a single order. I felt like going back to the blues."

About Dorsey

"The devil's music." That's what traditional church music lovers called Thomas A. Dorsey's early gospel songs. Dorsey combined sacred lyrics with jazz and blues melodies to produce a kind of gospel music that had never been heard before. His music slowly gained popularity, and at the time of his death, Dorsey was the acknowledged father of gospel music.

Dorsey began his musical career as Georgia Tom, a teenaged blues singer and composer. After a series of nervous breakdowns, Dorsey was persuaded by a minister to try to heal his emotional torment by composing church music. In 1932 Dorsey formed one of the first gospel music choirs at the Pilgrim Baptist Church in Chicago. A year later, he and several other gospel music performers established the National Convention of Gospel Choirs and Choruses.

Gospel Music

Gospel music has its roots in eighteenth-century spirituals, which married biblical and other religious texts with secular American and British folk music. By the nineteenth century, Pentecostal churches were on the rise, and in black communities, the services were often accompanied by pianos, organs, guitars, banjos, horns, and tambourines. "Shoutings" in these church services likely developed from the African tradition of "ring shouts," religious dances that featured singing and rhythmic clapping. From this rich mixture of African, British, American, and biblical influences emerged gospel music, which has continued to evolve as new musical styles emerge.

Take My Hand, Precious Lord

— *Thomas A. Dorsey*

Precious Lord, take my hand,
Lead me on, let me stand,
I am tired, I am weak, I am worn.
Through the storm, through the night
5   Lead me on to the light,
Take my hand, precious Lord,
Lead me home.

When my way grows drear,
Precious Lord, linger near.
10   When my life is almost gone,
Hear my cry, hear my call,
Hold my hand lest I fall.
Take my hand, precious Lord,
Lead me home.

15   When the darkness appears
And the night draws near,
And the day is past and gone,
At the river I stand,
Guide my feet, hold my hand.
20   Take my hand, precious Lord
Lead me home.

Responding to the Selection ————————

Questions for Discussion

1. Describe some of the feelings the speaker is expressing in these lyrics. Which words or phrases express these feelings?

2. What do you think the speaker is asking for?

3. Each stanza seems to have a slightly different focus. Based on your reading of the lyrics, what is the focus of each stanza?

Activities

Interpreting Gospel Music

1. Think about the African American experience during the eighteenth, nineteenth, and twentieth centuries. In a brief **essay,** explain how you think that experience is reflected in the lyrics of Dorsey's song.

Comparing Music

2. Find two or three different recordings of "Take My Hand, Precious Lord." After listening to each a few times, decide which version best captures the spirit and meaning of the song for you.

Before You Read

The Negro Speaks of Rivers

Langston Hughes
1902–1967

> *"An artist must be free to choose what he does, certainly, but he must also never be afraid to do what he might choose."*

About Hughes

One evening in Washington, D.C., the poet Vachel Lindsay was dining in a restaurant. A young African American busboy left three poems beside Lindsay's plate. Later that night, at a reading of his poetry, Lindsay recounted the story and read the poems. Newspapers throughout the country reported that Lindsay had discovered a busboy poet. But the busboy, Langston Hughes, had already been discovered by the editors of a prominent black magazine, *The Crisis,* who had published "The Negro Speaks of Rivers," a poem which Hughes had written the summer after he graduated from high school. Before Hughes received his college degree in 1929, he had already published two books of poetry.

During the 1920s, Hughes traveled extensively in Africa and Europe. He later settled in Manhattan's Harlem neighborhood, which he called "the greatest Negro city in the world." At the time, Harlem was experiencing an explosion of art, music, and literature that would revolutionize African American culture, and Hughes was part of that explosion. He infused his poetry and prose with the rhythms of jazz and blues as he gave voice to the fears, the anger, and the aspirations of black Americans. A fierce social critic, he often irritated both white and black Americans who preferred less confrontational literature. In 1943 Hughes introduced his most beloved fictional character, Jesse B. Semple, a Virginia-born Harlem resident affectionately known as "Simple." Simple served as an alter-ego for Hughes, through whom he could comment on issues of race, politics, and culture in the United States. Hughes's body of work includes poetry, novels, nonfiction, young adult literature, drama, songs, and the text for an opera.

The Negro Speaks of Rivers

— *Langston Hughes*

I've known rivers:
I've known rivers ancient as the world and older than the
    flow of human blood in human veins.

My soul has grown deep like the rivers.

I bathed in the Euphrates when dawns were young.
5   I built my hut near the Congo and it lulled me to sleep.
I looked upon the Nile and raised the pyramids above it.
I heard the singing of the Mississippi when Abe Lincoln
    went down to New Orleans, and I've seen its muddy
    bosom turn all golden in the sunset.

I've known rivers:
Ancient, dusky rivers.

10   My soul has grown deep like the rivers.

Responding to the Selection

Questions for Discussion

1. What does the speaker know about rivers?

2. How are rivers like the blood that flows through human veins?

3. Fossil evidence suggests that the earliest human beings first emerged from the plains of what is now central Africa. How does this knowledge deepen your understanding of the poem?

4. What does the line "My soul has grown deep like the rivers" mean to you?

Activities

Writing a Poem

1. Try writing a **poem** that echoes the thoughts and feelings of Hughes's poem. Begin your poem as Hughes does but choose a different aspect of nature to "know," such as mountains, forests, prairies, valleys, or canyons.

Exploring a River

2. Choose one of the rivers mentioned in the poem and write a brief **report** on its importance to the land and its people.

Before You Read

from *The Life of Olaudah Equiano*

Olaudah Equiano
1745–1797

". . . I might say my sufferings were great; but when I compare my lot with that of most of my countrymen, I regard myself as a particular favorite of heaven. . . ."

About Equiano

Olaudah Equiano, the son of a chieftain of the Igbo people, was born in 1745 in the African village of Essaka (now northeastern Nigeria). When he was only eleven years old, Equiano and his sister were kidnapped by slave traders. Separated from his sister, whom he would never see again, Equiano was shipped to the island of Barbados in the Caribbean Sea.

In Barbados, Equiano traded the "cheerfulness and affability . . . the leading characteristics of our nation" for the "shrieks of the women and the groans of the dying [that made] a scene of horror almost inconceivable."

Equiano had been in Barbados for nearly a year when an officer of the British Royal Navy bought him and renamed him Gustavus Vassa. By the age of twelve, Equiano had learned to read and write. At age twenty-one, he was finally able to buy his freedom. He settled in England and devoted himself to the antislavery movement. His autobiography, *The Interesting Narrative of the Life of Olaudah Equiano, or Gustavus Vassa, the African,* was first published in 1789. It would forever change the views of many Europeans and Americans about slavery.

About the Middle Passage

From the 1500s to the 1800s, about twelve million Africans suffered unspeakable horrors on the forced journey from their homes to enslavement in the Western Hemisphere. The longest and most arduous portion of the journey, known as the Middle Passage, was a two-month voyage from West Africa to the West Indies. Almost two million Africans died from malnutrition, disease, suffocation, beatings, and despair.

from The Life of Olaudah Equiano

— *Olaudah Equiano*

The first object which saluted my eyes when I arrived on the coast, was the sea, and a slave ship, which was then riding at anchor, and waiting for its cargo. These filled me with astonishment, which was soon converted into terror, when I was carried on board. I was immediately handled, and tossed up to see if I were sound, by some of the crew; and I was now persuaded that I had gotten into a world of bad spirits, and that they were going to kill me.

Their complexions, too, differing so much from ours, their long hair, and the language they spoke, (which was very different from any I had ever heard) united to confirm me in this belief. Indeed, such were the horrors of my views and fears at the moment, that, if ten thousand worlds had been my own, I would have freely parted with them all to have exchanged my condition with that of the meanest slave in my own country. When I looked round the ship too, and saw a large furnace of copper boiling, and a multitude of black people of every description chained together, every one of their countenances expressing dejection and sorrow, I no longer doubted of my fate; and, quite overpowered with horror and anguish, I fell motionless on the deck and fainted. When I recovered a little, I found some black people about me, who I believed were some of those who had brought me on board, and had been receiving their pay; they talked to me in order to cheer me, but all in vain. I asked them if we were not to be eaten by those white men with horrible looks, red faces, and long hair. They told me I was not: and one of the crew brought me a small portion of spirituous liquor in a wine glass, but, being afraid of him, I would not take it out of his hand. One of the blacks, therefore, took it from him and gave it to me, and I took a little down my palate, which, instead of reviving me, as they

from *The Life of Olaudah Equiano*

thought it would, threw me into the greatest consternation at the strange feeling it produced, having never tasted any such liquor before. Soon after this, the blacks who brought me on board went off, and left me abandoned to despair.

I now saw myself deprived of all chance of returning to my native country, or even the least glimpse of hope of gaining the shore, which I now considered as friendly; and I even wished for my former slavery in preference to my present situation, which was filled with horrors of every kind, still heightened by my ignorance of what I was to undergo. I was not long suffered to indulge my grief; I was soon put down under the decks, and there I received such a salutation in my nostrils as I had never experienced in my life: so that, with the loathsomeness of the stench, and crying together, I became so sick and low that I was not able to eat, nor had I the least desire to taste any thing. I now wished for the last friend, death, to relieve me; but soon, to my grief, two of the white men offered me eatables; and, on my refusing to eat, one of them held me fast by the hands, and laid me across, I think the windlass, and tied my feet, while the other flogged me severely. I had never experienced any thing of this kind before, and although not being used to the water, I naturally feared that element the first time I saw it, yet, nevertheless, could I have got over the nettings, I would have jumped over the side, but I could not; and besides, the crew used to watch us very closely who were not chained down to the decks, lest we should leap into the water; and I have seen some of these poor African prisoners most severely cut, for attempting to do so, and hourly whipped for not eating. This indeed was often the case with myself. In a little time after, amongst the poor chained men, I found some of my own nation, which in a small degree gave ease to my mind. I inquired of these what was to be done with us? They gave me to understand, we were to be carried to these white people's country to work for them. I then was a little revived, and thought, if it were no worse than working, my situation was not so desperate; but still I feared I should be put to death, the white people looked and acted, as I thought, in so savage a manner; for I had never seen among any people such instances of brutal cruelty; and this not only shown towards us blacks, but also to some of the whites themselves. One white man in particular I saw, when we were permitted to be on deck, flogged so unmercifully with a large rope near the foremast, that he died in consequence of it; and they tossed him over the side as they would have done a brute. This made me fear these people the more; and I expected nothing less than to be treated in the same manner. I could not help expressing my fears and apprehensions to some of my countrymen; I asked them if these people had no country, but lived in this hollow place? (the ship) they told me they did not, but came from a distant one. "Then," said I, "how comes it in all our country we never heard of them?" They told me because they lived so very far off. I then asked where were their women? had they any like themselves? I was told they had. "And why," said I, "do we not see them?" They answered, because they were left behind. I asked how the vessel could go? they told me they could not tell; but that there was cloth put upon the masts by the help of the ropes I saw, and then the vessel went on; and the white men had some spell or magic they put in the water when they liked, in order to stop the vessel. I was exceedingly amazed at this account, and really thought they were spirits. I therefore wished much to be from amongst them, for I expected they would sacrifice me; but my wishes were vain—for we were so quartered that it was impossible for any of us to make our escape.

While we stayed on the coast I was mostly on deck; and one day, to my great astonishment, I saw one of these vessels coming in with the sails up. As soon as the whites saw it, they gave a great shout, at which we were amazed; and the more so, as the vessel appeared larger by approaching nearer. At last, she came to an anchor in my sight, and when the anchor was let go, I and my countrymen who saw it, were lost in astonishment to observe the vessel stop—and were now convinced it was done by magic. Soon after this the other ship got her boats out, and they came on board of us, and the people of both ships seemed very glad to see each other. Several of the strangers also shook hands with us black people, and made motions with their hands, signifying I suppose, we were to go to their country, but we did not understand them.

At last, when the ship we were in, had got in all her cargo, they made ready with many fearful noises, and we were all put under deck, so that we could not see how they managed the vessel. But this disappointment was the least of my sorrow. The stench of the hold while we were on the coast was so intolerably loathsome, that it was dangerous to remain there for any time, and some of us had been permitted to stay on the deck for the fresh air; but now that the whole ship's cargo were confined together, it became absolutely pestilential. The closeness of the place, and the heat of the climate, added to the number in the ship, which was so crowded that each had scarcely room to turn himself, almost suffocated us. This produced copious perspirations, so that the air soon became unfit for respiration, from a variety of loathsome smells, and brought on a sickness among the slaves, of which many died—thus falling victims to the improvident avarice, as I may call it, of their purchasers. This wretched situation was again aggravated by the galling of the chains, now became insupportable; and the filth of the necessary tubs, into which the children often fell, and were almost suffocated. The shrieks of the women, and the groans of the dying, rendered the whole a scene of horror almost inconceivable. Happily perhaps, for myself, I was soon reduced so low here that it was thought necessary to keep me almost always on deck; and from my extreme youth I was not put in fetters. In this situation I expected every hour to share the fate of my companions, some of whom were almost daily brought upon deck at the point of death, which I began to hope would soon put an end to my miseries. Often did I think many of the inhabitants of the deep much more happy than myself. I envied them the freedom they enjoyed, and as often wished I could change my condition for theirs. Every circumstance I met with, served only to render my state more painful, and heightened my apprehensions, and my opinion of the cruelty of the whites.

One day they had taken a number of fishes; and when they had killed and satisfied themselves with as many as they thought fit, to our astonishment who were on deck, rather than give any of them to us to eat, as we expected, they tossed the remaining fish into the sea again, although we begged and prayed for some as well as we could, but in vain; and some of my countrymen, being pressed by hunger, took an opportunity, when they thought no one saw them, of trying to get a little privately; but they were discovered, and the attempt procured them some very severe floggings. One day, when we had a smooth sea and moderate wind, two of my wearied countrymen who were chained together, (I was near them at the time,) preferring death to such a life of misery, somehow made through the nettings and jumped into the sea: immediately, another quite dejected fellow, who, on account of his illness, was suffered to be out of irons, also followed their example; and I believe many more would very soon have done the same, if they had not been prevented by the ship's crew, who were instantly alarmed. Those of us that were the most active, were in a moment put down under the deck, and there was such a noise and confusion amongst the people of the ship as I never heard before, to stop her, and get the boat out to go after the slaves. However, two of the wretches were drowned, but they got the other, and afterwards flogged him unmercifully, for thus attempting to prefer death to slavery. In this manner we continued to undergo more hardships than I can now relate, hardships which are inseparable from this accursed trade. Many a time we were near suffocation from the want of fresh air, which we were often without for whole days together. This, and the stench of the necessary tubs, carried off many.

During our passage, I first saw flying fishes, which surprised me very much; they used frequently to fly across the ship, and many of them fell on the deck. I also now first saw the use of the quadrant; I had often with astonishment seen the mariners make observations with it, and I could not think what it meant. They at last took notice of my surprise;

and one of them, willing to increase it, as well as to gratify my curiosity, made me one day look through it. The clouds appeared to me to be land, which disappeared as they passed along. This heightened my wonder; and I was now more persuaded than ever, that I was in another world, and that every thing about me was magic. At last, we came in sight of the island of Barbadoes, at which the whites on board gave a great shout, and made many signs of joy to us. We did not know what to think of this; but as the vessel drew nearer, we plainly saw the harbor, and other ships of different kinds and sizes, and we soon anchored amongst them, off Bridgetown. Many merchants and planters now came on board, though it was in the evening. They put us in separate parcels, and examined us attentively. They also made us jump, and pointed to the land, signifying we were to go there. We thought by this, we should be eaten by these ugly men, as they appeared to us; and, when soon after we were all put down under the deck again, there was much dread and trembling among us, and nothing but bitter cries to be heard all the night from these apprehensions, insomuch, that at last the white people got some old slaves from the land to pacify us. They told us we were not to be eaten, but to work, and were soon to go on land, where we should see many of our country people. This report eased us much. And sure enough, soon after we were landed, there came to us Africans of all languages.

We were conducted immediately to the merchant's yard, where we were all pent up together, like so many sheep in a fold, without regard to sex or age. As every object was new to me, every thing I saw filled me with surprise. What struck me first, was, that the houses were built with bricks and stories, and in every other respect different from those I had seen in Africa; but I was still more astonished on seeing people on horseback. I did not know what this could mean; and, indeed, I thought these people were full of nothing but magical arts. While I was in this astonishment, one of my fellow-prisoners spoke to a countryman of his, about the horses, who said they were the same kind they had in their country. I understood them, though they were from a distant part of Africa; and I thought it odd I had not seen any horses there; but afterwards, when I came to converse with different Africans, I found they had many horses amongst them, and much larger than those I then saw.

We were not many days in the merchant's custody, before we were sold after their usual manner, which is this:—On a signal given, (as the beat of a drum,) the buyers rush at once into the yard where the slaves are confined, and make choice of that parcel they like best. The noise and clamor with which this is attended, and the eagerness visible in the countenances of the buyers, serve not a little to increase the apprehension of terrified Africans, who may well be supposed to consider them as the ministers of that destruction to which they think themselves devoted. In this manner, without scruple, are relations and friends separated, most of them never to see each other again. I remember, in the vessel in which I was brought over, in the men's apartment, there were several brothers, who, in the sale, were sold in different lots; and it was very moving on this occasion, to see and hear their cries at parting. O, ye nominal Christians! might not an African ask you— Learned you this from your God, who says unto you, Do unto all men as you would men should do unto you? Is it not enough that we are torn from our country and friends, to toil for your luxury and lust of gain? Must every tender feeling be likewise sacrificed to your avarice? Are the dearest friends and relations, now rendered more dear by their separation from their kindred, still to be parted from each other, and thus prevented from cheering the gloom of slavery, with the small comfort of being together, and mingling their sufferings and sorrows? Why are parents to lose their children, brothers their sisters, or husbands their wives? Surely, this is a new refinement in cruelty, which, while it has no advantage to atone for it, thus aggravates distress, and adds fresh horrors even to the wretchedness of slavery.

Responding to the Selection _____

Questions for Discussion

1. What does Equiano mean when he refers to his captors as "nominal Christians"?

2. Equiano writes of his first impressions upon boarding the slave ship, "I was now persuaded that I had gotten into a world of bad spirits, and that they were going to kill me." How do these words foreshadow both his voyage to the Caribbean and his experiences on Barbados?

3. What do you think is symbolic about the appearance of the flying fish?

Activities

Preparing an Illustrated Report

1. The voyage from Africa to the Americas was called the Middle Passage. Using primary sources such as Equiano's autobiography and illustrations from the time, prepare an **illustrated report** that details the horrors of the Middle Passage.

Writing a Persuasive Essay

2. Using this account from Equiano's autobiography, write a **persuasive essay** calling for an end to the slave trade and slavery.

Before You Read

Leaves

Countee Cullen
1903–1946

"I find that I am actuated by a strong sense of race consciousness."

About Cullen

One of the most celebrated poets of the Harlem Renaissance, Countee Cullen led a life marked by contradictions. He didn't want to be known as a "Negro poet," yet he wrote forcefully about racial injustice. An urban, black twentieth-century American, he wrote not in the rhythms and language of African Americans but rather in the highly structured traditional verse forms of eighteenth- and nineteenth-century European poets he studied while a graduate student at Harvard University. He modeled his work after that of John Keats, a British Romantic poet. Nevertheless, as noted Harlem Renaissance figure James Weldon Johnson pointed out, "the best of his poetry is motivated by race."

Cullen received a B.A. from New York University and an M.A. from Harvard. His first book of poems, *Color,* was published before he finished college and received critical praise, and his work appeared regularly in literary magazines. For a time, he was assistant editor of *Opportunity* magazine.

Cullen published several other books of poetry, but as the Harlem Renaissance waned, so, too, did his literary career. His marriage to Yolande DuBois, daughter of noted American black protest leader W. E. B. DuBois, ended in divorce in 1930. In his thirties, Cullen began teaching junior high school in New York City, a position he held until his death at age forty-three.

Leaves

— Countee Cullen

One, two, and three,
Dead leaves drift from a tree.

Yesterday they loved
Wind and rain, the brush
5   Of wings
Soft and clean, that moved
Through them beyond the crush
Of things.
Yesterday they loved.

10   Yesterday they sang
Silver symphonies,
Raised high
Holy chants that rang
Leaf-wise through their trees;
15   As I,
Yesterday they sang.

20   Unremembered now,
They will soon lie warm
With snow;
They could grace a bough
Once, and love and charm,
Although
Unremembered now.

Trees so soon forget
25   Little leaves they had
Before,
Knowing spring will let
Them wake, vernal clad
With more;
30   Trees so soon forget.

Man dreams that he
Is more than a leaf on a tree.

Responding to the Selection

Questions for Discussion

1. Is the poem literally about leaves and trees, or is it a **metaphor** for something else? Explain your reasoning.

2. The speaker says of the dead leaves, "They will soon lie warm / With snow." How might you explain the seeming contradiction between snow and warmth?

3. How do you think the poem reflects the rhythms of nature?

4. What do the last two lines of the poem mean to you?

Activities

Reflecting on the Past

1. In hindsight, "Leaves" could well be a metaphor for the arc of Cullen's life, from celebrated to forgotten poet. Write a reflective **essay** in which you use Cullen's life to interpret the meaning of the poem.

Comparing the Lives of Poets

2. Investigate the life of John Keats and read some of his poems. In what ways are Keats's and Cullen's lives and work similar and different?

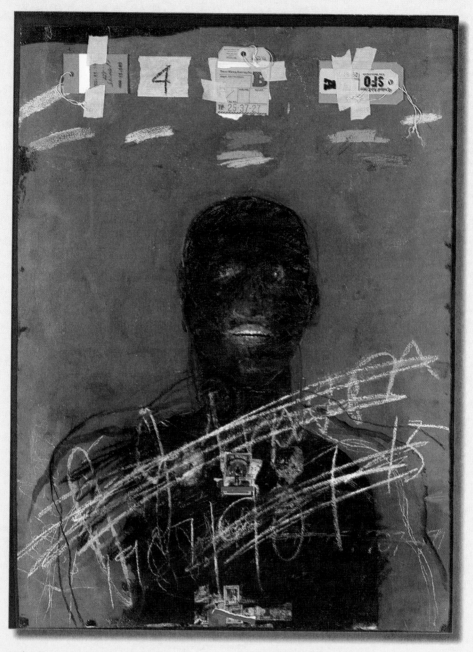

Jack Johnson, 1972. Raymond Saunders. Mixed media, 23 x 19 in. Stephen Wirtz Gallery, San Francisco.

Theme Two

Smoldering Embers

The civil rights movement called America to put a giant mirror before it and look at itself.

— Barbara Jordan

Before You Read

from *My Bondage and My Freedom*

Frederick Douglass
1818–1895

> *"Find out just what any people will quietly submit to and you have the exact measure of the injustice and wrong which will be imposed on them."*

About Douglass

Born on a Maryland plantation as Frederick Bailey, Fredrick Douglass never knew his white father and was separated from his enslaved mother soon after birth. At the age of eight, he was sent to the Auld family of Baltimore, where Mrs. Auld introduced him to the magic of reading. Realizing that education was a path to freedom, young Bailey taught himself to read and write. The more he learned, the more restless he became about his enslavement. To make him more obedient, Mrs. Auld sent Bailey to a "slave-breaker" who beat him for the slightest offense. Rather than breaking the young man's spirit, the experience made Bailey determined to be free.

At the age of twenty, Bailey finally escaped to freedom and changed his name to Douglass to avoid capture. His life changed dramatically in 1841 when he was asked to speak at an antislavery meeting. Douglass gave a moving speech and was persuaded to join the Massachusetts Anti-Slavery Society. Touring tirelessly for the society, he developed a reputation as a great orator.

Many of Douglass's listeners doubted that such an educated man could have been enslaved. Urged to document his experience, Douglass wrote *Narrative of the Life of Frederick Douglass.* Because the autobiography included information that might have led to his capture, Douglass fled to England.

In 1847 English friends raised money to purchase his freedom. He returned to the United States and began publishing an antislavery newspaper. He also expanded and republished his autobiography as *My Bondage and My Freedom* (1855) and again as *Life and Times of Frederick Douglass* (1881).

from

My Bondage
and
My Freedom

— Frederick Douglass

I lived in the family of Master Hugh, at Baltimore, seven years, during which time—as the almanac makers say of the weather—my condition was variable. The most interesting feature of my history here, was my learning to read and write, under somewhat marked disadvantages. In attaining this knowledge, I was compelled to resort to indirections by no means congenial to my nature, and which were really humiliating to me. My mistress—who, as the reader has already seen, had begun to teach me—was suddenly checked in her benevolent design, by the strong advice of her husband. In faithful compliance with this advice, the good lady had not only ceased to instruct me, herself, but had set her face as a flint against my learning to read by any means. It is due, however, to my mistress to say, that she did not adopt this course in all its stringency at the first. She either thought it unnecessary, or she lacked the depravity indispensable to shutting me up in mental darkness. It was, at least, necessary for her to have some training, and some hardening, in the exercise of the slaveholder's prerogative, to make her equal to forgetting my human nature and character, and to treating me as a thing destitute of a moral or an intellectual nature. Mrs. Auld—my mistress—was, as I have said, a most kind and tender-hearted woman; and, in the humanity of her heart, and the simplicity of her mind, she set out, when I first went to live with her, to treat me as she supposed one human being ought to treat another.

It is easy to see, that, in entering upon the duties of a slaveholder, some little experience is needed. Nature has done almost nothing to prepare men and women to be either slaves or slaveholders. Nothing but rigid training, long persisted in, can perfect the character of the one or the other. One cannot easily forget to love freedom; and it is as hard to cease to respect that natural love in our fellow creatures. On entering upon the career of a slaveholding mistress, Mrs. Auld was singularly deficient; nature, which fits nobody for such an office, had done less for her than any lady I had known. It was no easy matter to induce her to think and to feel that the curly-headed boy, who stood by her side, and even leaned on her lap; who was loved by little Tommy, and who loved little Tommy in turn; sustained to her only the relation of a chattel. I was *more* than that, and she felt me to be more than that. I could talk and sing; I could laugh and weep; I could reason and remember; I could love and hate. I was human, and she, dear lady, knew and felt me to be so. How could she, then, treat me as a brute, without a mighty struggle with all the noble powers of her own soul. That struggle came, and the will and power of the husband was victorious. Her noble soul was overthrown; but, he that overthrew it did not, himself, escape the consequences. He, not less than the other parties, was injured in his domestic peace by the fall.

When I went into their family, it was the abode of happiness and contentment. The mistress of the house was a model of affection and tenderness. Her fervent piety and watchful uprightness made it impossible to see her without thinking and feeling—*"that woman is a Christian."* There was no sorrow nor suffering for which she had not a tear, and there was no innocent joy for which she had not a smile. She had bread for the hungry, clothes for the naked, and comfort for every mourner that came within her reach. Slavery soon proved its ability to divest her of these excellent qualities, and her home of its early happiness. Conscience cannot stand much violence. Once thoroughly broken down, *who* is he that can repair the damage? It may be broken toward the slave, on Sunday, and toward the master on Monday. It cannot endure such shocks. It must stand entire, or it does not stand at all. If my condition waxed bad, that of the family waxed not better. The first step, in the wrong direction, was the violence done to nature and to conscience, in arresting the benevolence that would have enlightened my young mind. In ceasing to instruct me, she must begin to justify herself *to* herself; and, once consenting to take sides in such a debate, she was riveted to her position. One needs very little knowledge of moral philosophy, to see *where* my mistress now landed. She finally became even more violent in her opposition to my learning to read, than was her husband himself. She was not satisfied with simply doing as *well* as her husband had commanded her, but seemed resolved to better his instruction. Nothing appeared to make my poor mistress—after her turning toward the downward path—more angry, than seeing me, seated in some nook or corner, quietly reading a book or a newspaper. I have had her rush at me, with the utmost fury, and snatch from my hand such newspaper or book, with something of the wrath and consternation which a traitor might be supposed to feel on being discovered in a plot by some dangerous spy.

Mrs. Auld was an apt woman, and the advice of her husband, and her own experience, soon demonstrated, to her entire satisfaction, that education and slavery are incompatible with each other. When this conviction was thoroughly established, I was most narrowly watched in all my movements. If I remained in a separate room from the family for any considerable length of time, I was sure to be suspected of having a book, and was at once called upon to give an account of myself. All this, however, was entirely *too late*. The first, and never to be retraced, step had been taken. In teaching me the alphabet, in the days of her simplicity and kindness, my mistress had given me the *"inch,"* and now, no ordinary precaution could prevent me from taking the *"ell."*

Seized with a determination to learn to read, at any cost, I hit upon many expedients to accomplish the desired end. The plea which I mainly adopted, and the one by which I was most successful, was that of using my young white playmates, with whom I met in the street, as teachers. I used to carry, almost constantly, a copy of Webster's spelling book in my pocket; and, when sent of errands, or when play time was allowed me, I would step, with my young friends, aside, and take a lesson in spelling. I generally paid my *tuition fee* to the boys, with bread, which I also carried in my pocket. For a single biscuit, any of my hungry little comrades would give me a lesson more valuable to me than bread. Not every one, however, demanded this consideration, for there were those who took pleasure in teaching me, whenever I had a chance to be taught by them. I am strongly tempted to give the names of two or three of those little boys, as a slight testimonial of the gratitude and affection I bear them, but prudence forbids; not that it would injure me, but it might, possibly, embarrass them; for it is almost an unpardonable offense to do any thing, directly or indirectly, to promote a slave's freedom, in a slave state. It is enough to say, of my warm-hearted little play fellows, that they lived on Philpot street, very near Durgin & Bailey's shipyard.

Although slavery was a delicate subject, and very cautiously talked about among grown up people in Maryland, I frequently talked about it— and that very freely—with the white boys. I would, sometimes, say to them, while seated on a curb stone or a cellar door, "I wish I could be free, as you will be when you get to be men." "You will be free, you know, as soon as you are twenty-one, and can go where you like, but I am a slave for life. Have I not as good a right to be free as you have?" Words like these, I observed, always troubled them; and I had no small satisfaction in wringing from the boys, occasionally, that fresh and bitter condemnation of slavery, that springs from nature, unseared and unperverted. Of all consciences, let me have those to deal with which have not been bewildered by the cares of life. I do not remember ever to have met with a *boy*, while I was in slavery, who defended the slave system; but I have often had boys to console me, with the hope that something would yet occur, by which I might be made free. Over and over again, they have told me, that "they believed *I* had as good a right to be free as *they* had"; and that "they did not believe God ever made any one to be a slave." The reader will easily see, that such little conversations with my play fellows, had no tendency to weaken my love of liberty, nor to render me contented with my condition as a slave.

When I was about thirteen years old, and had succeeded in learning to read, every increase of knowledge, especially respecting the FREE STATES, added something to the almost intolerable burden of the thought—"I AM A SLAVE FOR LIFE." To my bondage I saw no end. It was a terrible reality, and I shall never be able to tell how sadly that thought chafed my young spirit. Fortunately, or unfortunately, about this time in my life, I had made enough money to buy what was then a very popular school book, viz: the "Columbian Orator." I bought this addition to my library, of Mr. Knight, on Thames street, Fell's Point, Baltimore, and paid him fifty cents for it. I was first led to buy this book, by hearing some little boys say that they were going to learn some little pieces out of it for the Exhibition. This volume was, indeed, a rich treasure, and every opportunity afforded me, for a time, was spent in diligently perusing it. Among much other interesting matter, that which I had perused and reperused with unflagging satisfaction, was a short dialogue between a master and his slave. The slave is represented as having been recaptured, in a second attempt to run away; and the master opens the dialogue with an upbraiding speech, charging the slave with ingratitude, and demanding to know what he has to say in his own defense. Thus upbraided, and thus called upon to reply, the slave rejoins, that he knows how little anything that he can say will avail, seeing that he is completely in the hands of his owner; and with noble resolution, calmly says, "I submit to my fate." Touched by the slave's answer, the master insists upon his further speaking, and recapitulates the many acts of kindness which he has performed toward the slave, and tells him he is permitted to speak for himself. Thus invited to the debate, the quondam slave made a spirited defense of himself, and thereafter the whole argument, for and against slavery, was brought out. The master was vanquished at every turn in the argument; and seeing himself to be thus vanquished, he generously and meekly emancipates the slave, with his best wishes for his prosperity. It is scarcely necessary to say, that a dialogue, with such an origin, and such an ending—read when the fact of my being a slave was a constant burden of grief—powerfully affected me; and I could not help feeling that the day might come, when the well-directed answers made by the slave to the master, in this instance, would find their counterpart in myself. . . .

I had now penetrated the secret of all slavery and oppression, and had ascertained their true foundation to be in the pride, the power and the avarice of man. The dialogue and the speeches were all redolent of the principles of liberty, and poured floods of light on the nature and character of slavery. . . . Nevertheless, the increase of knowledge was attended with bitter, as well as sweet results. The more I read, the more I was led to abhor and detest slavery, and my enslavers. "Slaveholders," thought I, "are only a band of successful robbers, who left their homes and went into Africa for the purpose of stealing and reducing my people to slavery." I loathed them as the meanest and the most wicked of men. As I read, behold! the very discontent so graphically predicted by Master Hugh, had already come upon me. I was no longer the light-hearted, gleesome boy, full of mirth and play, as when I landed first at Baltimore. Knowledge had come; light had penetrated the moral dungeon where I dwelt; and, behold! there lay the bloody whip, for my back, and here was the iron chain; and my good, *kind master,* he was the author of my situation. The revelation haunted me, stung me, and made me gloomy and miserable. As I writhed under the sting and torment of this knowledge, I almost envied my fellow slaves their stupid contentment. This knowledge opened my eyes to the horrible pit, and revealed the teeth of the frightful dragon that was ready to pounce upon me, but it opened no way for my escape. I have often wished myself a beast, or a bird—anything, rather than a slave. I was wretched and gloomy, beyond my ability to describe. I was too thoughtful to be happy. It was this everlasting thinking which distressed and tormented me; and yet there was no getting rid of the subject of my thoughts. All nature was redolent of it. Once awakened by the silver trump of knowledge, my spirit was roused to eternal wakefulness. Liberty! the inestimable birthright of every man, had, for me, converted every object into an asserter of this great right. It was heard in every sound, and beheld in every object. It was ever present, to torment me with a sense of my wretched condition. The more beautiful and charming were the smiles of nature, the more horrible and desolate was my condition. I saw nothing without seeing it, and I heard nothing without hearing it. I do not exaggerate, when I say, that it looked from every star, smiled in every calm, breathed in every wind, and moved in every storm.

I have no doubt that my state of mind had something to do with the change in the treatment adopted, by my once kind mistress toward me. I can easily believe, that my leaden, downcast, and discontented look, was very offensive to her. Poor lady! She did not know my trouble, and I dared not tell her. Could I have freely made her acquainted with the real state of my mind, and given her the reasons therefor, it might have been well for both of us. Her abuse of me fell upon me like the blows of the false prophet upon his ass; she did not know that an *angel* stood in the way; and—such is the relation of master and slave—I could not tell her. Nature had made us *friends*; slavery made us *enemies*. My interests were in a direction opposite to hers, and we both had our private thoughts and plans. She aimed to keep me ignorant; and I resolved to know, although knowledge only increased my discontent. My feelings were not the result of any marked cruelty in the treatment I received; they sprung from the consideration of my being a slave at all. It was *slavery*—not its mere *incidents*—that I hated. I had been cheated. I saw through the attempt to keep me in ignorance; I saw that slaveholders would have gladly made me believe that they were merely acting under the authority of God, in making a slave of me, and in making slaves of others; and I treated them as robbers and deceivers. The feeding and clothing me well, could not atone for taking my liberty from me. The smiles of my mistress could not remove the deep sorrow that dwelt in my young bosom. Indeed, these, in time, came only to deepen my sorrow. She had changed; and the reader will see that I had changed, too. We were both victims to the same over-shadowing evil—*she*, as mistress, *I*, as slave. I will not censure her harshly; she cannot censure me, for she knows I speak but the truth, and have acted in my opposition to slavery, just as she herself would have acted, in a reverse of circumstances.

Responding to the Selection ——————

Questions for Discussion

1. Why did Douglass's mistress, Mrs. Auld, stop teaching him to read and write? What does this suggest to you about the relationship between enslaved person and slaveholder?

2. Why does Douglass believe that Mrs. Auld is a true Christian? Quote from the text to support your answer.

3. Why do you suppose the young boys who were Douglass's playmates could not defend slavery? What does this tell you about the nature of prejudice and discrimination?

Activities

Writing a Reflective Essay

1. In a **reflective essay,** explain what you think Douglass means when he says, "Nature has done almost nothing to prepare men and women to be either slaves or slaveholders."

Telling the Truth

2. What does the saying "The truth shall set you free" mean to you? In a brief **personal narrative,** write about a time in your life when knowledge opened your eyes and freed you from some burden.

Before You Read

An Address Delivered at the Opening of the Cotton States' Exposition in Atlanta, Georgia, September, 1895

Booker T. Washington
1856–1915

*"You can't hold a man down
without staying down
with him."*

About Washington

Born into slavery only to be emancipated into poverty, Booker T. Washington spent his early years toiling in a salt furnace and a coal mine. He had, however, more ambitious goals for his life. Working as a janitor, Washington put himself through the Hampton Normal and Agricultural Institute in Virginia and later studied at the Wayland Seminary in Washington, D.C. He then joined the staff of the Hampton Institute.

Washington founded a new school for African Americans in Alabama in 1881. The Tuskegee Normal and Industrial Institute (now Tuskegee University), originally housed in two small buildings, with extremely limited resources, was transformed during Washington's thirty-four-year leadership. With an endowment approaching $2 million, the campus had expanded to over 100 buildings, serving nearly 1,500 students.

Throughout his life, Washington preached a philosophy of hard work and economic independence. He strongly believed that African Americans would gain the respect of other races and the benefits of full U.S. citizenship only if they were educated, industrious, and economically secure. Achieving these three goals, Washington reasoned, would lead naturally to civil rights.

By the turn of the century, Washington had become a powerful voice for African Americans. Harvard University and Dartmouth College awarded him honorary degrees, and in 1901 he published his autobiography, *Up from Slavery*, one of a dozen books he wrote during his life.

About the Address

"This was the first time in the history of the South that a Negro had been invited to take part on a program with white Southern people on any important and national occasion." So wrote Washington as he described how he came to deliver one of the opening addresses at the Cotton States' Exposition on September 18, 1895. Southern political leaders had planned this trade exposition in Atlanta to encourage industry and financial investors to bring their business to the South.

A special exhibit was created to show the progress African Americans had made in the thirty-some years since slavery had been abolished. The Negro Building, which had been constructed solely by African Americans, displayed agricultural and industrial products ranging from harnesses to wagons, along with academic papers and other publications.

Washington was invited to speak at the opening ceremony and spent the next month anxiously preparing an address that he was determined would underscore the achievements of his people but would not "give undue offense to the South." The speech was received with enthusiasm by the thousands, black and white, who attended the historic event.

The Atlanta Compromise

Although Booker T. Washington enjoyed the support of many African Americans, he had his critics as well. W. E. B. DuBois, an African American intellectual, dubbed Washington's address to the Cotton States' Exposition the "Atlanta Compromise." DuBois took issue with Washington's emphasis on the development of vocational skills over an immediate struggle for civil rights. Ironically, as Washington's stature grew, African Americans regularly were being denied the right to vote, the right to participate in politics, and the right to be treated equally alongside white Americans. Reality, it seemed, contradicted Washington's philosophy. He experienced the insult of institutionalized racism himself during a visit to the White House in 1901. Numerous protests erupted over what was deemed a "breach of racial etiquette."

An Address Delivered at the Opening of the

Cotton States' Exposition

in Atlanta, Georgia, September, 1895

— Booker T. Washington

Mr. President and Gentlemen of the Board of Directors and Citizens: One-third of the population of the South is of the Negro race. No enterprise seeking the material, civil, or moral welfare of this section can disregard this element of our population and reach the highest success. I but convey to you, Mr. President and Directors, the sentiment of the masses of my race when I say that in no way have the value and manhood of the American Negro been more fittingly and generously recognized than by the managers of this magnificent Exposition at every stage of its progress. It is a recognition that will do more to cement the friendship of the two races than any occurrence since the dawn of freedom.

Not only this, but the opportunity here afforded will awaken among us a new era of industrial progress. Ignorant and inexperienced, it is not strange that in the first years of our new life we began at the top instead of at the bottom; that a seat in Congress or the State Legislature was more sought than real estate or industrial skill; that the political convention or stump speaking had more attractions than starting a dairy farm or truck garden.

A ship lost at sea for many days suddenly sighted a friendly vessel. From the mast of the unfortunate vessel was seen a signal, "Water, water; we die of thirst!" The answer from the friendly vessel at once came back: "Cast down your bucket where you are." A second time the signal, "Water, water; send us water!" ran up from the distressed vessel, and was answered: "Cast down your bucket where you are." The captain of the distressed vessel, at last heeding the injunction, cast down his bucket, and it came up full of fresh, sparkling water from the mouth of the Amazon River. To those of my race who depend upon bettering their condition in a foreign land, or who underestimate the importance of cultivating friendly relations with the Southern white man, who is his next door neighbor, I would say: "Cast down your bucket where you are"—cast it down in making friends in every manly way of the people of all races by whom we are surrounded.

Cast it down in agriculture, mechanics, in commerce, in domestic service, and in the professions. And in this connection it is well to bear in mind that whatever other sins the South may be called to bear, when it comes to business, pure and simple, it is in the South that the Negro is given a man's chance in the commercial world, and in nothing is this Exposition more eloquent than in emphasizing this chance. Our greatest danger is, that in the great leap from slavery to freedom we may overlook the fact that the masses of us are to live by the productions of our hands, and fail to keep in mind that we shall prosper in proportion as we learn to dignify and glorify common labor, and put brains and skill into the common occupation of life; shall prosper in proportion as we learn to draw the line between the superficial and the substantial, the ornamental gewgaws of life and the useful. No race can prosper till it learns that there is as much dignity in tilling a field as in writing a poem. It is at the bottom of life we must begin, and not at the top. Nor should we permit our grievances to overshadow our opportunities.

To those of the white race who look to the incoming of those of foreign birth and strange tongue and habits for the prosperity of the South, were I permitted I would repeat what I say to my own race, "Cast down your bucket where you are." Cast it down among the 8,000,000 Negroes whose habits you know, whose fidelity and love you have tested in days when to have proved treacherous meant the ruin of your firesides. Cast down your bucket among these people who have, without strikes and labor wars, tilled your fields, cleared your forests, built your railroads and cities, and brought forth treasures from the bowels of the earth, and helped make possible this magnificent representation of the progress of the South. Casting down your bucket among my people, helping and encouraging them as you are doing on these grounds, and, with education of head, hand and heart, you will find that they will buy your surplus land, make blossom the waste places in your fields, and run your factories. While doing this, you can be sure in the future, as in the past, that you and your families will be surrounded by the most patient, faithful, law-abiding, and unresentful people that the world has seen. As we have proved our loyalty to you in the past, in nursing your children, watching by the sick bed of your mothers and fathers, and often following them with tear-dimmed eyes to their graves, so in the future, in our humble way, we shall stand by you with a devotion that no foreigner can approach, ready to lay down our lives, if need be, in defense of yours, interlacing our industrial, commercial, civil, and religious life with yours in a way that shall make the interests of both races one. In all things that are purely social we can be as separate as the fingers, yet one as the hand in all things essential to mutual progress.

There is no defense to security for any of us except in the highest intelligence and development of all. If anywhere there are efforts tending to curtail the fullest growth of the Negro, let these efforts be turned into stimulating, encouraging, and making him the most useful and intelligent citizen. Effort or means so invested will pay a thousand per cent interest. These efforts will be twice blessed—blessing him that gives and him that takes.

There is no escape through the law of man or God from the inevitable:

> The laws of changeless justice bind
> Oppressor with oppressed;
> And close as sin and suffering joined
> We march to fate abreast.

Nearly sixteen millions of hands will aid you in pulling the load upwards or they will pull against you the load downwards. We shall constitute one-third and more of the ignorance and crime of the South, or one-third its intelligence and progress; we shall contribute one-third to the business and industrial prosperity of the South, or we shall prove a veritable body of death, stagnating, depressing, retarding every effort to advance the body politic.

Gentlemen of the Exposition, as we present to you our humble effort at an exhibition of our progress, you must not expect overmuch. Starting thirty years ago with ownership here and there in a few quilts and pumpkins and chickens (gathered from miscellaneous sources), remember the path that has led from these to the invention and production of agricultural implements, buggies, steam engines, newspapers, books, statuary, carving, paintings, the management of drug stores and banks has not been trodden without contact with thorns and thistles. While we take pride in what we exhibit as a result of our independent efforts, we do not for a moment forget that our part in this exhibition would fall far short of your expectations but for the constant help that has come to our educational life, not only from the Southern States, but especially from Northern philanthropists, who have made their gifts a constant stream of blessing and encouragement.

The wisest among my race understand that the agitation of questions of social equality is the extremist folly, and that progress in the enjoyment of all the privileges that will come to us must be the result of severe and constant struggle rather than of artificial forcing. No race that has anything to contribute to the markets of the world is long in any degree ostracized. It is important and right that all privileges of the law be ours, but it is vastly more important that we be prepared for the exercise of those privileges. The opportunity to earn a dollar in a factory just now is worth infinitely more than the opportunity to spend a dollar in an opera house.

In conclusion, may I repeat that nothing in thirty years has given us more hope and encouragement, and drawn us so near to you of the white race, as this opportunity offered by the Exposition; and here bending, as it were, over the altar that represents the results of the struggles of your race and mine, both starting practically empty-handed three decades ago, I pledge that, in your effort to work out the great and intricate problem which God has laid at the doors of the South, you shall have at all times the patient, sympathetic help of my race; only let this be constantly in mind that, while from representations in these buildings of the products of field, of forest, of mine, of factory, letters, and art, much good will come, yet far above and beyond material benefits will be the higher good, that let us pray God will come, in a blotting out of sectional differences and racial animosities and suspicions, in a determination to administer absolute justice, in a willing obedience among all classes to the mandates of law. This, coupled with our material prosperity, will bring into our beloved South a new heaven and a new earth.

Responding to the Selection ────────

Questions for Discussion

1. What do you think Washington meant when he said, ". . . in the first years of our new life we began at the top instead of at the bottom"? Does Washington find this understandable? Does he believe it is good for African Americans? Why?

2. Washington tells both the newly emancipated African Americans and the white Southerners to "Cast down your bucket where you are." What is each group to find when they pull their buckets back up? Why might Washington use **repetition** in this way?

3. Discuss possible interpretations of the quotation that precedes Washington's biography.

Activities

Writing Persuasively

1. Washington says, "In all things that are purely social we can be as separate as the fingers, yet one as the hand in all things essential to human progress." Write a **persuasive essay** in which you first explain what Washington means and then describe why you agree or disagree.

Explaining Aphorisms

2. Washington's address is filled with **aphorisms**—brief statements of truth or principle. Choose one that you find especially appealing and write a brief explanation of what it means to you.

Before You Read

Of Mr. Booker T. Washington and Others

W. E. B. DuBois
1868–1963

> "One ever feels his
> twoness—an American,
> a Negro; two souls, two
> thoughts, two unreconciled
> strivings; two warring ideals in
> one dark body, whose dogged
> strength alone keeps it from
> being torn asunder."

About DuBois

W. E. B. DuBois has been called the most significant African American activist and intellectual of the first half of the twentieth century. Born into a middle-class Massachusetts family, DuBois was the first black person to graduate from his high school. He earned degrees from Fisk and Harvard Universities, where he studied the social sciences.

DuBois began teaching in 1897 at Atlanta University and while there wrote investigative research papers on the lives of African Americans. He cofounded the National Association for the Advancement of Colored People (NAACP) in 1909. For twenty-four years, he edited the NAACP's magazine, *The Crisis*.

In 1961 DuBois joined the Communist Party. He died shortly after immigrating to Ghana, in West Africa.

The Talented Tenth

Although DuBois and Booker T. Washington held many similar beliefs, they differed greatly when the subject was education. Washington wanted blacks to receive training in basic industrial skills that he believed would lead to employment, economic independence, and eventual full civil rights.

DuBois believed that higher education was necessary to develop African American leaders. He proposed that the most able ten percent of African Americans—the "Talented Tenth" as he called them—be educated for careers as teachers, ministers, and business professionals so that they could serve as role models for all African Americans.

Of Mr. Booker T. Washington and Others

— *W. E. B. DuBois*

From birth till death enslaved; in word, in deed, unmanned!
. . . .
Hereditary bondsmen! Know ye not
Who would be free themselves must strike the blow?

— BYRON

Easily the most striking thing in the history of the American Negro since 1876 is the ascendancy of Mr. Booker T. Washington. It began at the time when war memories and ideals were rapidly passing; a day of astonishing commercial development was dawning; a sense of doubt and hesitation overtook the freedmen's sons—then it was that his leading began. Mr. Washington came, with a single definite program, at the psychological moment when the nation was a little ashamed of having bestowed so much sentiment on Negroes, and was concentrating its energies on Dollars. His program of industrial education, conciliation of the South, and submission and silence as to civil and political rights, was not wholly original; the Free Negroes from 1830 up to war-time had striven to build industrial schools, and the American Missionary Association had from the first taught various trades; and Price and others had sought a way of honorable alliance with the best of the Southerners. But Mr. Washington first indissolubly linked these things; he put enthusiasm, unlimited energy, and perfect faith into his program, and changed it from a by-path into a veritable Way of Life. And the tale of the methods by which he did this is a fascinating study of human life.

It startled the nation to hear a Negro advocating such a program after many decades of bitter complaint; it startled and won the applause of the South, it interested and won the admiration of the North; and after a confused murmur of protest, it silenced if it did not convert the Negroes themselves.

To gain the sympathy and cooperation of the various elements comprising the white South was Mr. Washington's first task; and this, at the time Tuskegee was founded, seemed, for a black man, well-nigh impossible. And yet ten years later it was done in the word spoken at Atlanta: "In all things purely social we can be as separate as the five fingers, and yet one as the hand in all things essential to mutual progress." This "Atlanta Compromise" is by all odds the most notable thing in Mr. Washington's career. The South interpreted it in different ways: the radicals received it as a complete surrender of the demand for civil and political equality; the conservatives, as a generously conceived working basis for mutual understanding. So both approved it, and to-day its author is certainly the most distinguished Southerner since Jefferson Davis, and the one with the largest personal following.

Next to this achievement comes Mr. Washington's work in gaining place and consideration in the North. Others less shrewd and tactful had formerly essayed to sit on these two stools and had fallen between them; but as Mr. Washington knew the heart of the South from birth and training, so by singular insight he intuitively grasped the spirit of the age which was dominating the North. And so thoroughly did he learn the speech and thought of triumphant commercialism, and the ideals of material prosperity, that the picture of a lone black boy poring over a French grammar amid the weeds and dirt of a neglected home soon seemed to him the acme of absurdities. One wonders what Socrates and St. Frances of Assisi would say to this.

And yet this very singleness of vision and thorough oneness with his age is a mark of the successful man. It is as though Nature must needs make men narrow in order to give them force. So Mr. Washington's cult has gained unquestioning followers, his work has wonderfully prospered, his friends are legion, and his enemies are confounded. To-day he stands as the one recognized spokesman of his ten million fellows, and one of the most notable figures in a nation of seventy millions. One hesitates, therefore, to criticize a life which beginning with so little, has done so much. And yet the time is come when one may speak in all sincerity and utter courtesy of the mistakes and shortcomings of Mr. Washington's career, as well as of his triumphs, without being thought captious or envious, and without forgetting that it is easier to do ill than well in the world.

The criticism that has hitherto met Mr. Washington has not always been of this broad character. In the South especially has he had to walk warily to avoid the harshest judgments—and naturally so, for he is dealing with the one subject of deepest sensitiveness to that section. Twice—once when at the Chicago celebration of the Spanish-American War he alluded to the color-prejudice that is "eating away the vitals of the South," and once when he dined with President Roosevelt—has the resulting Southern criticism been violent enough to threaten seriously his popularity. In the North the feeling has several times forced itself into words, that Mr. Washington's counsels of submission overlooked certain elements of true manhood, and that his educational program was unnecessarily narrow. Usually, however, such criticism has not found open expression, although, too, the spiritual sons of the Abolitionists have not been prepared to acknowledge that the schools founded before Tuskegee, by men of broad ideals and self-sacrificing spirit, were wholly failures or worthy of ridicule. While, then, criticism has not failed to follow Mr. Washington, yet the prevailing public opinion of the land has been but too willing to deliver the solution of a wearisome problem into his hands, and say, "If that is all you and your race ask, take it."

Among his own people, however, Mr. Washington has encountered the strongest and most lasting opposition, amounting at times to bitterness, and even to-day continuing strong and insistent even though largely silenced in outward expression by the public opinion of the nation. Some of this opposition is, of course, mere envy; the disappointment of displaced demagogues and the spite of narrow minds. But aside from this, there is among educated and thoughtful colored men in all parts of the land a feeling of deep regret, sorrow, and apprehension at the wide currency and ascendancy which some of Mr. Washington's theories have gained. These same men admire his sincerity of purpose, and are willing to forgive much to honest endeavor which is doing something worth the doing. They coöperate with Mr. Washington as far as they conscientiously can; and, indeed, it is no ordinary tribute to this man's tact and power that, steering as he must between so many diverse interests and opinions, he so largely retains the respect of all.

But the hushing of the criticism of honest opponents is a dangerous thing. It leads some of the best of the critics to unfortunate silence and paralysis of effort, and others to burst into speech so passionately and intemperately as to lose listeners. Honest and earnest criticism from those whose interests are most nearly touched—criticism of writers by readers, of government by those governed, of leaders by those led—this is the soul of democracy and the safeguard of modern society. If the best of the American Negroes receive by outer pressure a leader whom they had not recognized before, manifestly there is here a certain palpable gain. Yet there is also irreparable loss—a loss of that peculiarly valuable education which a group receives when by search and criticism it finds and commissions its own leaders. The way in which this is done is at once the most elementary and the nicest problem of social growth. History is but the record of such group-leadership; and yet how infinitely changeful is its type and character! And of all types and kinds, what can be more instructive than the leadership of a group within a group?—that curious double movement where real progress may be negative and actual advance be relative retrogression. All this is the social student's inspiration and despair.

Of Mr. Booker T. Washington *and Others*

Now in the past the American Negro has had instructive experience in the choosing of group leaders, founding thus a peculiar dynasty which in the light of present conditions is worth while studying. When sticks and stones and beasts form the sole environment of a people, their attitude is largely one of determined opposition to and conquest of natural forces. But when to earth and brute is added an environment of men and ideas, then the attitude of the imprisoned group may take three main forms—a feeling of revolt and revenge; an attempt to adjust all thought and action to the will of the greater group; or, finally, a determined effort at self-realization and self-development despite environing opinion. The influence of all of these attitudes at various times can be traced to the history of the American Negro, and in the evolution of his successive leaders.

Before 1750, while the fire of African freedom still burned in the veins of the slaves, there was in all leadership or attempted leadership but the one motive of revolt and revenge—typified in the terrible Maroons, the Danish blacks, and Cato of Stono, and veiling all the Americans in fear of insurrection. The liberalizing tendencies of the latter half of the eighteenth century brought, along with kindlier relations between black and white, thoughts of ultimate adjustment and assimilation. Such aspiration was especially voiced in the earnest songs of Phyllis, in the martyrdom of Attucks, the fighting of Salem and Poor, the intellectual accomplishments of Banneker and Derham, and the political demands of the Cuffes.

Stern financial and social stress after the war cooled much of the previous humanitarian ardor. The disappointment and impatience of Negroes at the persistence of slavery and serfdom voiced itself in two movements. The slaves in the South, aroused undoubtedly by vague rumors of the Haytian revolt, made three fierce attempts at insurrection—in 1800 under Gabriel in Virginia, in 1822 under Vesey in Carolina, and in 1831 again in Virginia under the terrible Nat Turner. In the Free States, on the other hand, a new and curious attempt at self-development was made. In Philadelphia and New York color-prescription led to a withdrawal of Negro communicants from white churches and the formation of a peculiar socio-religious institution among the Negroes known as the African Church—an organization still living and controlling in its various branches over a million of men.

Walker's wild appeal against the trend of the times showed how the world was changing after the coming of the cotton-gin. By 1830 slavery seemed hopelessly fastened on the south and the slaves thoroughly cowed into submission. The free Negroes of the North, inspired by the mulatto immigrants from the West Indies, began to change the basis of their demands; they recognized the slavery of slaves, but insisted that they themselves were freemen, and sought assimilation and amalgamation with the nation on the same terms with other men. Thus, Forten and Purvis of Philadelphia, Shad of Wilmington, DuBois of New Haven, Barbadoes of Boston, and others, strove singly and together as men, they said, not as slaves: as "people of color," not as "Negroes." The trend of the times, however, refused them recognition save in individual and exceptional cases, considered them as one with all the despised blacks, and they soon found themselves striving to keep even the rights they formerly had of voting and working and moving as freemen. Schemes of migration and colonization arose among them; but these they refused to entertain, and they eventually turned to the Abolition movement as a final refuge.

Here, led by Remond, Nell, Wells-Brown, and Douglass, a new period of self-assertion and self-development dawned. To be sure, ultimate freedom and assimilation was the ideal before the leaders, but the assertion of the manhood rights of the Negro by himself was the main reliance, and John Brown's raid was the extreme of its logic. After the war and emancipation, the great form of Frederick Douglass, the greatest of American Negro leaders, still led the host. Self-assertion, especially in political lines, was the main program, and behind Douglass came Elliot, Bruce, and Langston, and the Reconstruction politicians, and, less conspicuous but of greater social significance, Alexander Crummell and Bishop Daniel Payne.

Then came the Revolution of 1876, the suppression of the Negro votes, the changing and shifting of ideals, and the seeking of new lights in the great night. Douglass, in his old age, still bravely stood for the ideals of his early manhood—ultimate assimilation *through* self-assertion, and on no other terms. For a time Price arose as a new leader, destined, it seemed, not to give up, but to re-state the old ideals in a form less repugnant to the white South. But he passed away in his prime. Then came the new leader. Nearly all the former ones had become leaders by the silent suffrage of their fellows, had sought to lead their own people alone, and were usually, save Douglass, little known outside their race. But Booker T. Washington arose as essentially the leader not of one race but of two—a compromiser between the South, the North, and the Negro. Naturally the Negroes resented, at first bitterly, signs of compromise which surrendered their civil and political rights, even though this was to be exchanged for larger chances of economic development. The rich and dominating North, however, was not only weary of the race problem, but was investing largely in Southern enterprises, and welcomed any method of peaceful coöperation. Thus, by national opinion, the Negroes began to recognize Mr. Washington's leadership; and the voice of criticism was hushed.

Mr. Washington represents in Negro thought the old attitude of adjustment and submission; but adjustment at such a peculiar time as to make his program unique. This is an age of unusual economic development, and

Of Mr. Booker T. Washington *and Others*

Mr. Washington's program naturally takes an economic cast, becoming a gospel of Work and Money to such an extent as apparently almost completely to overshadow the higher aims of life. Moreover, this is an age when the more advanced races are coming in closer contact with the less developed races, and the race-feeling is therefore intensified; and Mr. Washington's program practically accepts the alleged inferiority of the Negro races. Again, in our own land, the reaction from the sentiment of war times has given impetus to race-prejudice against Negroes, and Mr. Washington withdraws many of the high demands of Negroes as men and American citizens. In other periods of intensified prejudice all the Negro's tendency to self-assertion has been called forth; at this period a policy of submission is advocated. In the history of nearly all other races and peoples the doctrine preached at such crises has been that manly self-respect is worth more than lands and houses, and that a people who voluntarily surrender such respect, or cease striving for it, are not worth civilizing.

In answer to this, it has been claimed that the Negro can survive only through submission. Mr. Washington distinctly asks that black people give up, at least for the present, three things—

1. First, political power,
2. Second, insistence on civil rights,
3. Third, higher education of Negro youth—

and concentrate all their energies on industrial education, and accumulation of wealth, and the conciliation of the South. This policy has been courageously and insistently advocated for over fifteen years, and has been triumphant for perhaps ten years. As a result of this tender of the palm-branch, what has been the return? In these years there have occurred:

The disfranchisement of the Negro.

The legal creation of a distinct status of civil inferiority for the Negro.

The steady withdrawal of aid from institutions for the higher training of the Negro.

These movements are not, to be sure, direct results of Mr. Washington's teachings; but his propaganda has, without a shadow of doubt, helped their speedier accomplishment. The question then comes: Is it possible, and probable, that nine millions of men can make effective progress in economic lines if they are deprived of political rights, made a servile caste, and allowed only the most meagre chance for developing their exceptional men? If history and reason give any distinct answer to these questions, it is an emphatic *No*. And Mr. Washington thus faces the triple paradox of his career:

1. He is striving nobly to make Negro artisans business men and property-owners; but it is utterly impossible, under modern competitive methods, for workingmen and property-owners to defend their rights and exist without the right of suffrage.

Of Mr. Booker T. Washington *and Others*

2. He insists on thrift and self-respect, but at the same time counsels a silent submission of civic inferiority such as is bound to sap the manhood of any race in the long run.

3. He advocates common-school and industrial training, and depreciates institutions of higher learning; but neither the Negro common-schools, nor Tuskegee itself, could remain open a day were it not for teachers training in Negro colleges, or trained by their graduates.

This triple paradox in Mr. Washington's position is the object of criticism by two classes of colored Americans. One class is spiritually descended from Toussaint the Savior, through Gabriel, Vesey, and Turner, and they represent the attitude of revolt and revenge; they hate the white South blindly and distrust the white race generally, and so far as they agree on definite action, think that the Negro's only hope lies in emigration beyond the borders of the United States. And yet, by the irony of fate, nothing has more effectually made this program seem hopeless than the recent course of the United States toward weaker and darker peoples in the West Indies, Hawaii, and the Philippines—for where in the world may we go and be safe from lying and brute force?

The other class of Negroes who cannot agree with Mr. Washington has hitherto said little aloud. They deprecate the sight of scattered counsels, of internal disagreement; and especially they dislike making their just criticism of a useful and earnest man an excuse for a general discharge of venom from small-minded opponents. Nevertheless, the questions involved are so fundamental and serious that it is difficult to see how men like the Grimkes, Kelly Miller, J. W. E. Bowen, and other representatives of this group, can much longer be silent. Such men feel in conscience bound to ask of this nation three things:

1. The right to vote.
2. Civic equality.
3. The education of youth according to ability.

They acknowledge Mr. Washington's invaluable service in counseling patience and courtesy in such demands; they do not ask that ignorant black men vote when ignorant whites are debarred, or that any reasonable restrictions in the suffrage should not be applied; they know that the low social level of the mass of the race is responsible for much discrimination against it, but they also know, and the nation knows, that relentless color-prejudice is more often a cause than a result of the Negro's degradation; they seek the abatement of this relic of barbarism, and not its systematic encouragement and pampering by all agencies of social power from the Associated Press to the Church of Christ. They advocate, with Mr. Washington, a broad system of Negro common schools supplemented by thorough industrial training; but they are surprised that a man of Mr. Washington's insight cannot see that no

Of Mr. Booker T. Washington *and Others*

such educational system ever has rested or can rest on any other basis than
that of the well-equipped college and university, and they insist that there is
a demand for a few such institutions throughout the South to train the best
of the Negro youth as teachers, professional men, and leaders.

This group of men honor Mr. Washington for his attitude of conciliation toward the white South; they accept the "Atlanta Compromise" in its
broadest interpretation; they recognize, with him, many signs of promise,
many men of high purpose and fair judgment, in this section; they know
that no easy task has been laid upon a region already tottering under heavy
burdens. But, nevertheless, they insist that the way to truth and right lies in
straightforward honesty, not in indiscriminate flattery; in praising those of
the South who do well and criticizing uncompromisingly those who do ill;
in taking advantage of the opportunities at hand and urging their fellows to
do the same, but at the same time in remembering that only a firm adherence to their higher ideals and aspirations will ever keep those ideals within
the realm of possibility. They do not expect that the free right to vote, to
enjoy civic rights, and to be educated, will come in a moment; they do not
expect to see the bias and prejudices of years disappear at the blast of a
trumpet; but they are absolutely certain that the way for a people to gain
their reasonable rights is not by voluntarily throwing them away and insisting that they do not want them; that the way for a people to gain respect is
not by continually belittling and ridiculing themselves; that, on the contrary, Negroes must insist continually, in season and out of season, that voting is necessary to modern manhood, that color discrimination is barbarism,
and that black boys need education as well as white boys.

In failing thus to state plainly and unequivocally the legitimate
demands of their people, even at the cost of opposing an honored leader,
the thinking classes of American Negroes would shirk a heavy responsibility—a responsibility to themselves, a responsibility to the struggling
masses, a responsibility to the darker races of men whose future depends
so largely on this American experiment, but especially a responsibility to
this nation—this common Fatherland. It is wrong to encourage a man or
a people in evil-doing; it is wrong to aid and abet a national crime simply
because it is unpopular not to do so. The growing spirit of kindliness and
reconciliation between the North and South after the frightful differences
of a generation ago ought to be a source of deep congratulation to all, and
especially to those whose mistreatment caused the war; but if that reconciliation is to be marked by the industrial slavery and civic death of those
same black men, with permanent legislation into a position of inferiority,
then those black men, if they are really men, are called upon by every
consideration of patriotism and loyalty to oppose such a course by all civilized methods, even though such opposition involves disagreement with

Of Mr. Booker T. Washington *and Others*

Mr. Booker T. Washington. We have no right to sit silently by while the inevitable seeds are sown for a harvest of disaster to our children, black and white.

First, it is the duty of black men to judge the South discriminatingly. The present generation of Southerners are not responsible for the past, and they should not be blindly hated or blamed for it. Furthermore, to no class is the indiscriminate endorsement of the recent course of the South toward Negroes more nauseating than to the best thought of the South. The South is not "solid"; it is a land in the ferment of social change, wherein forces of all kinds are fighting for supremacy; and to praise the ill the South is today perpetrating is just as wrong as to condemn the good. Discriminating and broad-minded criticism is what the South needs— needs it for the sake of her own white sons and daughters, and for the insurance of robust, healthy mental and moral development.

To-day even the attitude of the Southern whites toward the blacks is not, as so many assume, in all cases the same; the ignorant Southerner hates the Negro, the workingmen fear his competition, the money-makers wish to use him as a laborer, some of the educated see a menace in his upward development, while others—usually the sons of the masters—wish to help him to rise. National opinion has enabled this last class to maintain the Negro common schools, and to protect the Negro partially in property, life, and limb. Through the pressure of money-makers, the Negro is in danger of being reduced to semi-slavery, especially in the country districts; the workingmen, and those of the educated who fear the Negro, have united to disfranchise him, and some have urged his deportation; while the passions of the ignorant are easily aroused to lynch and abuse any black man. To praise this intricate whirl of thought and prejudice is non-sense; to inveigh indiscriminately against "the South" is unjust; but to use the same breath in praising Governor Aycock, exposing Senator Morgan, arguing with Mr. Thomas Nelson Page, and denouncing Senator Ben Tillman, is not only sane, but the imperative duty of thinking black men.

It would be unjust to Mr. Washington not to acknowledge that in several instances he has opposed movements in the South which were unjust to the Negro; he sent memorials to the Louisiana and Alabama constitutional conventions, he has spoken against lynching, and in other ways has openly or silently set his influence against sinister schemes and unfortunate happenings. Notwithstanding this, it is equally true to assert that on the whole the distinct impression left by Mr. Washington's propaganda is first, that the South is justified in its present attitude toward the Negro because of the Negro's degradation; secondly, that the prime cause of the Negro's failure to rise more quickly is his wrong education in the past; and, thirdly, that his future rise depends primarily on his own efforts. Each of these propositions is a dangerous half-truth. The supplementary truths must never be lost sight of: first, slavery and race-prejudice are potent if not sufficient causes of the Negro's position, second, industrial and common-school training were necessarily slow in planting because they had to await the black teachers trained by higher institutions—it being extremely doubtful if any essentially different development was possible, and certainly a Tuskegee was unthinkable before 1880; and third, while it is a great truth to say that the Negro must strive and strive mightily to help himself it is equally true that unless his striving be not simply seconded, but rather aroused and encouraged, by the initiative of the richer and wiser environing group, he cannot hope for great success.

In his failure to realize and impress this last point, Mr. Washington is especially to be criticized. His doctrine has tended to make the whites, North and South, shift the burden of the Negro problem to the Negro's shoulders and stand aside as critical and rather pessimistic spectators; when in fact the burden belongs to the nation, and the hands of none of us are clean if we bend not our energies to righting these great wrongs.

The South ought to be led, by candid and honest criticism, to assert her better self and do her full duty to the race she has cruelly wronged and is still wronging. The North—her co-partner in guilt—cannot salve her conscience by plastering it with gold. We cannot settle this problem by diplomacy and suaveness, by "policy" alone. If worse comes to worst, can the moral fiber of this country survive the slow throttling and murder of nine millions of men?

The black men of America have a duty to perform, a duty stern and delicate—a forward movement to oppose a part of the work of their greatest leader. So far as Mr. Washington preaches Thrift, Patience, and Industrial Training for the masses, we must hold up his hands and strive with him, rejoicing in his honors and glorying in the strength of this Joshua called of God and of man to lead the headless host. But so far as Mr. Washington apologizes for injustice, North or South, does not rightly value the privilege and duty of voting, belittles the emasculating effects of caste distinctions, and opposes the higher training and ambition of our brighter minds—so far as he, the South, or the Nation, does this—we must unceasingly and firmly oppose them. By every civilized and peaceful method we must strive for the rights which the world accords to men, clinging unwaveringly to those great words which the sons of the Fathers would fain forget: "We hold these truths to be self-evident: That all men are created equal; that they are endowed by their Creator with certain unalienable rights; that among these are life, liberty, and the pursuit of happiness."

Responding to the Selection

Questions for Discussion

1. How does DuBois feel about Washington's leadership and his program for African Americans? Cite quotations from the essay that support your opinion.

2. According to DuBois, what three things is Washington asking African Americans to give up temporarily? What does DuBois say has resulted from Washington's request?

3. DuBois says that Washington's program for achieving progress for African Americans is marred by a triple paradox. Explain each of the three paradoxes.

4. An **epigraph** is a quotation placed at the beginning of a literary work, which usually highlights a theme in the work. Why might DuBois have chosen the quotation from British Romantic poet Lord Byron as his epigraph?

Activities

Researching Slave Revolts

1. Research one of the three slave rebellions that DuBois mentions and write a **report** explaining who led the rebellion, where and when it occurred, what actually happened during the rebellion, and the rebellion's aftermath.

Defining Liberty

2. DuBois once said, "The cost of liberty is less than the price of repression." In a brief **reflective essay,** explain what these words mean to you.

Before You Read

A Bronzeville Mother Loiters in Mississippi. Meanwhile, a Mississippi Mother Burns Bacon. and The Last Quatrain of the Ballad of Emmett Till

Gwendolyn Brooks
Born 1917

"I am interested in telling my particular truth as I have seen it."

About Brooks

Born in Topeka, Kansas, Gwendolyn Brooks was raised on Chicago's South Side by parents who had little money but who did have high expectations for their children and a deep love of literature.

Brooks had her first poem published at age fourteen and her first book published at twenty-eight. With the publication of her second book, *Annie Allen,* in 1949, she became the first African American poet to win a Pulitzer Prize. Brooks is poet laureate of Illinois and a member of the National Women's Hall of Fame.

Emmett Till

Brooks's and Aimé Césaire's poems (page 79) concern the violent death of Emmett Till, a fourteen-year-old boy from the Bronzeville neighborhood in Chicago, who in 1955 visited relatives in Mississippi. Two days after he dared speak to a white woman in a store, Till was taken from his relatives' home in the middle of the night, allegedly by the store's owner, Roy Bryant, and his brother-in-law, J. W. Milam. Three days later, Till's mutilated body was found in the Tallahatchie River. At his funeral in Chicago, Till's mother, Mamie Bradley, left his casket open to show "all the world . . . what they did to my son."

Till's murder and the trial of Bryant and Milam created a national sensation. Officials in Mississippi promised that justice would be served. Nevertheless, after four days of testimony, the all-white jury took just over one hour to reach a verdict—not guilty. Bryant and Milam went free.

A Bronzeville Mother Loiters in Mississippi. Meanwhile, a Mississippi Mother Burns Bacon.

— *Gwendolyn Brooks*

From the first it had been like a
Ballad. It had the beat inevitable. It had the blood.
A wildness cut up, and tied in little bunches,
Like the four-line stanzas of the ballads she had never quite
5   Understood—the ballads they had set her to, in school.

Herself: the milk-white maid, the "maid mild"
Of the ballad. Pursued
By the Dark Villain. Rescued by the Fine Prince.
The Happiness-Ever-After.
10   That was worth anything.
It was good to be a "maid mild."
That made the breath go fast.

Her bacon burned. She
Hastened to hide it in the step-on can, and
15   Drew more strips from the meat case. The eggs and sour-milk
      biscuits
Did well. She set out a jar
Of her new quince preserve.

. . . But there was a something about the matter of the Dark
   Villain.
He should have been older, perhaps.
20 The hacking down of a villain was more fun to think about
When his menace possessed undisputed breadth, undisputed
      height,
And a harsh kind of vice.
And best of all, when his history was cluttered
With the bones of many eaten knights and princesses.

25 The fun was disturbed, then all but nullified
When the Dark Villain was a blackish child
Of fourteen, with eyes still too young to be dirty,
And a mouth too young to have lost every reminder
Of its infant softness.

30 That boy must have been surprised! For
These were grown-ups. Grown-ups were supposed to be wise.
And the Fine Prince—and that other—so tall, so broad, so
Grown! Perhaps the boy had never guessed
That the trouble with grown-ups was that under the magnificent
      shell of adulthood, just under,
35 Waited the baby full of tantrums.
It occurred to her that there may have been something
Ridiculous in the picture of the Fine Prince
Rushing (rich with the breadth and height and
Mature solidness whose lack, in the Dark Villain, was im-
      pressing her,
40 Confronting her more and more as this first day after the
      trial
And acquittal wore on) rushing
With his heavy companion to hack down (unhorsed)
That little foe.
So much had happened, she could not remember now what
      that foe had done
45 Against her, or if anything had been done.
The one thing in the world that she did know and knew
With terrifying clarity was that her composition
Had disintegrated. That, although the pattern prevailed,
The breaks were everywhere. That she could think
50 Of no thread capable of the necessary
Sew-work.

She made the babies sit in their places at the table.
Then, before calling Him, she hurried
To the mirror with her comb and lipstick. It was necessary
55   To be more beautiful than ever.
The beautiful wife.
For sometimes she fancied he looked at her as though
Measuring her. As if he considered, Had she been worth It?
Had *she* been worth the blood, the cramped cries, the little
        stuttering bravado,
60   The gradual dulling of those Negro eyes,
The sudden, overwhelming *little-boyness* in that barn?
Whatever she might feel or half-feel, the lipstick necessity
        was something apart. He must never conclude
That she had not been worth It.

He sat down, the Fine Prince, and
65   Began buttering a biscuit. He looked at his hands.
He twisted in his chair, he scratched his nose.
He glanced again, almost secretly, at his hands.
More papers were in from the North, he mumbled. More meddling
        headlines.
With their pepper-words, "bestiality," and "barbarism," and
70   "Shocking."
The half-sneers he had mastered for the trial worked across
His sweet and pretty face.

What he'd like to do, he explained, was kill them all.
The time lost. The unwanted fame.
75   Still, it had been fun to show those intruders
A thing or two. To show that snappy-eyed mother,
That sassy, Northern, brown-black—

Nothing could stop Mississippi.
He knew that. Big Fella
80   Knew that.
And, what was so good, Mississippi knew that.
Nothing and nothing could stop Mississippi.
They could send in their petitions, and scar
Their newspapers with bleeding headlines. Their governors
85   Could appeal to Washington . . .

A Bronzeville Mother Loiters in Mississippi.
Meanwhile, a Mississippi Mother Burns Bacon.

"What I want," the older baby said, "is 'lasses on my jam."
Whereupon the younger baby
Picked up the molasses pitcher and threw
The molasses in his brother's face. Instantly
90   The Fine Prince leaned across the table and slapped
The small and smiling criminal.
She did not speak. When the Hand
Came down and away, and she could look at her child,
At her baby-child,
95   She could think only of blood.
Surely her baby's cheek
Had disappeared, and in its place, surely,
Hung a heaviness, a lengthening red, a red that had no end.
She shook her head. It was not true, of course.
100   It was not true at all. The
Child's face was as always, the
Color of the paste in her paste-jar.

She left the table, to the tune of the children's lamentations,
    which were shriller
Than ever. She
105   Looked out of a window. She said not a word. *That*
Was one of the new Somethings—
The fear,
Tying her as with iron.

Suddenly she felt his hands upon her. He had followed her
110   To the window. The children were whimpering now.
Such bits of tots. And she, their mother,
Could not protect them. She looked at her shoulders, still
Gripped in the claim of his hands. She tried, but could not
    resist the idea
That a red ooze was seeping, spreading darkly, thickly, slowly,
115   Over her white shoulders, her own shoulders,
And over all of Earth and Mars.

He whispered something to her, did the Fine Prince, something
About love, something about love and night and intention.
She heard no hoof-beat of the horse and saw no flash of the
    shining steel.

A Bronzeville Mother Loiters in Mississippi.
Meanwhile, a Mississippi Mother Burns Bacon.

120   He pulled her face around to meet
His, and there it was, close close,
For the first time in all those days and nights.
His mouth, wet and red,
So very, very, very red,
125   Closed over hers.

Then a sickness heaved within her. The courtroom Coca-Cola,
The courtroom beer and hate and sweat and drone,
Pushed like a wall against her. She wanted to bear it.
But his mouth would not go away and neither would the
130   Decapitated exclamation points in that Other Woman's eyes.

She did not scream.
She stood there.
But a hatred for him burst into glorious flower,
And its perfume enclasped them—big,
135   Bigger than all magnolias.

The last bleak news of the ballad.
The rest of the rugged music.
The last quatrain.

The Last Quatrain of the Ballad of Emmett Till

— *Gwendolyn Brooks*

after the murder,
after the burial

Emmett's mother is a pretty-faced thing;
      the tint of pulled taffy.
5   She sits in a red room,
      drinking black coffee.
She kisses her killed boy.
      And she is sorry.
Chaos in windy grays
10   through a red prairie.

Responding to the Selection

Questions for Discussion

1. In telling the story of Emmett Till, Brooks takes an unusual approach. What is that approach, and why is it unusual?

2. Who are the "maid mild," the "Fine Prince," and the "Dark Villain" in the first poem? To what is Brooks comparing these people and their situation?

3. Why does the Mississippi mother find it "necessary / To be more beautiful than ever"?

4. Describe what you think the Mississippi mother is experiencing emotionally.

5. Why do you think Brooks makes a point of using so many color descriptions in "The Last Quatrain of the Ballad of Emmett Till"?

6. Consider the differences in length and details between the two poems. Do you think "The Last Quatrain of the Ballad of Emmett Till" is as powerful as the first poem? Why or why not?

Activity

Writing About Ballads

In "A Bronzeville Mother," the Mississippi mother compares her experience to the **ballads** she read in school. Research what a ballad is and write an **expository essay** explaining how her story is like a ballad and how it is not. Discuss how "The Last Quatrain of the Ballad of Emmett Till" functions as part of the ballad.

Before You Read

State of the Union

Aimé Césaire
Born 1913

"It is no use painting the foot of the tree white, the strength of the bark cries out from beneath the paint."

About Césaire

Born in Martinique and educated in Paris, black poet, playwright, and politician Aimé Césaire played an important role in shaping the voice and themes of the literature written by French-speaking Africans. He cofounded the Négritude movement, which stressed the need for Africans to embrace the culture of their ancestors. He found expression in a surrealistic writing style, which lends an almost dreamlike intensity to his work.

Césaire was an active foe of French colonialism and saw politics as a way to compromise the system. In 1945 he became the mayor of Fort-de-France, the capital of Martinique, and later represented Martinique as a deputy in the French National Assembly. Césaire used his poetry and plays to vent his anger at colonialism and its supporters. He later abandoned Négritude in favor of black militancy, a position that was woven into the political tragedies he wrote during the 1960s.

State of the Union

— *Aimé Césaire*
Translated by Denis Kelly

Gentlemen,

the situation is tragic;
beneath our soil we have left
only 75 years of iron
5   only 50 years of cobalt;

but what of the
55 years of sulfur,
20 years of bauxite
in the heart?

10   nothing   zero,
mine without vein,
cave where no man moves,
not a drop left
of blood.

15   EMMET TILL,
your eyes were a conch where the bottle
of wine of your fifteen-year-old blood
bubbled,
never had any age, these young men,
20   or it weighed them down
more than skyscrapers,
five hundred years
             of torturers

                              of burners of witches
25   five hundred years

                              of bad gin
                              of big cigars
                              of fat bellies
                              filled with slices
30   of rancid bibles
     five hundred years

                              of mouths
                              of old women
                              bitter with sins
35   They've had five hundred years, EMMET TILL,
     five hundred years is the ageless age of the gallows of Cain.
     EMMET TILL I tell you
                              in the heart zero
                              not a drop left
40   of blood;

     and your heart,
     let it conceal my sun,
     let it mix with my bread.

     Boy from Chicago,
45   are you still worth
     as much as a white man?

     Spring, he believed in you,
     yes even on the levee of night,
     on the dikes of the MISSISSIPPI,
50   sweeping between high banks
     of racial hate its jails its barricades
     its tides of tombstones
     in spring, whose sounds flow
     in eyes of riverboats, the portholes.
55   In spring whistling stampedes
     on savannas of blood.
     In spring slipping its gloves from delicate hands
     in explosions of shells and silica
     which loosen the blood-clots of fear,
60   dissolve the blood-clots of hate,
     swelling with age in the thread of rivers of blood,
     rafting the hazardous rubric of beasts in ambush

But They
were invulnerable slow mounted massive
65 on sinister immemorial billygoats
BOY FROM CHICAGO
gone in the stuttering of racial winds
hear him in the blue grove of the veins
sing like the blood-bird
70 foretell above the banks of sleep
his climbing in the blue field grappling
Sun your furtive step vehement fish

Then night remembered in its arms,
soft flight of the vampire gliding suddenly
75 and the pistol of BIG MILLAM
wrote these words on a black living wall
in rusty letters wrote
State of the Union Message
zinc 20 years
80 copper 15 years
oil 15 years
and in the 180th year of these states
but what in the heart unfeeling clock
nothing zero what not a drop of blood
85 left in the putrid white and
antiseptic heart?

Responding to the Selection

Questions for Discussion

1. The beginning and the ending of Césaire's poem include a recitation of ores within the earth and how long each natural resource will last. What do these lines mean to you in the context of the poem as a whole? In what ways is the situation "tragic"?

2. What do you think the speaker means by references to "five hundred years / of torturers / of burners of witches . . . / of bad gin . . . / of mouths / of old women . . ."? What is the significance of "five hundred years"?

3. How would you characterize the **tone** of Brooks's and Césaire's poems?

4. What is the significance of blood in each poem?

5. From what cultural perspective is each poet writing? How do you think these two perspectives are alike?

Activities

Exploring Words About a Tragedy

1. In 1963 popular folk balladeer Bob Dylan recorded his song "The Death of Emmett Till." Search the Internet for the lyrics to Dylan's song. Locate a recording of the song and listen to it with your classmates. Then explore the ways in which Dylan's song compares with Césaire's and Brooks's poems.

Creating an Illustrated Report

2. Research the murder of Emmett Till and the subsequent trial. Use the Internet and print resources to find primary source documents—newspaper articles, editorials, and photographs, for example—and create an **illustrated report** about these events.

Focus on . . .
The Struggle for Civil Rights

Civil Rights marchers on highway, Brandon, Mississippi. May 27, 1965.

During the post–Civil War period, the Constitution was amended to ensure equality for all Americans. The Thirteenth Amendment (1865) outlawed slavery, the Fourteenth Amendment (1868) declared that all people born in the United States were citizens and were guaranteed equal protection under the law, and the Fifteenth Amendment (1870) stated that everyone was entitled to vote regardless of race. But these amendments did not alter the reality of being black in America—emancipation was not freedom, social justice could not be legislated, and the real struggle for dignity and equality was just beginning.

Jim Crow stalked the South. "Jim Crow" was the name for a body of laws that kept blacks segregated from whites. African Americans couldn't share taxi rides with whites, and they had to enter buildings through separate entrances, attend separate schools, drink from separate water fountains, and use separate restrooms.

Eventually, these laws and the injustices they mandated sparked protests. On December 1, 1955, Mrs. Rosa Parks boarded a bus in Montgomery, Alabama. She took a seat in the first row of the black section. As the bus filled with whites, the driver ordered her to move further back. Mrs. Parks refused and was arrested. This simple act of civil disobedience ignited a black boycott of the Montgomery bus system. For over a year, blacks and sympathetic whites refused to ride the buses. The Montgomery bus company suffered serious financial losses. In November 1956, the U.S. Supreme Court ruled that segregation on public transportation was unconstitutional. The boycott had been a success and was called off.

Many who struggled for justice and equality paid the ultimate price. In March 1965, on a freedom march from Selma to Montgomery, Alabama, the police savagely beat and teargassed the marchers, set vicious dogs upon them, and blasted them with high-pressure fire hoses. An especially horrific act of violence took place on Sunday, September 15, 1963, when members of the Ku Klux Klan bombed the Sixteenth Street Baptist Church in Birmingham, Alabama. Four young African American girls were killed in

the explosion. Much of the nation was shaken and disgusted by this act of cowardice and hate. Before the struggle was over, its leader, Martin Luther King Jr., would also give his life for the cause.

They did not die in vain. A nation's conscience had been moved by the struggle, and legislation was passed to guarantee equal rights. President Lyndon Johnson worked with Civil Rights leaders and Congress to craft the Civil Rights Act of 1964 and the Voting Rights Act of 1965. The struggle was not over, but critical battles had been fought and won.

The March on Washington, August 1963

Rosa Parks

Linking to . . .
• Keep this information about the Civil Rights movement in mind as you read the following selections.

Before You Read

Freedom Songs

If you miss me at the back of
  the bus,
And you can't find me
  nowhere,
Come on up to the front of
  the bus,
I'll be riding up there.

If you miss me in the cotton
  field,
And you can't find me
  nowhere,
Come on down to the
  courthouse,
I'll be voting right there.

> — from the song "If You Miss Me
> at the Back of the Bus"

About Freedom Songs

Music played an important role in the Civil Rights movement. Activists sang "freedom songs" to inspire themselves, to create a sense of community, and to let segregationists know, with music rather than violence, that African American demands for human dignity and social justice were not negotiable. Songs like "We Shall Overcome" and "We Shall Not Be Moved" helped to set the moral tone for the movement and gave followers a common vocabulary with which to sway popular opinion.

Freedom songs were not a product of the Civil Rights movement. African Americans had been singing such songs for well over a century. At first, the songs were mostly religious in content, focusing on salvation, the freedom from sin. Throughout the 1900s, however, lyrics to the songs were often changed to reflect current events. For example, "Keep Your Hand on the Plow" includes biblical references to Jesus and his mother, Mary, as well as to the early Christians, Paul, Silas, and Peter.

Years later, the lyrics were changed, and the song "Keep Your Eyes on the Prize" became one of the many anthems of hope that helped fuel the Civil Rights movement.

Keep Your Hand on the Plow

Mary wo' three links of chain,
Ev'ry link was Jesus' name.
Keep your hand on the plow,
Hold on.

CHORUS
5 Hold on, hold on,
Keep your hand on the plow,
Hold on.

Paul and Silas bound in jail,
Had nobody for to go their bail,
10 Keep your hand on the plow,
Hold on.

Paul and Silas began to shout,
Jail doors opened and they walked out . . .

Peter was so nice and neat,
15 Wouldn't let Jesus wash his feet . . .

Jesus said, "If I wash them not,
You'll have no father in this lot" . . .

Peter got anxious and he said,
"Wash my feet, my hands and head," . . .

20 Got my hand on the gospel plow,
Wouldn't take nothin' for my journey now, . . .

Keep Your Eyes on the Prize

Paul and Silas, bound in jail,
Had no money for to go their bail,
Keep your eyes on the prize, hold on, hold on.

CHORUS
Hold on, hold on,
5   Keep your eyes on the prize,
Hold on, hold on.

Paul and Silas begin to shout,
The jail door opened and they walked out,
Keep your eyes on the prize, hold on.

10   Freedom's name is mighty sweet,
Black and white are gonna meet.

Got my hand on the Gospel plow,
I wouldn't take nothin' for my journey now.

The only chain that a man can stand,
15   Is that chain of hand in hand.

The only thing that we did wrong,
Stayed in the wilderness a day too long.

But the one thing we did right,
Was the day we started to fight.

20   We're gonna board that big Greyhound,
Carryin' love from town to town.

88 Traditional

We're gonna ride for civil rights,
We're gonna ride both black and white.

We've met jail and violence too,
25   But God's love has seen us through.

Haven't been to heaven but I've been told,
Streets up there are paved with gold.

Albenny Georgia lives in race
We're goin' to fight it from place to place

30   I know what I think is right
Freedom in the souls of black and white

Singing and shouting is very well
Get off your seat and go to jail

Jordan River is deep and wide
35   We'll find freedom on the other side.

Responding to the Selection ———————

Questions for Discussion

1. What is the meaning of the repeated lyric "Keep your hand on the plow, / Hold on"?

2. How do "Keep your hand on the plow" and "Keep your eyes on the prize" differ in meaning?

3. Which verses in the Civil Rights version of the song suggest that the time for waiting is over and the time for action is now? Which verse suggests that it is time to move beyond singing?

Activities

Writing About Freedom

1. The verse "We're gonna board that big Greyhound, / Carryin' love from town to town" is a reference to the Freedom Riders. Who were they? What was their role in the Civil Rights movement? How were they treated by the people whose towns they rode into? Write a brief **report** that tells the story of the Freedom Riders.

Singing About Freedom

2. Use the Internet to research other freedom songs that were popular during the Civil Rights movement. Were they based on traditional songs? Were lyrics changed to reflect the struggle? If possible, listen to recordings of the songs. Discuss with your classmates the emotional impact these songs have on you.

Researching the References

3. Deepen your understanding of the meaning of these songs by researching the biblical references. What is the significance of Paul and Silas's imprisonment (Acts 16:16–40) and of Peter's refusal to let Jesus wash his feet (John 13:3–20)? Write an **expository essay** comparing and contrasting the meaning of the Paul and Silas references in the two versions of the song.

Before You Read

from *Stride Toward Freedom*

Martin Luther King Jr.
1929–1968

"Do your work so well that no one could do it better. Do it so well that all the hosts of heaven and earth will have to say: Here lived a man who did his job as if God Almighty called him at this particular time in history to do it."

About King

These words were King's advice to others, but they also describe King himself and his role in the Civil Rights movement.

Martin Luther King Jr., the son of a minister in Atlanta, Georgia, entered college at the age of fifteen. After receiving a Ph.D. in theology, he became a Baptist minister in Montgomery, Alabama. Shortly thereafter, in 1955, the first major nonviolent protest of the Civil Rights movement took place. Sparked by Rosa Parks's refusal to give up her seat to a white passenger, Montgomery's fifty thousand black citizens boycotted the city's buses for more than a year. The boycott was successful, and King's outstanding leadership and speaking skills drew national attention.

When the center of the Civil Rights struggle shifted to Birmingham, Alabama, King was there. He was jailed, and violence exploded in the streets. King, however, remained true to his belief in nonviolence. "We will go on," he told his supporters, "because we have started a fire in Birmingham that water cannot put out. We are going on because we love Birmingham and we love democracy. And we are going to remain nonviolent."

One of the enduring triumphs of the movement was the March on Washington in 1963. King delivered his "I Have a Dream" speech to about 250,000 people. One year later, he became the youngest person to win the Nobel Peace Prize.

Despite his commitment to nonviolence, King was the target of numerous threats and actual violence. In 1968, at the age of thirty-nine, King was assassinated in Memphis, Tennessee.

from

Stride
Toward
Freedom

— *Martin Luther King Jr.*

. . . Oppressed people deal with their oppression in three characteristic ways. One way is acquiescence: the oppressed resign themselves to their doom. They tacitly adjust themselves to oppression, and thereby become conditioned to it. In every movement toward freedom some of the oppressed prefer to remain oppressed. Almost 2,800 years ago Moses set out to lead the children of Israel from the slavery of Egypt to the freedom of the promised land. He soon discovered that slaves do not always welcome their deliverers. They become accustomed to being slaves. They would rather bear those ills they have, as Shakespeare pointed out, than flee to others that they know not of. They prefer the "fleshpots of Egypt" to the ordeals of emancipation.

There is such a thing as the freedom of exhaustion. Some people are so worn down by the yoke of oppression that they give up. A few years ago in the slum areas of Atlanta, a Negro guitarist used to sing almost daily: "Ben down so long that down don't bother me." This is the type of negative freedom and resignation that often engulfs the life of the oppressed.

But this is not the way out. To accept passively an unjust system is to cooperate with that system; thereby the oppressed become as evil as the oppressor. Noncooperation with evil is as much a moral obligation as is cooperation with good. The oppressed must never allow the conscience of the oppressor to slumber. Religion reminds every man that he is his brother's keeper. To accept injustice or segregation passively is to say to the oppressor that his actions are morally right. It is a way of allowing his conscience to fall asleep. At this moment the oppressed fails to be his brother's keeper. So acquiescence—while often the easier way—is not the moral way. It is the way of the coward. The Negro cannot win the respect of his oppressor by acquiescing; he merely increases the oppressor's arrogance and contempt. Acquiescence is interpreted as proof of the Negro's inferiority. The Negro cannot win the respect of the white people of the South or the peoples of the world if he is willing to sell the future of his children for his personal and immediate comfort and safety.

A second way that oppressed people sometimes deal with oppression is to resort to physical violence and corroding hatred. Violence often brings about momentary results. Nations have frequently won their independence in battle. But in spite of temporary victories, violence never brings permanent peace. It solves no social problem; it merely creates new and more complicated ones.

Violence as a way of achieving racial justice is both impractical and immoral. It is impractical because it is a descending spiral ending in destruction for all. The old law of an eye for an eye leaves everybody blind. It is immoral because it seeks to humiliate the opponent rather than win his understanding; it seeks to annihilate rather than to convert. Violence is immoral because it thrives on hatred rather than love. It destroys community and makes brotherhood impossible. It leaves society in monologue rather than dialogue. Violence ends by defeating itself. It creates bitterness in the survivors and brutality in the destroyers. A voice echoes through time saying to every potential Peter, "Put up your sword." History is cluttered with the wreckage of nations that failed to follow this command.

If the American Negro and other victims of oppression succumb to the temptation of using violence in the struggle for freedom, future generations will be the recipients of a desolate night of bitterness, and our chief legacy to them will be an endless reign of meaningless chaos. Violence is not the way.

The third way open to oppressed people in their quest for freedom is the way of nonviolent resistance. Like the synthesis in Hegelian philosophy, the principle of nonviolent resistance seeks to reconcile the truths of two opposites—acquiescence and violence—while avoiding the extremes and immoralities of both. The nonviolent resister agrees with the person who acquiesces that one should not be physically aggressive toward his opponent; but he balances the equation by agreeing with the person of violence that evil must be resisted. He avoids the nonresistance of the former and the violent resistance of the latter. With nonviolent resistance, no individual or group need submit to any wrong, nor need anyone resort to violence in order to right a wrong.

It seems to me that this is the method that must guide the actions of the Negro in the present crisis in race relations. Through nonviolent resistance the Negro will be able to rise to the noble height of opposing the unjust system while loving the perpetrators of the system. The Negro must work passionately and unrelentingly for full stature as a citizen, but he must not use inferior methods to gain it. He must never come to terms with falsehood, malice, hate, or destruction.

Nonviolent resistance makes it possible for the Negro to remain in the South and struggle for his rights. The Negro's problem will not be solved by running away. He cannot listen to the glib suggestion of those who would urge him to migrate en masse to other sections of the country. By grasping his great opportunity in the South he can make a lasting contribution to the moral strength of the nation and set a sublime example of courage for generations yet unborn.

By nonviolent resistance, the Negro can also enlist all men of good will in his struggle for equality. The problem is not a purely racial one, with Negroes set against whites. In the end, it is not a struggle between people at all, but a tension between justice and injustice. Nonviolent resistance is not aimed against oppressors but against oppression. Under its banner consciences, not racial groups, are enlisted.

If the Negro is to achieve the goal of integration, he must organize himself into a militant and nonviolent mass movement. All three elements are indispensable. The movement for equality and justice can only be a success if it has both a mass and militant character; the barriers to be overcome require both. Nonviolence is an imperative in order to bring about ultimate community.

A mass movement of a militant quality that is not at the same time committed to nonviolence tends to generate conflict, which in turn breeds anarchy. The support of the participants and the sympathy of the uncommitted are both inhibited by the threat that bloodshed will engulf the community. This reaction in turn encourages the opposition to threaten and resort to force. When, however, the mass movement repudiates violence while moving resolutely toward its goal, its opponents are revealed as the instigators and practitioners of violence if it occurs. Then public support is magnetically attracted to the advocates of nonviolence, while those who employ violence are literally disarmed by overwhelming sentiment against their stand.

Responding to the Selection

Questions for Discussion

1. Explain the three ways that King believes oppressed people respond to their oppression. What does he say about each type of response?

2. What do you think King means by "the freedom of exhaustion"?

3. Discuss the concept of nonviolent resistance. What is it? How does it work?

Activities

Reporting on Nonviolence

1. Both Mahatma Gandhi and Nelson Mandela also led struggles for freedom based on the principles of nonviolent resistance. Choose one of these two leaders and investigate the movement he led. Write a **report** that discusses the person, the movement, and the role played by nonviolent resistance. Also, write about his relationship to King. Did he influence King or was he influenced by him?

Speaking of Peace

2. Look for essays and speeches by, and interviews with, Mahatma Gandhi, Martin Luther King Jr., and Nelson Mandela. Compile a list of quotations that you find especially moving or revealing about these men and their beliefs. Share them with your classmates and use them to put together a booklet titled "Freedom and the Path of Nonviolent Resistance."

Connecting to the Civil Rights Movement

"Will the Circle Be Unbroken?"

Integrating schools during the 1950s and 1960s drew national attention and caused tension and problems in many towns across the country. In September, 1957, African American students attending Little Rock Central High in Little Rock, Arkansas, had to be escorted to an army station wagon in order to avoid an angry demonstration and get home safely.

NARRATOR: While demonstrations and boycotts proved effective in desegregating public facilities, schools were a different matter. In Columbia [South Carolina], a small group of parents began to organize.

BENJAMIN GLOVER: When the Supreme Court declared that the "separate" system was not the type of thing to be, we said that we were going to send our children to integrate the school.

BEATRICE MCKNIGHT: We had a meeting with the parents to discuss what our plans were. Uh, we first wanted to know who was interested in enrolling their children or their child into an all-white school.

HATTIE FRUSTER: We got together through the United Citizens Committee and decided that we were going to enroll our children in Richmond District No. 1 come

August 31. So we got petitions, I think it was 45 students all together was supposed to start the school that Monday morning. But by that Sunday afternoon, twenty-something dropped out because the parents was afraid. They said [they] didn't want to use their children for sacrificial lambs. So that by that Monday morning, we had 22 children to enroll in all-white schools, in which I had five school aged children at that time.

OLIVER WASHINGTON SR.: So I had a lot of white friends who had children at Drear High School. They brought me the message back on the job saying that your son registered at Drear High School, said, "But the teachers in Drear High School say you can send him there but they not going to teach him nothin." The teachers just kinda ignored him. Wouldn't, you know, wouldn't try to teach him nothin. He just was in the class. Wasn't teaching him anything. That's some of the teachers, now.

HATTIE FRUSTER: It was important to me because I felt that my children should get a quality education, 'cause I had to pay the same amount of taxes a white person was paying. And to bus my children 10 or 15 miles away to school when you have school right in walking distance, it was out of time with the tunes.

BEATRICE MCKNIGHT: We did integrate. But, at the same time, we're seeing now that the schools are almost back to the same place they were before integration.

NARRATOR: Private academies were created to separate black and white. Even within the public schools, systems were created that effectively maintained segregation.

BENJAMIN GLOVER: There's segregation of the rankest type existing, because in most of your schools now, they have what they call 'special education classes.' If a little black child is just, doesn't behave like the little affluent child that came out of some other area, he's sent to a special education class. There's no way anybody could make me believe that 85% of all the children in special classes would have to be black children.

NOBLE COOPER: We still have the very same problems that we had forty years ago. But it amazes me how they can't see that South Carolina can never be any better than its worst citizen. If I were to disregard one-third of my patients or throw away the money that they give to me, I wouldn't make it. The same thing with South Carolina.

Questions for Discussion
1. Imagine you were one of the twenty-two African American children enrolled in an all-white school. How would you feel about being a "sacrificial lamb"? What thoughts might enter your mind on the day before school starts?
2. Beatrice McKnight said schools in South Carolina are almost the same as they were before integration. How could something like this happen again?

Before You Read

from *Freedom's Children*

Sheyann Webb
Born 1956

> *"My feets and legs be tired,*
> *but my soul still feels like*
> *marchin'."*

About Webb

Sheyann Webb, born in Selma, Alabama, was the youngest girl of eight children. When she was eight years old, her curiosity led her to Civil Rights meetings being held at a church in her neighborhood. There, she met Martin Luther King Jr. and was introduced to the goals of the Civil Rights movement. Despite her parents' fear, and over their objections, Webb continued to attend meetings and soon joined the marchers as they protested racial segregation. She marched to the Edmund Pettus Bridge on Bloody Sunday, a defining moment in the movement, when marchers were beaten, teargassed, attacked by police dogs, and blasted by fire hoses. She shares her story in the following narrative.

Selma, Alabama, in 1962

In 1962 Alabama, like many southern states, vigorously enforced harsh segregation policies. African Americans were denied the right to vote and the right to equal employment and pay. They could be denied service in restaurants or hotels. They had to sit in "Colored" waiting rooms in train stations, drink from "Colored" water fountains, and use "Colored" bathrooms. Their children attended substandard schools and were taught to defer to demands of white people. Any African American who defied these policies risked arrest or even physical violence. If the "offense" was considered grievous enough, lynching by an angry mob of whites was still not uncommon.

from Freedom's Children

— *Sheyann Webb*

I am the seventh child of eight, and I'm the baby girl. We were very poor, living in the George Washington Carver homes.

My house was right behind the Brown Chapel AME Church. The civil rights movement in Selma really began at this church. I had to pass it to go to school, and this is where I played most of the time. I remember this particular morning, on my way to school, seeing something that was different. A lot of blacks and whites mingling together. That was unusual to me. I used to see black people sitting together, and whites where they were supposed to be. I had never seen them in a friendly or social environment where they were actually communicating.

As I began to cross the street, I was still watching and wondering what was going on. I looked back and saw them as they began to go into the church. I was so wondering about that, I decided I'd cross back over and follow behind them. I didn't think about what might happen if I was late to school. It didn't even cross my mind. I went into church and sat in the last pew in the back. I began to listen to what the people were saying on the pulpit. I remember Hosea Williams being the presiding officer that day. He began to talk about blacks in Selma not being registered voters. He talked about the numbers, how many blacks weren't registered. He talked about Dr. Martin Luther King. I didn't know anything about any of these things, but it was something that seemed exciting. It was like something was about to happen.

Finally I left and went on to school. When I got there, I realized I might be punished. I was very afraid to go into my classroom. I stood outside, and my teacher saw me peeking in. She told me to come in and she asked me in front of the classroom where I had been. I began to try to whisper to her and explain. The more I talked to her about what I saw and what I had heard, it became more interesting to her. I realized later on why. It was because at that time teachers weren't even registered. It was a time when nothing was happening in Selma in terms of the struggle.

As I talked she began to ask me question after question. Most questions I couldn't even answer. She told me they would have to contact my parents. And then she said I had no business being over there in that mess. As the day went on, I could see her whispering to other teachers about what I had told her.

When I got home that afternoon, of course they had talked with my mom and dad. All I could think about was being whipped. Then I began to see how inquisitive they were as they talked to me about what was going on. It made my parents nervous not only for me, but about what was about to happen in Selma. They were fearing something. This made it even more interesting to me.

I wanted to know about voting. I didn't know what that was about. And then I wanted to know who was this man Dr. Martin Luther King. Once Hosea Williams talked about him coming to Selma, you could tell in his expression and the way the people were applauding that he had to be somebody great. My parents knew of his name, but it was like I shouldn't know him or want to know him. This made me even more inquisitive. I was told to stay away from around there. I had no business being there.

Rachel, who was my best friend, lived right next door. After I saw I wasn't going to get a whipping, I was anxious to tell her about what happened. We talked, and I told her I was going back out there.

One day we were playing out in front of the church, and we saw some pretty cars drive up. In the sixties in our housing area, we didn't see many big cars ride through there like that. It caught our attention. We saw these black men get out of the cars, all dressed neat. And we saw them as they huddled and were talking among themselves. We went a little closer, and when we got near them, there was this man who spoke to us and asked us our names. We told him, and he told us his. That was Dr. King. I said to Rachel, "This is the man that they were talking about!" So we followed them all into the church.

There was this other man who said to us, "You all can go on now." Dr. King immediately told him, "No, let them stay. There's nothing we can do to harm them." So we went on inside and sat there.

Then before they got ready to leave, Dr. King came to us again and told us that he wanted to see us when he came back. This was exciting to us, especially to me, because this was the man Hosea Williams had been talking about. Just the idea that he had the patience. He didn't throw us aside, or anything. He gave us the attention.

I didn't start learning what freedom meant until later on. We went home and told our parents that we met Dr. Martin Luther King, and that they were talking about a mass meeting, whatever that was. It was going to be at Brown Chapel Church, and I wanted to be there.

It started off with Rachel and me going to mass meetings. We'd sit in the front row and sing. The first song we learned was "Ain't Gonna Let Nobody Turn Me 'Round." That song itself told me a lot about what freedom was. It naturally meant there was going to be a struggle for rights that were owed to the black race.

The more mass meetings I attended, the more I began to learn. The words equality and justice were mentioned so much. I put all the pieces together just with those words. I may not have understood it well, but I understood enough.

It was so visible with us being there as children, that they started asking us to come up and lead freedom songs. When Dr. Martin Luther King had first come to one of the mass meetings, we were sitting in the front row. We had already led a few freedom songs, and we inched up to the pulpit and sat on his lap. He remembered us, and every time he would come, we would go up there and sit on his lap. We looked forward to him being there. It was just a thrill. The more we saw him come, the more mass meetings I attended. I became a very disobedient child. That's how deep I got into it.

Teachers were afraid for a long time because they would definitely lose their jobs if they had got involved in any way. They would call on me sometimes just to ask me what was going on. It was a great day when I saw all of the teachers marching together. That was a beautiful day.

Before then I only recall one teacher that stood out among all of them. Her name was Margaret Moore. After I had made my own decision that I was going to do it anyway, even though my parents said not to, this is the lady I would look to, Margaret Moore. On the demonstrations I would always go with her. I felt I was safe then. She was not my teacher. She was a teacher at another school.

I remember the first march I went on very well. I had gone to a mass meeting, and they were talking about marching to the Dallas County courthouse. It was a march about blacks getting registered to vote, and you had to register at the courthouse. I wasn't sure that I really wanted to go because it just wasn't clear what could happen. But I also wanted to be there. As I got ready for school, this was on my mind. I stopped at the church.

After I had gotten there and they began to prepare to march, I got with Margaret Moore. It was exciting to me, seeing all the people walking. We sang as we marched. Looking at the hostility, now that was a little frightening. You could see it and feel it as you walked. You know, whites standing at the side and looking and saying nasty things. I remember the policemen having their billy clubs. On this one march we went to a certain point, and we prayed and then turned back around.

With my family, it was always that fear factor. This lasted a long time. Everything that I saw and everything that I really wanted to talk about was almost being pushed aside. I recall one time as I really began to grow into the movement, coming and talking to my mom about what they were saying at the meetings. I remember her telling me that I could cause her to lose her job. I didn't understand that, and I began to ask her how could she lose her job with me being there. "White folks don't like that. If they knew that you were involved and you're my child, they would fire me."

But I didn't have any fear. I used to tell my momma, "I want you and Daddy to be free. I want you to be able to vote just like the white folks." They couldn't do it. They just couldn't do it. "We ain't free. We're not gonna be free." This really made me be motivated more and more.

My parents had given me the example of the four girls killed in the church bombing in Birmingham to keep me from being involved. They said it could happen in Selma at Brown Chapel Church. And there were several bomb threats.

Why children? Why us? It made me realize that it didn't matter who you were. If you were black and you were in an area they didn't like or where the cause for freedom was being fought, you were at risk. It didn't matter—children, boy, girl, or whatever.

My father and I went to Jimmie Lee Jackson's funeral. There were a number of situations that I knew of as a kid where death actually happened. Jimmie Lee Jackson, James Reeb, Jonathan Daniels, Viola Liuzzo, the four kids in Birmingham. Three of the people were white, but they were part of the struggle. And in the struggle it didn't matter if you were black or white, we were all just like a big family.

I remember being afraid on the first attempt of the Selma-to-Montgomery march [March 7, 1965]. That was the first time that I was really afraid. The night before the march I slipped to the mass meeting. They began to talk about the strategies, like not fighting back. That right there told me that there was a possibility that there could be some fights. They were saying if you're hit, or if something is said to you, just bow down. Out of all the times my parents had talked to me about what could happen, this is when it really came to me. But somehow I was still determined to go.

I got up the next morning, frightened to march. This was on a Sunday. I remember very well my mom and dad trying to ensure that I was in the house. I slipped out the back door and I ran down.

The people began to congregate and line up. I was looking for Mrs. Moore and I found her. I remember not wanting to get close to the front of the line because I was afraid. I remember Mrs. Moore telling me that I should go back home, and I was saying I was going to march. I got in the midway of the march. As usual we knelt down to pray, and after we had prayed, we began to sing. A little of that fear began to leave me as we sang, because people were still joyful.

As we marched down the street to the downtown area, I began to see more spectators, black as well as whites, and this was different to me. Normally you didn't see a whole lot of spectators. And I began to see more police officers riding around on motorcycles. It was a little bit more exciting. We still clapped, and we sang all the way down. The closer we got to the bridge, the more I began to get frightened. At this time I could see hundreds of policemen. The helmets, state troopers, dogs and horses, police cars. I got even more frightened then. I began to hold Mrs. Moore's hand tighter, and the person's hand on the other side of me. My heart was beginning to beat real, real fast. I looked up at Mrs. Moore, and I wanted to say, "I want to go home," but I didn't. She was looking straight ahead. Then the people began to kneel down and pray again.

We were still on the Edmund Pettus bridge. Going up, you can't see what's at the bottom on the other side. But I had gotten up to the top, which is midway on the bridge, and you could see down. The big picture that I saw frightened me more. When we were asked to kneel down and pray, I knelt down with everybody. Shortly after we got up, a burst of tear gas began. I could see the troopers and policemen swinging their billy clubs. People began to run, and dogs and horses began to trample them. You could hear people screaming and hollering. And I began to run. I don't know what happened with Mrs. Moore. All I wanted to do was make my way back home. As I got almost down to the bottom of the bridge, Hosea Williams picked me up. I told him to put me down 'cause he wasn't running fast enough. I just continued to run.

You began to hear sirens. You could still see the dogs and horses trampling people, who were running all the way back from the Edmund Pettus bridge to Brown Chapel Church. When I made my way back home, I saw my mother and father and even my sisters and brothers there. My father was standing in the doorway. They were just waiting for me to get home. I remember him opening up the door and taking a deep breath seeing me, that I was safe. I went straight upstairs. He stood at the door watching what else was happening after I had come in. I was crying, and my mother came upstairs to comfort me. I was shocked at what I had seen.

I was still determined to go back out to Brown Chapel Church, but my parents wouldn't let me. I was shut up in my room. I remember taking a

from Freedom's Children

pencil and writing down how I felt and what I saw. Then I wrote down my funeral arrangements because even with what I saw, I still wanted to go out and fight. And I said if I did that, I would probably die. So I wrote my funeral arrangements.

I realized on that day everything about what Dr. Martin Luther King was trying to say. It was wrong to be beaten for something that you was trying to fight for that was right. I realized it more on that day than on any other day. It all came together.

I didn't get out that night, but I went to the next meeting, and this is when other people who hadn't the slightest idea of getting involved in the movement came to get involved. It had made so many people angry about what took place in Selma on that day, that it really helped mobilize and bring blacks together.

Meetings after that were filled with people. They were fired up. Teachers, the ministers, the grass roots from all walks of life. People began to come from all over the world. I remember the first mass meeting my parents came to. My mom and dad, they were telling me that they were gonna come to one of the mass meetings. I was already there, and it was a great thrill for me to look back and see them. Then after they had gone to the meeting, we talked about them getting registered to vote. They promised me for my birthday that they would be registered. That was going to be my birthday present.

The second Selma-to-Montgomery march began on March 21, 1965. Sheyann participated.

It was almost like preparing for a picnic. I remember getting some sandwiches. I still wasn't supposed to be on that march. When I saw Dr. King, he asked me who was I with, and I said, "Nobody." So immediately I was in his group's care. They put me in a van and I came on over to Montgomery with one of his secretaries. Dr. King told his assistant that my parents had to be contacted and told that I was in their care, and that I was okay.

We went to this hotel up on a hill. It was my first time going in a hotel. We were sitting in the hotel room, and they had asked me what I wanted to eat. I didn't know what to tell them. They said, "Get her a club sandwich." I didn't know what a club sandwich was. It was the biggest sandwich I had ever seen, and it was with chips and a pickle.

I felt I was part of the change. Really, anyone who was a part of the struggle at that time contributed to a change. So I think anyone, young or old, who participated in the movement was a contributing factor to the good things that are happening as a result of the Selma movement.

from Freedom's Children

But now [25 years later], right here in Selma where the struggle actually took place, it looks like voter registration is declining. There are a lot of reasons why people don't vote. Some people say they don't like who's running, but that's not the point. When I went to register, that was something I looked forward to. When I go vote, I probably don't feel like most people feel. When I pull the switch, I just feel good about it. It's like a proud thing to me because I know what happened for us to get that.

Responding to the Selection

Questions for Discussion

1. Discuss Sheyann Webb's character. What kind of child was she? How did her personality influence her behavior?

2. A verse from the Bible says, "A little child shall lead them." Discuss how this verse applies to Sheyann Webb's story. Why are children sometimes able to do and see what adults cannot?

3. What portrait of Dr. King emerges in Webb's story? How would you characterize him?

Activities

Preparing a Multimedia Report

1. Research the events that led to Bloody Sunday in Selma. Prepare a **multimedia report** that shows and tells about that day and its aftermath. Your report might include photographs, videotapes, print text, audiotapes, and music, for example.

Reflecting Courage

2. Sheyann Webb displayed a great deal of courage for a young girl. What do you think inspired her? Why wouldn't she let her fears overwhelm her? In a **reflective essay,** write about the nature of courage and how Webb and the others who marched for racial justice defined courage.

Before You Read

Death of Dr. King

Sam Cornish
Born 1935

"Cornish shows that America has always been a land of crisis and social chaos. His work is an individual's record of tragic events."

— Jon Woodson

About Cornish

Sam Cornish is a poet, teacher, and author. In his native Baltimore, Cornish worked as a writing specialist with the Neighborhood Centers and coedited a collection of writings by Baltimore youth called *Chicory: Young Voices from the Black Ghetto* (1969). That same year he wrote a children's book, *Your Hand in Mine.* In 1970 Cornish published a collection of his poems, *Generations*, and in 1996, *Cross a Parted Sea.* His poetry has appeared in many publications, including *Journal of Black Poetry, Massachusetts*

Review, and *New American Review.* Cornish has taught literature and writing at the university level and was formerly literature director of the Massachusetts Council on the Arts and Humanities.

About the Assassination

On April 4, 1968, Martin Luther King Jr. was in Memphis, Tennessee, to march in support of striking sanitation workers. As he was standing on the balcony of his room at the Lorraine Motel, King was shot by a sniper and died soon after in a hospital emergency room.

Millions of Americans mourned his death, but it seemed in the ensuing days that his message of nonviolence would be lost in the chaos that erupted in cities throughout the country. Over several days in Sam Cornish's native Baltimore, for example, 4 people were killed (2 shot by police) and more than 250 injured. Thousands of troops were sent to keep order after rioters destroyed much of the black section of the city. While many in their rage and grief forgot King's philosophy of radical change by nonviolent means, many others purposefully turned to violence.

Death of Dr. King

— *Sam Cornish*

1

we sit outside
the bars   the dime stores
everything is closed today

we are mourning
5   our hands filled with bricks
a brother is dead

my eyes are white and cold
water is in my hands

this is grief

2

10   after the water
the broken bread
we return
to our separate
places

15   in our heads
bodies collapse
and grow again

the city boils
black men
20   jump out of trees

Responding to the Selection

Questions for Discussion

1. The speaker says, "everything is closed today." What is the speaker referring to? What else closed with the death of Dr. King?

2. How would you characterize the speaker in part 1 of the poem? Why?

3. Describe the "separate places" to which the speaker and others return.

Activities

Interpreting a Poem

1. Write an **interpretive essay** in which you explain your interpretation of part 2 of the poem and how it relates to part 1. Use quotations from the poem to enhance your interpretation.

Summarizing History

2. In the days after Dr. King's murder, many U.S. cities experienced severe violence and property destruction. Research this period in U.S. history and write a brief **summary** of what you find. Then write a **persuasive essay** in which you either defend or criticize the reactions to Dr. King's death. What do you think Dr. King would have said about the reactions?

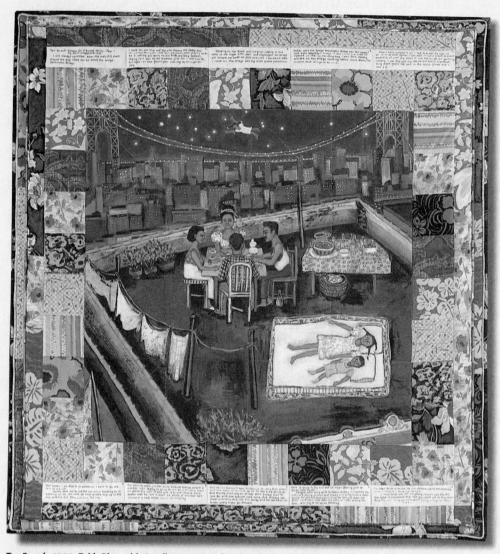

Tar Beach, 1988. Faith Ringgold. Acrylic on canvas bordered with printed, painted, quilted and pieced cloth, 74⅝ x 68½ in. Solomon R. Guggenheim Museum, New York. Gift of Mr. and Mrs. Gus and Judith Lieber, 1988.

Theme Three

Scattered Branches

A tree cannot stand without roots.

— *Mayombe proverb*

Before You Read

Southern Road

Sterling A. Brown
1901–1989

"I was first attracted [to African American language and folklore] by certain qualities that I thought the speech of the people had, and I wanted to get for my own writing a flavor, a color, a pungency of speech. Then later, I came to something more important—I wanted to get an understanding of people, to acquire an accuracy in the portrayal of their lives."

About Brown

The Harlem Renaissance was both a flowering and a celebration of African American culture, and Sterling A. Brown was one of the many writers who contributed to the richness of that period. Born into the African American middle class in Washington, D.C., Brown distinguished himself by winning honors in high school and college. After receiving his master's degree from Harvard University, he began a career in teaching. He taught at Howard University until his retirement in 1969.

Brown's first collection of poetry, *Southern Road* (1932), was greatly influenced by spirituals, work songs, jazz, and the blues and often spoke of racial concerns. He concentrated on teaching and on writing essays about African American literature and the impact of African American culture on American life. Brown published his second and final book of verse, *The Last Ride of Wild Bill,* in 1975.

Work Songs

Enslaved Africans in the South sang a wide array of original songs as they toiled for their white owners. Some of these songs were intended to relieve the boredom of such repetitive tasks as picking cotton. Others told stories that had little to do with work but expressed such emotions as anger or sorrow. Many work songs included the physical sounds of labor, such as grunts. Work songs were the forerunners of spirituals and, later, blues music.

Southern Road

— *Sterling A. Brown*

Swing dat hammer—hunh—
Steady, bo';
Swing dat hammer—hunh—
Steady, bo';
5 Ain't no rush, bebby,
Long ways to go.

Burner tore his—hunh—
Black heart away;
Burner tore his—hunh—
10 Black heart away;
Got me life, bebby,
An' a day.

Gal's on Fifth Street—hunh—
Son done gone;
15 Gal's on Fifth Street—hunh—
Son done gone;
Wife's in the de ward, bebby,
Babe's not bo'n.

My ole man died—hunh—
20 Cussin' me;
My ole man died—hunh—
Cussin' me;
Ole lady rocks, bebby,
Huh misery.

25   Doubleshackled—hunh—
       Guard behin';
       Doubleshackled—hunh—
       Guard behin';
       Ball an' chain, bebby,
30   On my min'.

       White man tells me—hunh—
       Damn yo' soul;
       White man tells me—hunh—
       Damn yo' soul;
35   Got no need, bebby,
       To be tole.

       Chain gang nevah—hunh—
       Let me go;
       Chain gang nevah—hunh—
40   Let me go;
       Po' los' boy, bebby,
       Evahmo'. . . .

Responding to the Selection

Questions for Discussion

1. Where is the speaker and what is he doing?
2. What does the repetition of "hunh" signify in the poem? What else does it add to the poem?
3. Who do you think "bebby" is?
4. What has happened to the speaker's family? Why?
5. How does the speaker sum up his own situation?

Activities

Writing an Essay

1. Brown's poetry was influenced greatly by music, including the blues. Research blues music, especially the structure of the lyrics. Then write an **expository essay** that discusses the blues and how Brown's poem was influenced by that musical genre.

Interpreting Poetry

2. Along with your classmates, create an **oral interpretation** of "Southern Road." As you work together, think about ways that you can use individual voices, groups of voices, and other sounds or music to enhance your interpretation. Tape-record or videotape your class's performance.

Before You Read

Isis

Zora Neale Hurston
1903(?)–1960

"I am not tragically colored.
There is no great sorrow
dammed up in my soul, nor
lurking behind my eyes. . . .
I do not weep at the world—
I am too busy sharpening my
oyster knife."

About Hurston

Zora Neale Hurston was born in the
African American town of Eatonville,
Florida, and soared to prominence as one
of the most distinguished writers of the
Harlem Renaissance. As a young woman,
Hurston followed a traveling theater
troupe to Baltimore, where she stayed and
earned her high school diploma. After
attending Howard University for several
years, she won a scholarship to Barnard
College, earning a degree in anthropology.

Hurston put her education to good use
during field trips she took to the rural
South. Her travels resulted in a pioneering
collection of African American folklore,
Mules and Men, published in 1935. Two
years later Hurston published her best-
loved novel, *Their Eyes Were Watching
God.* Although she was poor and largely
unknown when she died in 1960, Hurston
gained a new generation of admirers in
later years. Today, the adventurous girl
who left Eatonville to explore America is
widely considered one of the most important African American writers of the twentieth century.

Hurston's Southern World

Zora Neale Hurston was greatly influenced
by her upbringing in Eatonville. Because
the town's residents were all African
American, Hurston was not exposed to the
caustic racism prevalent in other parts of
the country. During the 1930s and 1940s,
some critics objected to her refusal to por-
tray African Americans as victims. At the
same time, she was praised for the vitality
of her characters and for her celebration of
African American culture. Much of her fiction, including "Isis," is set in small towns
reminiscent of Eatonville.

Isis

— Zora Neale Hurston

"You Isie Watts! Git 'own offen dat gate post an' rake up dis yahd!"

The small brown girl perched upon the gate post looked yearningly up the gleaming shell road that led to Orlando. After awhile, she shrugged her thin shoulders. This only seemed to heap still more kindling on Grandma Potts' already burning ire.

"Lawd a-mussy!" she screamed, enraged—"Heah Joel, gimme dat wash stick. Ah'll show dat limb of Satan she cain't shake herself at *me*. If she ain't down by the time Ah gets dere, Ah'll break huh down in de lines."

"Aw Gran'ma, Ah see Mist' George and Jim Robinson comin' and Ah wanted to wave at 'em," the child said impatiently.

"You jes' wave dat rake at dis heah yahd, madame, else Ah'll take you down a button hole lower. Youse too 'oomanish jumpin' up in everybody's face dat pass."

This struck the child sorely for nothing pleased her so much as to sit atop of the gate post and hail the passing vehicles on their way South to Orlando, or North to Sanford. That white shell road was her great attraction. She raced up and down the stretch of it that lay before her gate like a round-eyed puppy hailing gleefully all travelers. Everybody in the country, white and colored, knew little Isis Watts, Isis the Joyful. The Robinson brothers, white cattlemen, were particularly fond of her and always extended a stirrup for her to climb up behind one of them for a short ride, or let her try to crack the long bull whips and *yee whoo* at the cows.

Grandma Potts went inside and Isis literally waved the rake at the 'chaws' of ribbon cane that lay so bountifully about the yard in company with the knots and peelings, with a thick sprinkling of peanut hulls.

The herd of cattle in their envelope of gray dust came alongside and Isis dashed out to the nearest stirrup and was lifted up.

"Hello theah Snidlits, I was wonderin' wheah you was," said Jim Robinson as she snuggled down behind him in the saddle. They were almost out of the danger zone when Grandma emerged. "You Isie," she bawled.

Isis

The child slid down on the opposite side of the house and executed a flank movement through the corn patch that brought her into the yard from behind the privy.

"You li'l hasion you! Wheah you been?"

"Out in de back yahd," Isis lied and did a cart wheel and a few fancy steps on her way to the front again.

"If you doan git in dat yahd, Ah make a mommuk of you!" Isis observed that Grandma was cutting a fancy assortment of switches from peach, guana and cherry trees.

She finished the yard by raking everything under the edge of the porch and began a romp with the dogs, those lean, floppy-eared hounds that all country folks keep. But Grandma vetoed this also.

"Isie, you set on dat porch! Uh great big 'leben yeah ole gal racin' an' rompin' lak dat—set 'own!"

Isis flung herself upon the steps.

"Git up offa dem steps, you aggravatin' limb, 'fore Ah git dem hick'ries tuh you, an' set yo' seff on a cheah."

Isis arose, and then sat down as violently as possible in the chair. She slid down, and down, until she all but sat on her own shoulder blades.

"Now look atcher," Grandma screamed, "Put yo' knees together, an' git up offen yo' backbone! Lawd, you know dis hellion is gwine make me stomp huh insides out."

Isis sat bolt upright as if she wore a ramrod down her back and began to whistle. Now there are certain things that Grandma Potts felt no one of this female persuasion should do—one was to sit with the knees separated, 'settin' brazen' she called it; another was whistling, another playing with boys. Finally, a lady must never cross her legs.

Grandma jumped up from her seat to get the switches.

"So youse whistlin' in mah face, huh!" She glared till her eyes were beady and Isis bolted for safety. But the noon hour brought John Watts the widowed father, and this excused the child from sitting for criticism.

Being the only girl in the family, of course she must wash the dishes, which she did in intervals between frolics with the dogs. She even gave Jake, the puppy, a swim in the dishpan by holding him suspended above the water that reeked of 'pot likker'—just high enough so that his feet would be immersed. The deluded puppy swam and swam without ever crossing the pan, much to his annoyance. Hearing Grandma she hurriedly dropped him on the floor, which he tracked-up with feet wet with dishwater.

Grandma took her patching and settled down in the front room to sew. She did this every afternoon, and invariably slept in the big red rocker with her head lolled back over the back, the sewing falling from her hand.

Isis

Isis had crawled under the center table with its red plush cover with little round balls for fringe. She was lying on her back imagining herself various personages. She wore trailing robes, golden slippers with blue bottoms. She rode white horses with flaring pink nostrils to the horizon, for she still believed that to be land's end. She was picturing herself gazing over the edge of the world into the abyss when the spool of cotton fell from Grandma's lap and rolled away under the whatnot. Isis drew back from her contemplation of the nothingness at the horizon and glanced up at the sleeping woman. Her head had fallen far back. She breathed with a regular 'mark' intake and 'poosah' exhaust. But Isis was a visual-minded child. She heard the snores only subconsciously but she saw the straggling beard on Grandma's chin, trembling a little with every 'mark' and 'poosah'. They were long gray hairs curled every here and there against the dark brown skin. Isis was moved with pity for her mother's mother.

"Poah Gran-ma needs a shave," she murmured, and set about it. Just then Joel, next older than Isis, entered with a can of bait.

"Come on Isie, les' we all go fishin'. The Perch is bitin' fine in Blue Sink."

"Sh-sh—" cautioned his sister, "Ah got to shave Gran'ma."

"Who say so?" Joel asked, surprised.

"Nobody doan hafta tell me. Look at her chin. No ladies don't weah whiskers if they kin help it. Bur Gran-ma gittin ole an' she doan know how to shave lak *me*."

The conference adjourned to the back porch lest Grandma wake.

"Aw, Isie, you doan know nothin' 'bout shavin' a-tall—but a *man* lak *me*—"

"Ah do so know."

"You don't not. Ah'm goin' shave her mahseff."

"Naw, you won't neither, Smarty. Ah saw her first an' thought it all up first," Isis declared, and ran to the calico-covered box on the wall above the wash basin and seized her father's razor. Joel was quick and seized the mug and brush.

"Now!" Isis cried defiantly, "Ah got the razor."

"Goody, goody, goody, pussy cat, Ah got th' brush an' you can't shave 'thout lather—see! Ah know mo' than you," Joel retorted.

"Aw, who don't know dat?" Isis pretended to scorn. But seeing her progress blocked from lack of lather she compromised.

"Ah know! Les' we all shave her. You lather an' Ah shave."

This was agreeable to Joel. He made mountains of lather and anointed his own chin, and the chin of Isis and the dogs, splashed the wall and at last was persuaded to lather Grandma's chin. Not that he was loath but he wanted his new plaything to last as long as possible.

Isis

Isis stood on one side of the chair with the razor clutched cleaver fashion. The niceties of razor-handling had passed over her head. The thing with her was to *hold* the razor—sufficient in itself.

Joel splashed on the lather in great gobs and Grandma awoke.

For one bewildered moment she stared at the grinning boy with the brush and mug but sensing another presence, she turned to behold the business face of Isis and the razor-clutching hand. Her jaw dropped and Grandma, forgetting years and rheumatism, bolted from the chair and fled the house, screaming.

"She's gone to tell papa, Isie. You didn't have no business wid his razor and he's gonna lick yo' hide," Joel cried, running to replace mug and brush.

"You too, chuckle-head, you too," retorted Isis. "You was playin' wid his brush and put it all over the dogs—Ah seen you put it on Ned an' Beulah." Isis shaved and replaced it in the box. Joel took his bait and pole and hurried to Blue Sink. Isis crawled under the house to brood over the whipping she knew would come. She had meant well.

But sounding brass and tinkling cymbal drew her forth. The local lodge of the Grand United Order of Odd Fellows, led by a braying, thudding band, was marching in full regalia down the road. She had forgotten the barbecue and log-rolling to be held today for the benefit of the new hall.

Music to Isis meant motion. In a minute razor and whipping forgotten, she was doing a fair imitation of a Spanish dancer she had seen in a medicine show some time before. Isis' feet were gifted—she could dance most anything she saw.

Up, up, went her spirits, her small feet doing all sorts of intricate things and her body in rhythm, hand curving above her head. But the music was growing faint. Grandma was nowhere in sight. Isis stole out of the gate, running and dancing after the band.

Not far down the road, Isis stopped. She realized she couldn't dance at the carnival. Her dress was torn and dirty. She picked a long-stemmed daisy, and placed it behind her ear, but her dress remained torn and dirty just the same. Then Isis had an idea. Her thoughts returned to the battered, round-topped trunk back in the bedroom. She raced back to the house; then, happier, she raced down the white dusty road to the picnic grove, gorgeously clad. People laughed good-naturedly at her, the band played and Isis danced because she couldn't help it. A crowd of children gathered admiringly about her as she wheeled lightly about, hand on hip, flower between her teeth with the red and white fringe of the tablecloth— Grandma's new red tablecloth that she wore in lieu of a Spanish shawl— trailing in the dust. It was too ample for her meager form, but she wore it like a gypsy. Her brown feet twinkled in and out of the fringe. Some grown

Isis

people joined the children about her. The Grand Exalted Ruler rose to speak; the band was hushed, but Isis danced on, the crowd clapping their hands for her. No one listened to the Exalted one, for little by little the multitude had surrounded the small brown dancer.

An automobile drove up to the Crown and halted. Two white men and a lady got out and pushed into the crowd, suppressing mirth discretely behind gloved hands. Isis looked up and waved them a magnificent hail and went on dancing until—

Grandma had returned to the house, and missed Isis. She straightaway sought her at the festivities, expecting to find her in her soiled dress, shoeless, standing at the far edge of the crowd. What she saw now drove her frantic. Here was her granddaughter dancing before a gaping crowd in her brand new red tablecloth, and reeking of lemon extract. Isis had added the final touch to her costume. Of course she must also have perfume.

When Isis saw her Grandma, she bolted. She heard her Grandma cry—"Mah Gawd, mah brand new tablecloth Ah just bought f'um O'landah!"—as Isis fled through the crowd and on into the woods.

Isis followed the little creek until she came to the ford in a rutty wagon road that led to Apopka and laid down on the cool grass at the roadside. The April sun was quite warm.

Misery, misery and woe settled down upon her. The child wept. She knew another whipping was in store.

"Oh, Ah wish Ah could die, then Gran'ma an' papa would be sorry they beat me so much. Ah b'leeve Ah'll run away and never go home no mo'. Ah'm goin' drown mahseff in th' creek!"

Isis got up and waded into the water. She routed out a tiny 'gator and a huge bullfrog. She splashed and sang. Soon she was enjoying herself immensely. The purr of a motor struck her ear and she saw a large, powerful car jolting along the rutty road toward her. It stopped at the water's edge.

"Well, I declare, it's our little gypsy," exclaimed the man at the wheel. "What are you doing here, now?"

"Ah'm killin' mahseff," Isis declared dramatically, "Cause Gran'ma beats me too much."

There was a hearty burst of laughter from the machine.

"You'll last some time the way you are going about it. Is this the way to Maitland? We want to go to the Park Hotel."

Isis saw no longer any reason to die. She came up out of the water, holding up the dripping fringe of the tablecloth.

"Naw, indeedy. You go to Maitlan' by the shell road—it goes by mah house—an' turn off at Lake Sebelia to the clay road that takes you right to the do.'"

Isis

"Well," went on the driver, smiling furtively, "Could you quit dying long enough to go with us?"

"Yessuh," she said thoughtfully, "Ah wanta go wid you."

The door of the car swung open. She was invited to a seat beside the driver. She had often dreamed of riding in one of these heavenly chariots but never thought she would, actually.

"Jump in then, Madame Tragedy, and show us. We lost ourselves after we left your barbecue."

During the drive Isis explained to the kind lady who smelt faintly of violets and to the indifferent men that she was really a princess. She told them about her trips to the horizon, about the trailing gowns, the gold shoes with blue bottoms—she insisted on the blue bottoms—the white charger, the time when she was Hercules and had slain numerous dragons and sundry giants. At last the car approached her gate over which stood the umbrella chinaberry tree. The car was abreast of the gate and had all but passed when Grandma spied her glorious tablecloth lying back against the upholstery of the Packard.

"You Isie-e!" she bawled, "You li'l wretch you! Come heah *dis instant.*"

"That's me," the child confessed, mortified, to the lady on the rear seat.

"Oh Sewell, stop the car. This is where the child lives. I hate to give her up though."

"Do you wanta keep me?" Isis brightened.

"Oh, I wish I could. Wait, I'll try to save you a whipping this time."

She dismounted with the gaudy lemon-flavored culprit and advanced to the gate where Grandma stood glowering, switches in hand.

"You're gointuh ketchit f'um yo' haid to yo' heels m'lady. Jes' come in heah."

"Why, good afternoon," she accosted the furious grandparent. "You're not going to whip this poor little thing, are you?" the lady asked in conciliatory tones.

"Yes, Ma'am. She's de wustest li'l limb dat ever drawed bref. Jes' look at mah new tablecloth, dat ain't never been washed. She done traipsed all over de woods, uh dancin' an' uh prancin' in it. She done took a razor to me t'day an' Lawd knows whut mo'."

Isis clung to the stranger's hand fearfully.

"Ah wuzn't gointer hurt Gran'ma, miss—Ah wuz just gointer shave her whiskers fuh huh 'cause she's old an' can't."

The white hand closed tightly over the little brown one that was quite soiled. She could understand a voluntary act of love even though it miscarried.

"Now, Mrs. er-er-I didn't get the name—how much did your table-cloth cost?"

Isis

"One whole big silvah dollar down at O'landah—ain't had it a week yit."

"Now here's five dollars to get another one. I want her to go to the hotel and dance for me. I could stand a little light today—"

"Oh, yessum, yessum," Grandma cut in, "Everything's alright, sho' she kin go, yessum."

Feeling that Grandma had been somewhat squelched did not detract from Isis' spirit at all. She pranced over to the waiting motor-car and this time seated herself on the rear seat between the sweet-smiling lady and the rather aloof man in gray.

"Ah'm gointer stay wid you all," she said with a great deal of warmth, and snuggled up to her benefactress. "Want me tuh sing a song fuh you?"

"There, Helen, you've been adopted," said the man with a short, harsh laugh.

"Oh, I hope so, Harry." She put her arm about the red-draped figure at her side and drew it close until she felt the warm puffs of the child's breath against her side. She looked hungrily ahead of her and spoke into space rather than to anyone in the car. "I would like just a little of her sunshine to soak into my soul. I would like that a lot."

Responding to the Selection

Questions for Discussion

1. Do you admire Isis? Explain why.

2. Do you think Grandma Potts would treat Isis differently if she were a boy? What evidence in the story supports your opinion?

3. What do Isis and Zora Neale Hurston have in common?

4. Predict what Isis will be doing when she's eighteen. What makes you think so?

Activities

Writing a Monologue

1. What do you imagine will happen when Isis and her new friends go to the hotel? Write a **monologue** in which she describes her experience there.

Writing a Paragraph

2. Reread the quotation at the start of the brief biography of Hurston. Write a paragraph that explains your interpretation of what Hurston meant when she said, "I do not weep at the world—I am too busy sharpening my oyster knife"? How do these words help explain the character of Isis?

MEDIA connection

Newspaper Article

Zora Neale Hurston's works have experienced a renaissance, due in large part to an important biography written by Robert Hemenway.

Hemenway Sets Author's Story Straight

from the Lawrence (Kansas) Journal-World

by Jan Biles, Journal-World *Arts Editor*

Nearly 30 years ago, Robert Hemenway read the book *Their Eyes Were Watching God*—and before long he had packed his bags, bought a pickup camper and was crisscrossing the United States to dig up the truth about the book's author, Zora Neale Hurston.

"I thought, 'This is a fantastic novel'," Hemenway, now chancellor at Kansas University, said, recalling the first time he read Hurston's book. "I wanted to learn more about the person who wrote it."

What he discovered was contradiction. Some researchers said Hurston had been married once; others said twice or not at all. Some biographers swore the writer and folklorist was from Florida; others said New York.

"There was mass confusion about the biographical facts about this writer, and that intrigued me," Hemenway said. "I decided to write a book and get the true facts."

With a National Endowment for the Humanities grant funding his research, Hemenway set out in 1970 to explore the places where Hurston had lived and talk to the people Hurston had known.

He went from Key West, Fla., to White Sulphur Springs, Mont., to New Haven, Conn., in search of tidbits about the Harlem Renaissance writer of the 1930s. He parked his camper in a Yale University lot for six weeks so he could immerse himself in the books at its Beinecke Rare Book and Manuscript Library.

By 1977, Hemenway had found most of the answers to his questions, and the book *Zora Neale Hurston: A Literary Biography* was completed. Today the biography is considered an academic best-seller.

"Bob Hemenway is the author of the standard biography of Zora Neale Hurston" said Bill Andrews, director of the Hall Center for the Humanities. "When he started doing his research, she had been largely forgotten. Interest in her work has been developed over the last 20 years. . . . His book has been praised for its scholarship and literary interpretation, and it's a pivotal book in black women's studies."

Hemenway's book also had a profound impact

on author Alice Walker, who later wrote in its foreword:

"Robert Hemenway was the first critic I had read who seemed indignant that Zora's life ended in poverty and obscurity, that her last days were spent in a welfare home, and that her burial was paid for by 'subscription'; though Zora herself—as he is careful to point out in this book—remained gallant and unbowed until the end."

Hemenway said what intrigued him most about Hurston—a rural Florida native who briefly married twice, wrote seven books, maintained a long friendship with poet Langston Hughes and traveled the South collecting massive amounts of African American folklore—was her insight into human behavior, her rich use of metaphor and imagery and her dynamic personality.

Her novels were reviewed by the *New York Times* and *Saturday Review*, and she was considered to be a "real talent" of her time, he said. However, because of racial discrimination and prejudice, she was denied commercial success.

"Nine hundred and forty-five dollars was the most money one of her novels made," Hemenway said. "Many bookstores wouldn't even stock her books. . . . They didn't want to imply equality."

ZORA NEALE HURSTON

A NOVEL

THEIR EYES WERE WATCHING GOD

"There is no book more important to me than this one."—Alice Walker

Hemenway said his intent in penning the 353-page biography—which is available at local bookstores—was always simple.

[He wrote,] "She deserves an important place in American literary history. I have tried to demonstrate why this is so, not in the interests of producing a 'definitive' book—that book remains to be written, and by a black woman—but in order to contribute to a new, closer examination of the unusual career of this complex author. This book provides an order to Hurston's life and an interpretation of her art; there are more biographical facts to be discovered, different interpretations to come."

Questions for Discussion

1. Hurston lived a full life, wrote seven books, yet died poor and forgotten. In spite of this, Alice Walker writes she "remained gallant and unbowed until the end." Why, do you think, she was able to do so?

2. A writer wants to pen a biography of your life. What parts would you share? What parts would you leave out? Explain.

Before You Read

November Cotton Flower

Jean Toomer
1894–1967

"I was neither white nor black, but simply an American."

where he absorbed the sights and sounds that went into *Cane*. After settling in Harlem and contributing to a variety of literary journals, Toomer became interested in religion and philosophy, and he wrote a number of essays on these subjects. Ultimately, Toomer became a Quaker and lived his last years as a recluse.

Today, Toomer is recognized as one of the most talented figures of the Harlem Renaissance for his experimental style and his success in capturing both southern culture and the spiritual confusion experienced by many of his generation.

About Toomer

Jean Toomer wrote only one major work, but it has been called "the most impressive product" of the Harlem Renaissance. Published in 1923, *Cane* is an experimental mixture of drama, prose, and poetry that includes the poem you are about to read. In *Cane* Toomer describes African American culture in both the rural South and the industrial North, using rich, musical language.

Toomer was born in Washington, D.C., and attended college in several parts of the country. He taught school in Georgia,

Cotton Crop Disaster

For two months in the summer of 1921, Jean Toomer served as acting head of an agricultural school in Georgia. Traditionally, Georgia had depended heavily on cotton as a major crop, but during the 1920s, the state's cotton crop was devastated by boll weevils—destructive insects that attack cotton plants. Because so much of the cotton crop was destroyed, many farmers were ruined financially, and agricultural workers, many of them African American, were forced to migrate to the North in search of employment.

November
Cotton Flower

— *Jean Toomer*

Boll weevil's coming, and the winter's cold,
Made cotton stalks look rusty, seasons old,
And cotton, scarce as any southern snow,
Was vanishing; the branch, so pinched and slow,
5   Failed in its function as the autumn rake;
Drought fighting soil had caused the soil to take
All water from the streams; dead birds were found
In wells a hundred feet below the ground—
Such was the season when the flower bloomed.
10   Old folks were startled, and it soon assumed
Significance. Superstition saw
Something it had never seen before:
Brown eyes that loved without a trace of fear,
Beauty so sudden for that time of year.

Responding to the Selection

Questions for Discussion

1. What two things, according to lines 1–2, make the cotton look rusty? What happens to the cotton in lines 3–4?

2. What event startles "old folks"? Why might the event take on significance?

3. What two things has "Superstition" never seen before? What do these two things suggest about the effect of the sudden bloom on most people? What might the cotton flower symbolize? Explain.

4. The poem is a **Petrarchan sonnet,** a verse form consisting of an eight-line section (octave) that presents a problem or a situation, followed by a six-line section (sestet) that provides an answer or resolution to the problem. What change in thinking takes place from the first section to the second? Is the change significant? Explain.

Activities

Exploring Images

1. Jean Toomer uses imagery and rhyme to present the contrast of beauty against the grey of winter. Write a **descriptive essay** exploring contrasting images of winter in your neighborhood.

Comparing Images

2. Write a **poem** comparing a flower with something very different from a flower. Try to include details that appeal to at least two senses.

Before You Read

The Preserving

Kevin Young
Born 1970

"I wanted to preserve this way of life that was leaving us."

About Young

Kevin Young is an award-winning poet and an assistant professor in the University of Georgia's Creative Writing Program. A graduate of Harvard and Brown universities, Young has had work published in *The New Yorker,* the *Kenyon Review,* and other literary journals. At Harvard he won the Academy of American Poets Prize, and his first collection of poetry, *Most Way Home,* published in 1995, was awarded the John Zacharis Award by *Ploughshares* magazine. In 1998 *Swing* magazine named Young one of the thirty most powerful people under thirty in the United States.

About Preserving Food

People have always sought ways to preserve food. In the days before refrigeration, when a harvest was bountiful or game had been killed, much of the food may have been eaten immediately, but the rest had to be preserved for later—both to prevent waste and to provide for lean times. Particularly in rural or small town cultures, people have traditionally gardened or have grown fruit trees to supply much of the food for their families through the winter.

The foods produced in a garden may be preserved by drying or freezing, but they often are cooked and processed and then stored in jars. Some fruits, especially, are used to make wine.

These ways of preserving food, besides being practical, also fulfill a social function. They provide a way for people to share with each other the results of their labor and of their love.

The Preserving

— *Kevin Young*

Summer meant peeling: peaches,
pears, July, all carved up. August
was a tomato dropped
in boiling water, my skin coming
5   right off. And peas, Lord,
after shelling all summer, if I never
saw those green fingers again
it would be too soon. We'd also
make wine, gather up those peach
10   scraps, put them in jars & let them
turn. Trick was enough air.

Eating something boiled each meal,
my hair in coils by June first, Mama
could barely reel me in from the red
15   clay long enough to wrap my hair
with string. So tight
I couldn't think. But that was far
easier to take care of, lasted all
summer like ashy knees.
20   One Thanksgiving, while saying grace
we heard what sounded like a gunshot
ran to the back porch to see
peach glass everywhere. Reckon
someone didn't give the jar enough
25   room to breathe. Only good thing
bout them saving days was knowing
they'd be over, that by Christmas
afternoons turned to cakes: coconut
yesterday, fruitcake today, fresh

30   cushaw pie to start tomorrow.
On Jesus' Day we'd go house
to house tasting each family's peach
brandy. You know you could stand
only so much, a taste. Time we weaved
35   back, it had grown cold as war.
Huddling home, clutching each
other in our handed down hand-
me-downs, we felt we was dying
like a late fire; we prayed
40   those homemade spirits
would warm most way home.

Responding to the Selection ——————

Questions for Discussion

1. Describe the situation in which the speaker is involved.

2. Consider the title of the poem. What do you think it means? What is being preserved?

3. A **simile** is a comparison between two unlike things, using *like* or *as*. Find three similes in the poem and explain the comparisons being made.

4. At the end of the poem, the speaker says, "we prayed / those homemade spirits / would warm most way home." What do these words mean literally? Do you think they have other meanings as well?

Activity
Interpreting Poetry

The speaker says the trick to turning peach scraps into wine is "enough air." Later, the speaker says of a bottle of exploded peach wine, "Reckon / someone didn't give the jar enough / room to breathe." What else might be "turning" in the poem? What happens when there is not enough room to breathe? Write an **interpretive essay** in which you talk about these aspects of meaning in "The Preserving."

Before You Read

Blues Ain't No Mockin Bird

Toni Cade Bambara
1939–1995

"My mother never interrupted either my brother or me if we were daydreaming. She recognized that as important work to do."

About Bambara

Throughout her childhood, Toni Cade Bambara was encouraged to be creative, and she wrote on any slip of paper she could find. Her mother and other adults in her life not only encouraged her writing and daydreaming; they also said she had an important role in life. As proof of that special role, Bambara went on to publish short stories, essays, screenplays, and novels that reflect her African American heritage.

About the Title

The characters in this story probably live on a farm in a poor, rural southern county, during the late 1940s or the 1950s. It is winter, near Christmas, but the weather is still mild enough to play outdoors.

- Blues is an American original—a style of music with its roots in the rural South. The blues were first sung by African Americans as a way to express their troubles. "Singing the blues" means singing with deep feeling, often with sadness, about life's experiences. The blues can express a range of other emotions, too, from anger to joy.

- The mockingbird is a songbird that mimics, or imitates, the songs of other birds. While it communicates with other mockingbirds using songs of its own, it mimics other sounds as a survival mechanism. For example, it hides from its predators by mimicking their calls. The mockingbird is also highly territorial, fiercely defending its nest and environment by swooping down on its enemies.

Blues Ain't No Mockin Bird

— *Toni Cade Bambara*

The puddle had frozen over, and me and Cathy went stompin in it. The twins from next door, Tyrone and Terry, were swingin so high out of sight we forgot we were waitin our turn on the tire. Cathy jumped up and came down hard on her heels and started tap-dancin. And the frozen patch splinterin every which way underneath kinda spooky. "Looks like a plastic spider web," she said. "A sort of weird spider, I guess, with many mental problems." But really it looked like the crystal paperweight Granny kept in the parlor. She was on the back porch, Granny was, making the cakes drunk. The old ladle dripping rum into the Christmas tins, like it used to drip maple syrup into the pails when we lived in the Judson's woods, like it poured cider into the vats when we were on the Cooper place, like it used to scoop buttermilk and soft cheese when we lived at the dairy.

"Go tell that man we ain't a bunch of trees."

"Ma'am?"

"I said to tell that man to get away from here with that camera." Me and Cathy look over toward the meadow where the men with the station wagon'd been roamin around all mornin. The tall man with a huge camera lassoed to his shoulder was buzzin our way.

"They're makin movie pictures," yelled Tyrone, stiffenin his legs and twistin so the tire'd come down slow so they could see.

"They're makin movie pictures," sang out Terry.

"That boy don't never have anything original to say," say Cathy grown-up.

By the time the man with the camera had cut across our neighbor's yard, the twins were out of the trees swingin low and Granny was onto the steps, the screen door bammin soft and scratchy against her palms. "We thought we'd get a shot or two of the house and everything and then—"

"Good mornin," Granny cut him off. And smiled that smile.

"Good mornin," he said, head all down the way Bingo does when you yell at him about the bones on the kitchen floor. "Nice place you got here, aunty. We thought we'd take a—"

"Did you?" said Granny with her eyebrows. Cathy pulled up her socks and giggled.

"Nice things here," said the man, buzzin his camera over the yard. The pecan barrels, the sled, me and Cathy, the flowers, the printed stones along the driveway, the trees, the twins, the toolshed.

"I don't know about the thing, the it, and the stuff," said Granny, still talkin with her eyebrows. "Just people here is what I tend to consider."

Camera man stopped buzzin. Cathy giggled into her collar.

"Mornin, ladies," a new man said. He had come up behind us when we weren't lookin. "And gents," discoverin the twins givin him a nasty look. "We're filmin for the county," he said with a smile. "Mind if we shoot a bit around here?"

"I do indeed," said Granny with no smile. Smilin man was smiling up a storm. So was Cathy. But he didn't seem to have another word to say, so he and the camera man backed on out the yard, but you could hear the camera buzzin still. "Suppose you just shut that machine off," said Granny real low through her teeth, and took a step down off the porch and then another.

"Now, aunty," Camera said, pointin the thing straight at her.

"Your mama and I are not related."

Smilin man got his notebook out and a chewed-up pencil. "Listen," he said movin back into our yard, "we'd like to have a statement from you . . . for the film. We're filmin for the county, see. Part of the food stamp campaign. You know about the food stamps?"

Granny said nuthin.

"Maybe there's somethin you want to say for the film. I see you grow your own vegetables," he smiled real nice. "If more folks did that, see, there'd be no need—"

Granny wasn't sayin nuthin. So they backed on out, buzzin at our clothesline and the twins' bicycles, then back on down to the meadow. The twins were danglin in the tire, lookin at Granny. Me and Cathy were waitin, too, cause Granny always got somethin to say. She teaches steady with no let-up. "I was on this bridge one time," she started off. "Was a crowd cause this man was goin to jump, you understand. And a minister was there and the police and some other folks. His woman was there, too."

"What was they doin?" asked Tyrone.

Blues Ain't No Mockin Bird

"Tryin to talk him out of it was what they was doin. The minister talkin about how it was a mortal sin, suicide. His woman takin bites out of her own hand and not even knowin it, so nervous and cryin and talkin fast."

"So what happened?" asked Tyrone.

"So here comes . . . this person . . . with a camera, takin pictures of the man and the minister and the woman. Takin pictures of the man in his misery about to jump, cause life so bad and people been messin with him so bad. This person takin up the whole roll of film practically. But savin a few, of course."

"Of course," said Cathy, hatin the person. Me standin there wonderin how Cathy knew it was "of course" when I didn't and it was *my* grandmother.

After a while Tyrone say, "Did he jump?"

"Yeh, did he jump?" say Terry all eager.

And Granny just stared at the twins till their faces swallow up the eager and they don't even care any more about the man jumpin. Then she goes back onto the porch and lets the screen door go for itself. I'm lookin to Cathy to finish the story cause she knows Granny's whole story before me even. Like she knew how come we move so much and Cathy ain't but a third cousin we picked up on the way last Thanksgivin visitin. But she knew it was on account of people drivin Granny crazy till she'd get up in the night and start packin. Mumblin and packin and wakin everybody up sayin, "Let's get on away from here before I kill me somebody." Like people wouldn't pay her for things like they said they would. Or Mr. Judson bringin us boxes of old clothes and raggedy magazines. Or Mrs. Cooper comin in our kitchen and touchin everything and sayin how clean it all was. Granny goin crazy, and Granddaddy Cain pullin her off the people, sayin, "Now, now, Cora." But next day loadin up the truck, with rocks all in his jaw, madder than Granny in the first place.

"I read a story once," said Cathy soundin like Granny teacher. "About this lady Goldilocks who barged into a house that wasn't even hers. And not invited, you understand. Messed over the people's groceries and broke up the people's furniture. Had the nerve to sleep in the folks' bed."

"Then what happened?" asked Tyrone. "What they do, the folks, when they come in to all this mess?"

"Did they make her pay for it?" asked Terry, makin a fist. "I'd've made her pay me."

I didn't even ask. I could see Cathy actress was very likely to just walk away and leave us in mystery about this story which I heard was about some bears.

"Did they throw her out?" asked Tyrone, like his father sounds when he's bein extra nasty-plus to the washin-machine man.

"Woulda," said Terry. "I woulda gone upside her head with my fist and—"

"You woulda done whatcha always do—go cry to Mama, you big baby," said Tyrone. So naturally Terry starts hittin on Tyrone, and next thing you

Blues Ain't No Mockin Bird   135

know they tumblin out the tire and rollin on the ground. But Granny didn't say a thing or send the twins home or step out on the steps to tell us about how we can't afford to be fightin amongst ourselves. She didn't say nuthin. So I get into the tire to take my turn. And I could see her leanin up against the pantry table, starin at the cakes she was puttin up for the Christmas sale, mumblin real low and grumpy and holdin her forehead like it wanted to fall off and mess up the rum cakes.

Behind me I hear before I can see Granddaddy Cain comin through the woods in his field boots. Then I twist around to see the shiny black oilskin cuttin through what little left there was of yellows, reds, and oranges. His great white head not quite round cause of this bloody thing high on his shoulder, like he was wearin a cap on sideways. He takes the shortcut through the pecan grove, and the sound of twigs snapping overhead and underfoot travels clear and cold all the way up to us. And here comes Smilin and Camera up behind him like they was goin to do somethin. Folks like to go for him sometimes. Cathy say it's because he's so tall and quiet and like a king. And people just can't stand it. But Smilin and Camera don't hit him in the head or nuthin. They just buzz on him as he stalks by with the chicken hawk slung over his shoulder, squawkin, drippin red down the back of the oilskin. He passes the porch and stops a second for Granny to see he's caught the hawk at last, but she's just starin and mumblin, and not at the hawk. So he nails the bird to the toolshed door, the hammerin crackin through the eardrums. And the bird flappin himself to death and droolin down the door to paint the gravel in the driveway red, then brown, then black. And the two men movin up on tiptoe like they was invisible or we were blind, one.

"Get them persons out of my flower bed, Mister Cain," say Granny moanin real low like at a funeral.

"How come your grandmother calls her husband 'Mister Cain' all the time?" Tyrone whispers all loud and noisy and from the city and don't know no better. Like his mama, Miss Myrtle, tell us never mind the formality as if we had no better breeding than to call her Myrtle, plain. And then this awful thing—a giant hawk—come wailin up over the meadow, flyin low and tilted and screamin, zigzaggin through the pecan grove, breakin branches and hollerin, snappin past the clothesline, flyin every which way, flyin into things reckless with crazy.

"He's come to claim his mate," say Cathy fast, and ducks down. We all fall quick and flat into the gravel driveway, stones scrapin my face. I squinch my eyes open again at the hawk on the door, tryin to fly up out of her death like it was just a sack flown into by mistake. Her body holdin her there on that nail, though. The mate beatin the air overhead and clutchin for hair, for heads, for landin space.

The camera man duckin and bendin and runnin and fallin, jigglin the camera and scared. And Smilin jumpin up and down swipin at the huge bird, tryin to bring the hawk down with just his raggedy ole cap. Granddaddy Cain straight up and silent, watchin the circles of the hawk, then aimin the hammer off his wrist. The giant bird fallin, silent and slow. Then here comes Camera and Smilin all big and bad now that the awful screechin thing is on its back and broken, here they come. And Granddaddy Cain looks up at them like it was the first time noticin, but not payin them too much mind cause he's listenin, we all listenin, to that low groanin music comin from the porch. And we figure any minute, somethin in my back tells me any minute now, Granny gonna bust through that screen with somethin in her hand and murder on her mind. So Granddaddy say above the buzzin, but quiet, "Good day, gentlemen." Just like that. Like he'd invited them in to play cards and they'd stayed too long and all the sandwiches were gone and Reverend Webb was droppin by and it was time to go.

They didn't know what to do. But like Cathy say, folks can't stand Granddaddy tall and silent and like a king. They can't neither. The smile the men smilin is pullin the mouth back and showin the teeth. Lookin like the wolf man, both of them. Then Granddaddy holds his hand out—this huge hand I used to sit in when I was a baby and he'd carry me through the house to my mother like I was a gift on a tray. Like he used to on the trains. They called the other men just waiters. But they spoke of Granddaddy separate and said, The Waiter. And said he had engines in his feet and motors in his hands and couldn't no train throw him off and couldn't nobody turn him round. They were big enough for motors, his hands were. He held that one hand out all still and it gettin to be not at all a hand but a person in itself.

"He wants you to hand him the camera," Smilin whispers to Camera, tiltin his head to talk secret like they was in the jungle or somethin and come upon a native that don't speak the language. The men start untyin the straps, and they put the camera into that great hand speckled with the hawk's blood all black and crackly now. And the hand don't even drop with the weight, just the fingers move, curl up around the machine. But Granddaddy lookin straight at the men. They lookin at each other and everywhere but at Granddaddy's face.

"We filmin for the county, see," say Smilin. "We puttin together a movie for the food stamp program . . . filmin all around these parts. Uhh, filmin for the county."

"Can I have my camera back?" say the tall man with no machine on his shoulder, but still keepin it high like the camera was still there or needed to be. "Please, sir."

Then Granddaddy's other hand flies up like a sudden and gentle bird, slaps down fast on top of the camera and lifts off half like it was a calabash cut for sharing.

"Hey," Camera jumps forward. He gathers up the parts into his chest and everything unrollin and fallin all over. "Whatcha tryin to do? You'll ruin the film." He looks down into his chest of metal reels and things like he's protectin a kitten from the cold.

"You standin in the misses' flower bed," say Granddaddy. "This is our own place."

The two men look at him, then at each other, then back at the mess in the camera man's chest, and they just back off. One sayin over and over all the way down to the meadow, "Watch it, Bruno. Keep ya fingers off the film." Then Granddaddy picks up the hammer and jams it into the oilskin pocket, scrapes his boots, and goes into the house. And you can hear the squish of his boots headin through the house. And you can see the funny shadow he throws from the parlor window onto the ground by the string-bean patch. The hammer draggin the pocket of the oilskin out so Granddaddy looked even wider. Granny was hummin now—high, not low and grumbly. And she was doin the cakes again, you could smell the molasses from the rum.

"There's this story I'm goin to write one day," say Cathy dreamer. "About the proper use of the hammer."

"Can I be in it?" Tyrone say with his hand up like it was a matter of first come, first served.

"Perhaps," say Cathy, climbin onto the tire to pump us up. "If you there and ready."

Responding to the Selection

Questions for Discussion

1. Until now, where has the Cain family lived? How does their current home differ from the places the family has lived before?

2. What does Granny's story about the man's suicide attempt reveal about her and her reaction to the men? Use details from the story in your answer.

3. How are the two hawks like Granny and Granddaddy Cain? How are they like Camera and Smilin? Consider what kind of message their deaths might have sent to these men.

4. Do you think "Blues Ain't No Mockin Bird" is an appropriate **title** for this story? Why or why not?

5. Why did the author choose to tell the story from the child's **point of view?**

6. How did the **dialect** affect your reading and understanding of the story? How does dialect make the story's characters and events seem more real?

Before You Read

I've Got a Home in That Rock

Raymond Patterson
Born 1929

"Good men holding their
   courage slack
In their frightened pockets see
   how weak
The work that is done; and
   feel the weight
Of your blood on the ground for
   their spirits' sake . . ."

About Patterson

Raymond Patterson is a New York City poet who has spent his life teaching others about the craft of poetry. His work has appeared in many poetry anthologies, including *For Malcolm* (1967), *I Am the Darker Brother* (1968), and *Black Out Loud* (1970). Patterson edits a newsletter for poets and has traveled to schools and libraries throughout the state of New York as part of a poetry project sponsored by the New York State Council on the Arts. A volume of Patterson's poems, *26 Ways of Looking at a Black Man,* was published in 1969.

I've Got a Home in That Rock

— Raymond Patterson

I had an uncle once who kept a rock in his pocket—
Always did, up to the day he died.
And as far as I know, that rock is still with him,
Holding down some dust of his thighbone.

5   From Mississippi he'd got that rock, he'd say—
Or, sometimes, from Tennessee: a different place each time
He told it, how he'd picked it up when he first left home—
Running, he'd say—to remind him when times got hard
Enough to make him homesick, what home was really like.

Responding to the Selection

Questions for Discussion

1. What does the rock **symbolize** in this poem?

2. Why do you suppose the uncle kept the rock in his pocket, perhaps even in death?

3. The speaker says that the uncle left home "running." How would you interpret this behavior?

4. What do you think "home" was really like? Why do you think so?

Activities

Writing About Personal Objects

1. Physical objects can remind you of good times and bad times. Write a **personal narrative** or a **poem** about an object that you've kept for a long time. What does it symbolize to you? Why have you held onto it?

Interpreting Poetry

2. In a paragraph or two, explain how you think the title of the poem relates to its meaning.

Before You Read

from *The Autobiography of Malcolm X*

Malcolm X (with Alex Haley)
1925–1965

"Early in life, I had learned that if you want something, you had better make some noise."

About Malcolm X

Malcolm Little joined the Nation of Islam, a religious community that originally espoused black nationalism, in 1946, while serving a ten-year prison sentence for burglary in New York. After his release in 1952, he met Elijah Muhammad, the Nation's leader, and took the name "Malcolm X." He became a minister in Harlem and founded the newspaper *Muhammad Speaks.* Malcolm X was one of the Nation's most effective leaders and organizers.

Malcolm X eventually broke from the Nation of Islam, although he continued to practice the Islamic faith, and adopted a less militant, more inclusive point of view.

He still advocated racial solidarity for African Americans but encouraged them to work to end racial discrimination.

While speaking at a rally in 1965, Malcolm X was assassinated. The three men convicted of his murder had ties to the Nation of Islam. Some scholars and followers of Malcolm X suspect that the leadership of the Nation had ordered the murder. In 2000, Louis Farrakhan, the current leader of the Nation, conceded that he and others may have contributed to the climate of hate within the Nation that culminated in Malcolm X's death.

About Alex Haley

Alex Haley (1921–1992), a journalist and novelist, wrote *The Autobiography of Malcolm X* based on a series of interviews with Malcolm X. First published in 1965, the book provides an authoritative account of this man's early life of poverty and crime, through his religious conversion, reflecting as well his profound commitment to the African American community.

Haley is also known for his novel *Roots: The Saga of an American Family* (1976), in which he tells the story of his own family's history over seven generations, from the first enslaved African member of his family brought to the United States.

from The Autobiography of Malcolm X

from

The Autobiography of Malcolm X

— *Malcolm X*

When my mother was pregnant with me, she told me later, a party of hooded Ku Klux Klan riders galloped up to our home in Omaha, Nebraska, one night. Surrounding the house, brandishing their shotguns and rifles, they shouted for my father to come out. My mother went to the front door and opened it. Standing where they could see her pregnant condition, she told them that she was alone with her three small children, and that my father was away, preaching, in Milwaukee. The Klansmen shouted threats and warnings at her that we had better get out of town because "the good Christian white people" were not going to stand for my father's "spreading trouble" among the "good" Negroes of Omaha with the "back to Africa" preachings of Marcus Garvey.

My father, the Reverend Earl Little, was a Baptist minister, a dedicated organizer for Marcus Aurelius Garvey's U.N.I.A. (Universal Negro Improvement Association). With the help of such disciples as my father, Garvey, from his headquarters in New York City's Harlem, was raising the banner of black-race purity and exhorting the Negro masses to return to their ancestral African homeland—a cause which had made Garvey the most controversial black man on earth.

Still shouting threats, the Klansmen finally spurred their horses and galloped around the house, shattering every window pane with their gun butts. Then they rode off into the night, their torches flaring, as suddenly as they had come.

My father was enraged when he returned. He decided to wait until I was born—which would be soon—and then the family would move. I am not sure why he made this decision, for he was not a frightened Negro, as most then were, and many still are today. My father was a big, six-foot-four, very black man. He had only one eye. How he had lost the other one I have never known. He was from Reynolds, Georgia, where he had left school after the third or maybe fourth grade. He believed, as did Marcus Garvey, that freedom, independence and self-respect could never be achieved by the Negro in America, and that therefore the Negro should leave America to the white man and return to his African land of origin. Among the reasons my father had decided to risk and dedicate his life to help disseminate this philosophy among his people was that he had seen four of his six brothers die by violence, three of them killed by white men, including one by lynching. What my father could not know then was that of the remaining three, including himself, only one, my Uncle Jim, would die in bed, of natural causes. Northern white police were later to shoot my Uncle Oscar. And my father was finally himself to die by the white man's hands.

It has always been my belief that I, too, will die by violence. I have done all that I can to be prepared.

I was my father's seventh child. He had three children by a previous marriage—Ella, Earl, and Mary, who lived in Boston. He had met and married my mother in Philadelphia, where their first child, my oldest full brother, Wilfred, was born. They moved from Philadelphia to Omaha, where Hilda and then Philbert were born.

I was next in line. My mother was twenty-eight when I was born on May 19, 1925, in an Omaha hospital. Then we moved to Milwaukee, where Reginald was born. From infancy, he had some kind of hernia condition which was to handicap him physically for the rest of his life.

Louise Little, my mother, who was born in Grenada, in the British West Indies, looked like a white woman. Her father *was* white. She had straight black hair, and her accent did not sound like a Negro's. Of this white father of hers, I know nothing except her shame about it. I remember hearing her say she was glad that she had never seen him. It was, of course, because of him that I got my reddish-brown "mariny" color of skin, and my hair of the same color. I was the lightest child in our family. (Out in the world later on, in Boston and New York, I was among the millions of Negroes who were insane enough to feel that it was some kind of status symbol to be light-complexioned—that one was actually fortunate to be born thus. But, still later, I learned to hate every drop of that white rapist's blood that is in me.)

Our family stayed only briefly in Milwaukee, for my father wanted to find a place where he could raise our own food and perhaps build a business. The teaching of Marcus Garvey stressed becoming independent of the white man. We went next, for some reason, to Lansing, Michigan. My father bought a house and soon, as had been his pattern, he was doing free-lance Christian preaching in local Negro Baptist churches, and during the week he was roaming about spreading word of Marcus Garvey.

He had begun to lay away savings for the store he had always wanted to own when, as always, some stupid local Uncle Tom Negroes began to funnel stories about his revolutionary beliefs to the local white people. This time, the get-out-of-town threats came from a local hate society called The Black Legion. They wore black robes instead of white. Soon, nearly everywhere my father went, Black Legionnaires were reviling him as an "uppity nigger" for wanting to own a store, for living outside the Lansing Negro district, for spreading unrest and dissension among "the good niggers."

As in Omaha, my mother was pregnant again, this time with my youngest sister. Shortly after Yvonne was born came the nightmare night in 1929, my earliest vivid memory. I remember being suddenly snatched awake into a frightening confusion of pistol shots and shouting and smoke and flames. My father had shouted and shot at the two white men who had set the fire and were running away. Our home was burning down around us. We were lunging and bumping and tumbling all over each other trying to escape. My mother, with the baby in her arms, just made it into the yard before the house crashed in, showering sparks. I remember we were outside in the night in our underwear, crying and yelling our heads off. The white police and firemen came and stood around watching as the house burned down to the ground.

My father prevailed on some friends to clothe and house us temporarily; then he moved us into another house on the outskirts of East Lansing. In those days Negroes weren't allowed after dark in East Lansing proper. There's where Michigan State University is located; I related all of this to an audience of students when I spoke there in January, 1963 (and had the first reunion in a long while with my younger brother, Robert, who was there doing postgraduate studies in psychology). I told them how East Lansing harassed us so much that we had to move again, this time two miles out of town, into the country. This was where my father built for us with his own hands a four-room house. This is where I really begin to remember things—this home where I started to grow up.

After the fire, I remember that my father was called in and questioned about a permit for the pistol with which he had shot at the white men who set the fire. I remember that the police were always dropping by our house, shoving things around, "just checking" or "looking for a gun." The pistol they were looking for—which they never found, and for which they wouldn't issue a permit—was sewed up inside a pillow. My father's .22 rifle and his shotgun, though, were right out in the open; everyone had them for hunting birds and rabbits and other game.

After that, my memories are of the friction between my father and mother. They seemed to be nearly always at odds. Sometimes my father would beat her. It might have had something to do with the fact that my mother had a pretty good education. Where she got it I don't know. But an educated woman, I suppose, can't resist the temptation to correct an uneducated man. Every now and then, when she put those smooth words on him, he would grab her.

My father was also belligerent toward all of the children, except me. The older ones he would beat almost savagely if they broke any of his rules—and he had so many rules it was hard to know them all. Nearly all my whippings came from my mother. I've thought a lot about why. I actually believe that as anti-white as my father was, he was subconsciously so afflicted with the white man's brainwashing of Negroes that he inclined to favor the light ones, and I was his lightest child. Most Negro parents in those days would almost instinctively treat any lighter children better than they did the darker ones. It came directly from the slavery tradition that the "mulatto," because he was visibly nearer to white, was therefore "better."

My two other images of my father are both outside the home. One was his role as a Baptist preacher. He never pastored in any regular church of his own; he was always a "visiting preacher." I remember especially his favorite sermon: "That little *black* train is a-comin' . . . an' you better get all your business right!" I guess this also fit his association with the back-to-Africa movement, with Marcus Garvey's "Black Train Homeward." My brother Philbert, the one just older than me, loved church, but it confused and amazed me. I would sit goggle-eyed at my father jumping and shouting as he preached, with the congregation jumping and shouting behind him, their souls and bodies devoted to singing and praying. Even at that young age, I just couldn't believe in the Christian concept of Jesus as someone divine. And no religious person, until I was a man in my twenties—and then in prison—could tell me anything. I had very little respect for most people who represented religion.

It was in his role as a preacher that my father had most contact with the Negroes of Lansing. Believe me when I tell you that those Negroes were in bad shape then. They are still in bad shape—though in a different way. By that I mean that I don't know a town with a higher percentage of complacent and misguided so-called "middle-class" Negroes—the typical status-symbol-oriented, integration-seeking type of Negroes. Just recently, I was standing in a lobby at the United Nations talking with an African ambassador and his wife, when a Negro came up to me and said, "You know me?" I was a little embarrassed because I thought he was someone I should remember. It turned out that he was one of those bragging, self-satisfied, "middle-class" Lansing Negroes. I wasn't ingratiated. He was the type who would never have been associated with Africa, until the fad of having African friends became a status-symbol for "middle-class" Negroes.

from The Autobiography of Malcolm X

Back when I was growing up, the "successful" Lansing Negroes were such as waiters and bootblacks. To be a janitor at some downtown store was to be highly respected. The real "elite," the "big shots," the "voices of the race," were the waiters at the Lansing Country Club and the shoeshine boys at the state capitol. The only Negroes who really had any money were the ones in the numbers racket, or who ran the gambling houses, or who in some other way lived parasitically off the poorest ones, who were the masses. No Negroes were hired then by Lansing's big Oldsmobile plant, or the Reo plant. (Do you remember the Reo? It was manufactured in Lansing, and R. E. Olds, the man after whom it was named, also lived in Lansing. When the war came along, they hired some Negro janitors.) The bulk of the Negroes were either on Welfare, or W.P.A., or they starved.

The day was to come when our family was so poor that we would eat the hole out of a doughnut; but at that time we were much better off than most town Negroes. The reason was we raised much of our own food out there in the country where we were. We were much better off than the town Negroes who would shout, as my father preached, for the pie-in-the-sky and their heaven in the hereafter while the white man had his here on earth.

I knew that the collections my father got for his preaching were mainly what fed and clothed us, and he also did other odd jobs, but still the image of him that made me proudest was his crusading and militant campaigning with the words of Marcus Garvey. As young as I was then, I knew from what I overheard that my father was saying something that made him a "tough" man. I remember an old lady, grinning and saying to my father, "You're scaring these white folks to death!"

One of the reasons I've always felt that my father favored me was that to the best of my remembrance, it was only me that he sometimes took with him to the Garvey U.N.I.A. meetings which he held quietly in different people's homes. There were never more than a few people at any one time—twenty at most. But that was a lot, packed into someone's living room. I noticed how differently they all acted, although sometimes they were the same people who jumped and shouted in church. But in these meetings both they and my father were more intense, more intelligent and down to earth. It made me feel the same way.

I can remember hearing of "Adam driven out of the garden into the caves of Europe," "Africa for the Africans," "Ethiopians, Awake!" And my father would talk about how it would not be much longer before Africa would be completely run by Negroes—"by black men," was the phrase he always used. "No one knows when the hour of Africa's redemption cometh. It is in the wind. It is coming. One day, like a storm, it will be here."

I remember seeing the big, shiny photographs of Marcus Garvey that were passed from hand to hand. My father had a big envelope of them that he always took to these meetings. The pictures showed what seemed to me millions of Negroes thronged in parade behind Garvey riding in a fine car, a big black man dressed in a dazzling uniform with gold braid on it, and he was wearing a thrilling hat with tall plumes. I remember hearing that he had black followers not only in the United States but all around the world, and I remember how the meetings always closed with my father saying, several times, and the people chanting after him, "Up, you mighty race, you can accomplish what you will!"

I have never understood why, after hearing as much as I did of these kinds of things, I somehow never thought, then, of the black people in Africa. My image of Africa, at that time, was of naked savages, cannibals, monkeys and tigers and steaming jungles.

My father would drive in his old black touring car, sometimes taking me, to meeting places all around the Lansing area. I remember one day-time meeting (most were at night) in the town of Owosso, forty miles from Lansing, which the Negroes called "White City." (Owosso's greatest claim to fame is that it is the home town of Thomas E. Dewey.) As in East Lansing, no Negroes were allowed on the streets there after dark—hence the daytime meeting. In point of fact, in those days lots of Michigan towns were like that. Every town had a few "home" Negroes who lived there. Sometimes it would be just one family, as in the nearby county seat, Mason, which had a single Negro family named Lyons. Mr. Lyons had been a famous football star at Mason High School, was highly thought of in Mason, and consequently he now worked around that town in menial jobs.

My mother at this time seemed to be always working—cooking, washing, ironing, cleaning, and fussing over us eight children. And she was usually either arguing with or not speaking to my father. One cause of friction was that she had strong ideas about what she wouldn't eat—and didn't want *us* to eat—including pork and rabbit, both of which my father loved dearly. He was a real Georgia Negro, and he believed in eating plenty of what we in Harlem today call "soul food."

I've said that my mother was the one who whipped me—at least she did whenever she wasn't ashamed to let the neighbors think she was killing me. For if she even acted as though she was about to raise her hand to me, I would open my mouth and let the world know about it. If anybody was passing by out on the road, she would either change her mind or just give me a few licks.

Thinking about it now, I feel definitely that just as my father favored me for being lighter than the other children, my mother gave me more hell for the same reason. She was very light herself but she favored the ones who were darker. Wilfred, I know, was particularly her angel. I remember that she would tell me to get out of the house and "Let the sun shine on you so you can get some color." She went out of her way never to let me become afflicted with a sense of color-superiority. I am sure that she treated me this way partly because of how she came to be light herself.

I learned early that crying out in protest could accomplish things. My older brothers and sister had started to school when, sometimes, they would come in and ask for a buttered biscuit or something and my mother, impatiently, would tell them no. But I would cry out and make a fuss until I got what I wanted. I remember well how my mother asked me why I couldn't be a nice boy like Wilfred; but I would think to myself that Wilfred, for being so nice and quiet, often stayed hungry. So early in life, I had learned that if you want something, you had better make some noise.

Not only did we have our big garden, but we raised chickens. My father would buy some baby chicks and my mother would raise them. We all loved chicken. That was one dish there was no argument with my father about. One thing in particular that I remember made me feel grateful toward my mother was that one day I went and asked her for my own garden, and she did let me have my own little plot. I loved it and took care of it well. I loved especially to grow peas. I was proud when we had them on our table. I would pull out the grass in my garden by hand when the first little blades came up. I would patrol the rows on my hands and knees for any worms and bugs, and I would kill and bury them. And sometimes when I had everything straight and clean for my things to grow, I would lie down on my back between two rows, and I would gaze up in the blue sky at the clouds moving and think all kinds of things.

At five, I, too, began to go to school, leaving home in the morning along with Wilfred, Hilda, and Philbert. It was the Pleasant Grove School that went from kindergarten through the eighth grade. It was two miles outside the city limits, and I guess there was no problem about our attending because we were the only Negroes in the area. In those days white people in the North usually would "adopt" just a few Negroes; they didn't see them as any threat. The white kids didn't make any great thing about us, either. They called us "nigger" and "darkie" and "Rastus" so much that we thought those were our natural names. But they didn't think of it as an insult; it was just the way they thought about us.

One afternoon in 1931 when Wilfred, Hilda, Philbert, and I came home, my mother and father were having one of their arguments. There had lately been a lot of tension around the house because of Black Legion threats. Anyway, my father had taken one of the rabbits which we were raising, and ordered my mother to cook it. We raised rabbits, but sold them to whites. My father had taken a rabbit from the rabbit pen. He had pulled off the rabbit's head. He was so strong, he needed no knife to behead chickens or rabbits. With one twist of his big black hands he simply twisted off the head and threw the bleeding-necked thing back at my mother's feet.

My mother was crying. She started to skin the rabbit, preparatory to cooking it. But my father was so angry he slammed on out of the front door and started walking up the road toward town.

It was then that my mother had this vision. She had always been a strange woman in this sense, and had always had a strong intuition of things about to happen. And most of her children are the same way, I think. When something is about to happen, I can feel something, sense something. I never have known something to happen that has caught me completely off guard—except once. And that was when, years later, I discovered facts I couldn't believe about a man who, up until that discovery, I would gladly have given my life for.

My father was well up the road when my mother ran screaming out onto the porch. *"Early! Early!"* She screamed his name. She clutched up her apron in one hand, and ran down across the yard and into the road. My father turned around. He saw her. For some reason, considering how angry he had been when he left, he waved at her. But he kept on going.

She told me later, my mother did, that she had a vision of my father's end. All the rest of the afternoon, she was not herself, crying and nervous and upset. She finished cooking the rabbit and put the whole thing in the warmer part of the black stove. When my father was not back home by our bedtime, my mother hugged and clutched us, and we felt strange, not knowing what to do, because she had never acted like that.

I remember waking up to the sound of my mother's screaming again. When I scrambled out, I saw the police in the living room; they were trying to calm her down. She had snatched on her clothes to go with them. And all of us children who were staring knew without anyone having to say it that something terrible had happened to our father.

My mother was taken by the police to the hospital, and to a room where a sheet was over my father in a bed, and she wouldn't look, she was afraid to look. Probably it was wise that she didn't. My father's skull, on one side, was crushed in, I was told later. Negroes in Lansing have always whispered that he was attacked, and then laid across some tracks for a streetcar to run over him. His body was cut almost in half.

He lived two and a half hours in that condition. Negroes then were stronger than they are now, especially Georgia Negroes. Negroes born in Georgia had to be strong simply to survive.

It was morning when we children at home got the word that he was dead. I was six. I can remember a vague commotion, the house filled up with people crying, saying bitterly that the white Black Legion had finally gotten him. My mother was hysterical. In the bedroom, women were holding smelling salts under her nose. She was still hysterical at the funeral.

I don't have a very clear memory of the funeral, either. Oddly, the main thing I remember is that it wasn't in a church, and that surprised me, since my father was a preacher, and I had been where he preached people's funerals in churches. But his was in a funeral home.

And I remember that during the service a big black fly came down and landed on my father's face, and Wilfred sprang up from his chair and he shooed the fly away, and he came groping back to his chair—there were folding chairs for us to sit on—and the tears were streaming down his face. When we went by the casket, I remember that I thought that it looked as if my father's strong black face had been dusted with flour, and I wished they hadn't put on such a lot of it.

Back in the big four-room house, there were many visitors for another week or so. They were good friends of the family, such as the Lyons from Mason, twelve miles away, and the Walkers, McGuires, Liscoes, the Greens, Randolphs, and the Turners, and others from Lansing, and a lot of people from other towns, whom I had seen at the Garvey meetings.

We children adjusted more easily than our mother did. We couldn't see, as clearly as she did, the trials that lay ahead. As the visitors tapered off, she became very concerned about collecting the two insurance policies that my father had always been proud he carried. He had always said that families should be protected in case of death. One policy apparently paid off without any problem—the smaller one. I don't know the amount of it. I would imagine it was not more than a thousand dollars, and maybe half of that.

But after that money came, and my mother had paid out a lot of it for the funeral and expenses, she began going into town and returning very upset. The company that had issued the bigger policy was balking at paying off. They were claiming that my father had committed suicide. Visitors came again, and there was bitter talk about white people: how could my father bash himself in the head, then get down across the streetcar tracks to be run over?

So there we were. My mother was thirty-four years old now, with no husband, no provider or protector to take care of her eight children. But some kind of a family routine got going again. And for as long as the first insurance money lasted, we did all right.

Wilfred, who was a pretty stable fellow, began to act older than his age. I think he had the sense to see, when the rest of us didn't, what was in the wind for us. He quietly quit school and went to town in search of work. He took any kind of job he could find and he would come home, dog-tired, in the evenings, and give whatever he had made to my mother.

Hilda, who always had been quiet, too, attended to the babies. Philbert and I didn't contribute anything. We just fought all the time—each other at home, and then at school we would team up and fight white kids. Sometimes the fights would be racial in nature, but they might be about anything.

Reginald came under my wing. Since he had grown out of the toddling stage, he and I had become very close. I suppose I enjoyed the fact that he was the little one, under me, who looked up to me.

My mother began to buy on credit. My father had always been very strongly against credit. "Credit is the first step into debt and back into slavery," he had always said. And then she went to work herself. She would go into Lansing and find different jobs—in housework, or sewing— for white people. They didn't realize, usually, that she was a Negro. A lot of white people around there didn't want Negroes in their houses.

She would do fine until in some way or other it got to people who she was, whose widow she was. And then she would be let go. I remember how she used to come home crying, but trying to hide it, because she had lost a job that she needed so much.

Once when one of us—I cannot remember which—had to go for something to where she was working, and the people saw us, and realized she was actually a Negro, she was fired on the spot, and she came home crying, this time not hiding it.

When the state Welfare people began coming to our house, we would come from school sometimes and find them talking with our mother, asking a thousand questions. They acted and looked at her, and at us, and around in our house, in a way that had about it the feeling—at least for me—that we were not people. In their eyesight we were just *things*, that was all.

My mother began to receive two checks—a Welfare check and, I believe, a widow's pension. The checks helped. But they weren't enough, as many of us as there were. When they came, about the first of the month, one always was already owed in full, if not more, to the man at the grocery store. And, after that, the other one didn't last long.

We began to go swiftly downhill. The physical downhill wasn't as quick as the psychological. My mother was, above everything else, a proud woman, and it took its toll on her that she was accepting charity. And her feelings were communicated to us.

She would speak sharply to the man at the grocery store for padding the bill, telling him that she wasn't ignorant, and he didn't like that. She would talk back sharply to the state Welfare people, telling them that she was a grown woman, able to raise her children, that it wasn't necessary for them to keep coming around so much, meddling in our lives. And they didn't like that.

from The Autobiography of Malcolm X

But the monthly Welfare check was their pass. They acted as if they owned us, as if we were their private property. As much as my mother would have liked to, she couldn't keep them out. She would get particularly incensed when they began insisting upon drawing us older children aside, one at a time, out on the porch or somewhere, and asking us questions, or telling us things—against our mother and against each other.

We couldn't understand why, if the state was willing to give us packages of meat, sacks of potatoes and fruit, and cans of all kinds of things, our mother obviously hated to accept. We really couldn't understand. What I later understood was that my mother was making a desperate effort to preserve her pride—and ours.

Pride was just about all we had to preserve, for by 1934, we really began to suffer. This was about the worst depression year, and no one we knew had enough to eat or live on. Some old family friends visited us now and then. At first they brought food. Though it was charity, my mother took it.

Wilfred was working to help. My mother was working, when she could find any kind of job. In Lansing, there was a bakery where, for a nickel, a couple of us children would buy a tall flour sack of day-old bread and cookies, and then walk the two miles back out into the country to our house. Our mother knew, I guess, dozens of ways to cook things with bread and out of bread. Stewed tomatoes with bread, maybe that would be a meal. Something like French toast, if we had any eggs. Bread pudding, sometimes with raisins in it. If we got hold of some hamburger, it came to the table more bread than meat. The cookies that were always in the sack with the bread, we just gobbled down straight.

But there were times when there wasn't even a nickel and we would be so hungry we were dizzy. My mother would boil a big pot of dandelion greens, and we would eat that. I remember that some small-minded neighbor put it out, and children would tease us, that we ate "fried grass." Sometimes, if we were lucky, we would have oatmeal or cornmeal mush three times a day. Or mush in the morning and cornbread at night.

Philbert and I were grown up enough to quit fighting long enough to take the .22 caliber rifle that had been our father's, and shoot rabbits that some white neighbors up or down the road would buy. I know now that they just did it to help us, because they, like everyone, shot their own rabbits. Sometimes, I remember, Philbert and I would take little Reginald along with us. He wasn't very strong, but he was always so proud to be along. We would trap muskrats out in the little creek in back of our house. And we would lie quiet until unsuspecting bullfrogs appeared, and we would spear them, cut off their legs, and sell them for a nickel a pair to people who lived up and down the road. The whites seemed less restricted in their dietary tastes.

from The Autobiography of Malcolm X

Then, about in late 1934, I would guess, something began to happen. Some kind of psychological deterioration hit our family circle and began to eat away our pride. Perhaps it was the constant tangible evidence that we were destitute. We had known other families who had gone on relief. We had known without anyone in our home ever expressing it that we had felt prouder not to be at the depot where the free food was passed out. And, now, we were among them. At school, the "on relief" finger suddenly was pointed at us, too, and sometimes it was said aloud.

It seemed that everything to eat in our house was stamped Not To Be Sold. All Welfare food bore this stamp to keep the recipients from selling it. It's a wonder we didn't come to think of Not To Be Sold as a brand name.

Sometimes, instead of going home from school, I walked the two miles up the road into Lansing. I began drifting from store to store, hanging around outside where things like apples were displayed in boxes and barrels and baskets, and I would watch my chance and steal me a treat. You know what a treat was to me? Anything!

Or I began to drop in about dinnertime at the home of some family that we knew. I knew that they knew exactly why I was there, but they never embarrassed me by letting on. They would invite me to stay for supper, and I would stuff myself.

Especially, I liked to drop in and visit at the Gohannas' home. They were nice, older people, and great churchgoers. I had watched them lead the jumping and shouting when my father preached. They had, living with them—they were raising him—a nephew whom everyone called "Big Boy," and he and I got along fine. Also living with the Gohannas was old Mrs. Adcock, who went with them to church. She was always trying to help anybody she could, visiting anyone she heard was sick, carrying them something. She was the one who, years later, would tell me something that I remembered a long time: "Malcolm, there's one thing I like about you. You're no good, but you don't try to hide it. You are not a hypocrite."

The more I began to stay away from home and visit people and steal from the stores, the more aggressive I became in my inclinations. I never wanted to wait for anything.

I was growing up fast, physically more so than mentally. As I began to be recognized more around the town, I started to become aware of the peculiar attitude of white people toward me. I sensed that it had to do with my father. It was an adult version of what several white children had said at school, in hints, or sometimes in the open, which really expressed what their parents had said—that the Black Legion or the Klan had killed my father, and the insurance company had pulled a fast one in refusing to pay my mother the policy money.

from The Autobiography of Malcolm X

When I began to get caught stealing now and then, the state Welfare people began to focus on me when they came to our house. I can't remember how I first became aware that they were talking of taking me away. What I first remember along that line was my mother raising a storm about being able to bring up her own children. She would whip me for stealing, and I would try to alarm the neighborhood with my yelling. One thing I have always been proud of is that I never raised my hand against my mother.

In the summertime, at night, in addition to all the other things we did, some of us boys would slip out down the road, or across the pastures, and go "cooning" watermelons. White people always associated watermelons with Negroes, and they sometimes called Negroes "coons" among all the other names, and so stealing watermelons became "cooning" them. If white boys were doing it, it implied that they were only acting like Negroes. Whites have always hidden or justified all of the guilts they could by ridiculing or blaming Negroes.

One Halloween night, I remember that a bunch of us were out tipping over those old country outhouses, and one old farmer—I guess he had tipped over enough in his day—had set a trap for us. Always, you sneak up from behind the outhouse, then you gang together and push it, to tip it over. This farmer had taken his outhouse off the hole, and set it just in *front* of the hole. Well, we came sneaking up in single file, in the darkness, and the two white boys in the lead fell down into the outhouse hole neck deep. They smelled so bad it was all we could stand to get them out, and that finished us all for that Halloween. I had just missed falling in myself. The whites were so used to taking the lead, this time it had really gotten them in the hole.

Thus, in various ways, I learned various things. I picked strawberries, and though I can't recall what I got per crate for picking, I remember that after working hard all one day, I wound up with about a dollar, which was a whole lot of money in those times. I was so hungry, I didn't know what to do. I was walking away toward town with visions of buying something good to eat, and this older white boy I knew, Richard Dixon, came up and asked me if I wanted to match nickels. He had plenty of change for my dollar. In about a half hour, he had all the change back, including my dollar, and instead of going to town to buy something, I went home with nothing, and I was bitter. But that was nothing compared to what I felt when I found out later that he had cheated. There is a way that you can catch and hold the nickel and make it come up the way you want. This was my first lesson about gambling: if you see somebody winning all the time, he isn't gambling, he's cheating. Later on in life, if I were continuously losing in any gambling situation, I would watch very closely. It's like the Negro in America seeing the white man win all the time. He's a professional

from **The Autobiography of Malcolm X**   155

gambler; he has all the cards and the odds stacked on his side, and he has always dealt to our people from the bottom of the deck.

About this time, my mother began to be visited by some Seventh Day Adventists who had moved into a house not too far down the road from us. They would talk to her for hours at a time, and leave booklets and leaflets and magazines for her to read. She read them, and Wilfred, who had started back to school after we had begun to get the relief food sup-plies, also read a lot. His head was forever in some book.

Before long, my mother spent much time with the Adventists. It's my belief that what mostly influenced her was that they had even more diet restrictions than she always had taught and practiced with us. Like us, they were against eating rabbit and pork; they followed the Mosaic dietary laws. They ate nothing of the flesh without a split hoof, or that didn't chew a cud. We began to go with my mother to the Adventist meetings that were held further out in the country. For us children, I know that the major attraction was the good food they served. But we listened, too. There were a handful of Negroes, from small towns in the area, but I would say that it was ninety-nine percent white people. The Adventists felt that we were living at the end of time, that the world soon was coming to an end. But they were the friendliest white people I had ever seen. In some ways, though, we children noticed, and, when we were back at home, discussed, that they were different from us—such as the lack of enough seasoning in their food, and the different way that white people smelled.

Meanwhile, the state Welfare people kept after my mother. By now, she didn't make it any secret that she hated them, and didn't want them in her house. But they exerted their right to come, and I have many, many times reflected upon how, talking to us children, they began to plant the seeds of division in our minds. They would ask such things as who was smarter than the other. And they would ask me why I was "so different."

I think they felt that getting children into foster homes was a legiti-mate part of their function, and the result would be less troublesome, how-ever they went about it.

And when my mother fought them, they went after her—first, through me. I was the first target. I stole; that implied that I wasn't being taken care of by my mother.

All of us were mischievous at some time or another, I more so than any of the rest. Philbert and I kept a battle going. And this was just one of a dozen things that kept building up the pressure on my mother.

I'm not sure just how or when the idea was first dropped by the Welfare workers that our mother was losing her mind.

But I can distinctly remember hearing "crazy" applied to her by them when they learned that the Negro farmer who was in the next house down the road from us had offered to give us some butchered pork—a whole pig, maybe even two of them—and she had refused. We all heard them call my mother "crazy" to her face for refusing good meat. It meant nothing to them even when she explained that we had never eaten pork, that it was against her religion as a Seventh Day Adventist.

They were as vicious as vultures. They had no feelings, understanding, compassion, or respect for my mother. They told us, "She's crazy for refusing food." Right then was when our home, our unity, began to disintegrate. We were having a hard time, and I wasn't helping. But we could have made it, we could have stayed together. As bad as I was, as much trouble and worry as I caused my mother, I loved her.

The state people, we found out, had interviewed the Gohannas family, and the Gohannas' had said that they would take me into their home. My mother threw a fit, though, when she heard that—and the home wreckers took cover for a while.

Responding to the Selection —————

Questions for Discussion

1. Why did Marcus Garvey advocate that African Americans return to Africa?

2. What very personal reason did Malcolm's father have for preaching the philosophy of Marcus Garvey?

3. Malcolm X perceived that both his father and his mother treated him differently than they treated his siblings. What is his explanation for their differing treatment?

4. What role did the state welfare investigators play in the disintegration of the Little family, according to Malcolm X? Why did his mother think it necessary to resign herself to their visits?

Activities

Researching Marcus Garvey

1. Marcus Garvey was a colorful and highly influential African American leader. Research his life and his philosophy and write a **report** about what you discover. How did Garvey come by his beliefs? Was he successful?

Researching the Nation of Islam

2. Malcolm X rose to public prominence after he became a minister in the Nation of Islam. What is the Nation of Islam? Who were and are its leaders? What are its religious and political beliefs? After learning about the Nation of Islam, create a **fact sheet,** a list of twenty statements that relate important information about this organization.

Before You Read ———————

I Know Why the Caged Bird Sings

Maya Angelou
Born 1928

"If one is lucky, a solitary fantasy can totally transform one million realities."

About Angelou

Maya Angelou's childhood experiences in St. Louis and rural Arkansas are the basis for her autobiography, *I Know Why the Caged Bird Sings*. Born Marguerite Johnson, Angelou is an author, poet, actress, historian, playwright, film director, and civil rights activist. She has written ten best-selling books and has received Pulitzer Prize and National Book Award nominations.

Angelou's remarkable talents have been recognized by several U.S. presidents. President Jimmy Carter appointed her to the National Commission on the Observance of International Women's Year, and President Gerald Ford invited her to join the American Revolutionary Bicentennial Commission. President Bill Clinton asked her to compose and read a poem, "On the Pulse of Morning," for his first inauguration in 1993. Since 1981 she has held the title of Reynolds Professor of American Studies at Wake Forest University in North Carolina.

The Caged Bird

The title for Angelou's autobiographical narrative was taken from Paul Laurence Dunbar's poem "Sympathy," which includes the following stanza:

I know why the caged bird sings, ah me,
  When his wing is bruised and his bosom
    sore—
When he beats his bars and would be free;
It is not a carol of joy or glee,
  But a prayer that he sends from his heart's
    deep core,
But a plea, that upward to Heaven, he flings—
I know why the caged bird sings!

from
I Know Why the Caged Bird Sings

— *Maya Angelou*

1

When I was three and Bailey four, we had arrived in the musty little town, wearing tags on our wrists which instructed—"To Whom It May Concern"—that we were Marguerite and Bailey Johnson Jr., from Long Beach, California, en route to Stamps, Arkansas, c/o Mrs. Annie Henderson.

Our parents had decided to put an end to their calamitous marriage, and Father shipped us home to his mother. A porter had been charged with our welfare—he got off the train the next day in Arizona—and our tickets were pinned to my brother's inside coat pocket.

I don't remember much of the trip, but after we reached the segregated southern part of the journey, things must have looked up. Negro passengers, who always traveled with loaded lunch boxes, felt sorry for "the poor little motherless darlings" and plied us with cold fried chicken and potato salad.

Years later I discovered that the United States had been crossed thousands of times by frightened Black children traveling alone to their newly affluent parents in Northern cities, or back to grandmothers in Southern towns when the urban North reneged on its economic promises.

The town reacted to us as its inhabitants had reacted to all things new before our coming. It regarded us a while without curiosity but with caution, and after we were seen to be harmless (and children) it closed in around us, as a real mother embraces a stranger's child. Warmly, but not too familiarly.

We lived with our grandmother and uncle in the rear of the Store (it was always spoken of with a capital s), which she had owned some twenty-five years.

Early in the century, Momma (we soon stopped calling her Grandmother) sold lunches to the sawmen in the lumberyard (east Stamps) and the seedmen at the cotton gin (west Stamps). Her crisp meat pies and cool lemonade, when joined to her miraculous ability to be in two places at the same time, assured her business success. From being a mobile lunch counter, she set up a stand between the two points of fiscal interest and supplied the workers' needs for a few years. Then she had the Store built in the heart of the Negro area. Over the years it became the lay center of activities in town. On Saturdays, barbers sat their customers in the shade on the porch of the Store, and troubadours on their ceaseless crawlings through the South leaned across its benches and sang their sad songs of The Brazos while they played juice harps and cigar-box guitars.

The formal name of the Store was the Wm. Johnson General Merchandise Store. Customers could find food staples, a good variety of colored thread, mash for hogs, corn for chickens, coal oil for lamps, light bulbs for the wealthy, shoestrings, hair dressing, balloons, and flower seeds. Anything not visible had only to be ordered.

Until we became familiar enough to belong to the Store and it to us, we were locked up in a Fun House of Things where the attendant had gone home for life.

Each year I watched the field across from the Store turn caterpillar green, then gradually frosty white. I knew exactly how long it would be before the big wagons would pull into the front yard and load on the cotton pickers at daybreak to carry them to the remains of slavery's plantations.

During the picking season my grandmother would get out of bed at four o'clock (she never used an alarm clock) and creak down to her knees and chant in a sleep-filled voice, "Our Father, thank you for letting me see this New Day. Thank you that you didn't allow the bed I lay on last night to be my cooling board, nor my blanket my winding sheet. Guide my feet this day along the straight and narrow, and help me to put a bridle on my tongue. Bless this house, and everybody in it. Thank you, in the name of your Son, Jesus Christ, Amen."

Before she had quite arisen, she called our names and issued orders, and pushed her large feet into homemade slippers and across the bare lye-washed wooden floor to light the coal-oil lamp.

The lamplight in the Store gave a soft make-believe feeling to our world which made me want to whisper and walk about on tiptoe. The odors of onions and oranges and kerosene had been mixing all night and wouldn't be disturbed until the wooded slat was removed from the door and the early morning air forced its way in with the bodies of people who had walked miles to reach the pickup place.

from I Know Why the Caged Bird Sings

"Sister, I'll have two cans of sardines."

"I'm gonna work so fast today I'm gonna make you look like you standing still."

"Lemme have a hunk uh cheese and some sody crackers."

"Just gimme a coupla them fat peanut paddies." That would be from a picker who was taking his lunch. The greasy brown paper sack was stuck behind the bib of his overalls. He'd use the candy as a snack before the noon sun called the workers to rest.

In those tender mornings the Store was full of laughing, joking, boasting and bragging. One man was going to pick two hundred pounds of cotton, and another three hundred. Even the children were promising to bring home fo' bits and six bits.

The champion picker of the day before was the hero of the dawn. If he prophesied that the cotton in today's field was going to be sparse and stick to the bolls like glue, every listener would grunt a hearty agreement.

The sound of the empty cotton sacks dragging over the floor and the murmurs of waking people were sliced by the cash register as we rang up the five-cent sales.

If the morning sounds and smells were touched with the supernatural, the late afternoon had all the features of the normal Arkansas life. In the dying sunlight the people dragged, rather than their empty cotton sacks.

Brought back to the Store, the pickers would step out of the backs of trucks and fold down, dirt-disappointed, to the ground. No matter how much they had picked, it wasn't enough. Their wages wouldn't even get them out of debt to my grandmother, not to mention the staggering bill that waited on them at the white commissary downtown.

The sounds of the new morning had been replaced with grumbles about cheating houses, weighted scales, snakes, skimpy cotton and dusty rows. In later years I was to confront the stereotyped picture of gay song-singing cotton pickers with such inordinate rage that I was told even by fellow Blacks that my paranoia was embarrassing. But I had seen the fingers cut by the mean little cotton bolls, and I had witnessed the backs and shoulders and arms and legs resisting any further demands.

Some of the workers would leave their sacks at the Store to be picked up the following morning, but a few had to take them home for repairs. I winced to picture them sewing the coarse material under a coal-oil lamp with fingers stiffening from the day's work. In too few hours they would have to walk back to Sister Henderson's Store, get vittles and load, again, onto the trucks. Then they would face another day of trying to earn enough for the whole year with the heavy knowledge that they were going to end the season as they started it. Without the money or credit necessary to sustain a family for three months. In cotton-picking time the late afternoons

from I Know Why the Caged Bird Sings

revealed the harshness of Black Southern life, which in the early morning had been softened by nature's blessing of grogginess, forgetfulness and the soft lamplight.

2

When Bailey was six and I a year younger, we used to rattle off the times tables with the speed I was later to see Chinese children in San Francisco employ on their abacuses. Our summer-gray pot-bellied stove bloomed rosy red during winter, and became a severe disciplinarian threat if we were so foolish as to indulge in making mistakes.

Uncle Willie used to sit, like a giant black Z (he had been crippled as a child), and hear us testify to the Lafayette County Training Schools' abilities. His face pulled down on the left side, as if a pulley had been attached to his lower teeth, and his left hand was only a mite bigger than Bailey's, but on the second mistake or on the third hesitation his big overgrown right hand would catch one of us behind the collar, and in the same moment would thrust the culprit toward the dull red heater, which throbbed like a devil's toothache. We were never burned, although once I might have been when I was so terrified I tried to jump onto the stove to remove the possibility of its remaining a threat. Like most children, I thought if I could face the worst danger voluntarily, and *triumph*, I would forever have power over it. But in my case of sacrificial effort I was thwarted. Uncle Willie held tight to my dress and I only got close enough to smell the clean dry scent of hot iron. We learned the times tables without understanding their grand principle, simply because we had the capacity and no alternative.

The tragedy of lameness seems so unfair to children that they are embarrassed in its presence. And they, most recently off nature's mold, sense that they have only narrowly missed being another of her jokes. In relief at the narrow escape, they vent their emotions in impatience and criticism of the unlucky cripple.

Momma related times without end, and without any show of emotion, how Uncle Willie had been dropped when he was three years old by a woman who was minding him. She seemed to hold no rancor against the baby-sitter, nor for her just God who allowed the accident. She felt it necessary to explain over and over again to those who knew the story by heart that he wasn't "born that way."

In our society, where two-legged, two-armed strong Black men were able at best to eke out only the necessities of life, Uncle Willie, with his starched shirts, shined shoes and shelves full of food, was the whipping boy and butt of jokes of the underemployed and underpaid. Fate not only disabled him but laid a double-tiered barrier in his path. He was also proud and sensitive. Therefore he couldn't pretend that he wasn't crippled, nor could he deceive himself that people were not repelled by his defect.

Only once in all the years of trying not to watch him, I saw him pretend to himself and others that he wasn't lame.

Coming home from school one day, I saw a dark car in our front yard. I rushed in to find a strange man and woman (Uncle Willie said later they were schoolteachers from Little Rock) drinking Dr. Pepper in the cool of the Store. I sensed a wrongness around me, like an alarm clock that had gone off without being set.

I knew it couldn't be the strangers. Not frequently, but often enough, travelers pulled off the main road to buy tobacco or soft drinks in the only Negro store in Stamps. When I looked at Uncle Willie, I knew what was pulling my mind's coattails. He was standing erect behind the counter, not leaning forward or resting on the small shelf that had been built for him. Erect. His eyes seemed to hold me with a mixture of threats and appeal.

I dutifully greeted the strangers and roamed my eyes around for his walking stick. It was nowhere to be seen. He said, "Uh . . . this this . . . this . . . uh, my niece. She's . . . uh . . . just come from school." Then to the couple—"You know . . . how, uh, children are . . . th-th-these days . . . they play all d-d-day at school and c-c-can't wait to get home and pl-play some more."

The people smiled, very friendly.

He added, "Go on out and pl-play, Sister."

The lady laughed in a soft Arkansas voice and said, "Well, you know, Mr. Johnson, they say, you're only a child once. Have you children of your own?"

Uncle Willie looked at me with an impatience I hadn't seen in his face even when he took thirty minutes to loop the laces over his high-topped shoes. "I . . . I thought I told you to go . . . go outside and play."

Before I left I saw him lean back on the shelves of Garret Snuff, Prince Albert, and Spark Plug chewing tobacco.

"No, ma'am . . . no ch-children and no wife." He tried a laugh. "I have an old m-m-mother and my brother's t-two children to l-look after."

I didn't mind his using us to make himself look good. In fact, I would have pretended to be his daughter if he wanted me to. Not only did I not feel any loyalty to my own father, I figured that if I had been Uncle Willie's child I would have received much better treatment.

The couple left after a few minutes, and from the back of the house I watched the red car scare chickens, raise dust and disappear toward Magnolia.

Uncle Willie was making his way down the long shadowed aisle between the shelves and the counter—hand over hand, like a man climbing out of a dream. I stayed quiet and watched him lurch from one side, bumping to the other, until he reached the coal-oil tank. He put his hand behind that dark recess and took his cane in the strong fist and shifted his weight on the wooden support. He thought he had pulled it off.

I'll never know why it was important to him that the couple (he said later that he'd never seen them before) would take a picture of a whole Mr. Johnson back to Little Rock.

He must have tired of being crippled, as prisoners tire of penitentiary bars and the guilty tire of blame. The high-topped shoes and the cane, his uncontrollable muscles and thick tongue, and the looks he suffered of either contempt or pity had simply worn him out, and for one afternoon, one part of an afternoon, he wanted no part of them.

I understood and felt closer to him at that moment than ever before or since.

Responding to the Selection ———

Questions for Discussion

1. When the train carrying the narrator and her brother began crossing the southern states, the way they were treated by those on board changed. How? What does this tell you about the people's sense of community? Where might you find the roots of this community?

2. How does the success of the Wm. Johnson General Merchandise Store relate to the events in the story?

3. The cotton pickers are not slaves, yet they remain enslaved. Explain how.

4. Discuss Uncle Willie's encounter with the school teachers from Little Rock. Why do you think he was so insistent about not appearing disabled?

Activities

Interpreting Poetry

1. Write an **interpretive essay** in which you explain what the stanza from Paul Laurence Dunbar's poem means to you.

The Southern Christian Leadership Conference

2. During the 1960s, Maya Angelou was asked by Dr. Martin Luther King Jr. to become the northern coordinator for his landmark Civil Rights organization, the Southern Christian Leadership Conference. Research this chapter in Angelou's life and write a brief **report** about her experiences.

Focus on . . .
The Great Migration

African American night club in New York

The Promised Land. That's what enslaved African Americans called the North during the late-eighteenth and nineteenth centuries. Despite the overseers, the Southern militias, the bloodhounds, and the bounty hunters, many blacks slipped their shackles and headed north, some on their own and others under the guidance of conductors on the Underground Railroad, all of them risking their lives for a taste of freedom. After the Civil War their numbers swelled, and by the first decade of the twentieth century, a historic migration north had begun.

They came in waves, by the hundreds of thousands, in search of what the South would not provide: opportunity, dignity, equality. Between the First World War and the start of the Great Depression, more than 1.25 million African American men, women, and children made the journey. The *Chicago Defender,* an African American news weekly that was available in the South, urged them on in editorials and advertisements. And they responded, as in this letter to the *Defender* dated May 13, 1917, from Lutcher, Louisiana:

> Dear Sir: I have been reading the *Chicago Defender* and seeing so many advertisements about the work in the North that I thought to write you concerning my condition. I am working hard in the

South and can hardly earn a living. I have a wife and one child and can hardly feed them. . . . Please sir let me hear from you as soon as possible.

Not unlike the pioneers who were certain their dreams would blossom in the West, African Americans streamed north to stake their claim to a better life. They filled the row houses of Harlem, the tenements of Chicago's South Side, the flats in Scranton, Pennsylvania. They found jobs in factories, on the railroads, in hospitals, and as domestics. Charles Johnson of the Chicago Urban League began interviewing migrants in 1917. He wrote of one family:

They are from Meridian, Mississippi. Mr. Cole came to Chicago in May. Family came in August. At home he earned $1.00 per day. Here he now makes $3.75 a day, at Marks Mfg. Co., Indiana Harbor.

Many southerners, particularly those with business interests, saw in the migration the loss of their cheap labor force. They tried to discourage those heading north by claiming that northern recruiters offered nothing more than false hope.

True enough, some who migrated were disappointed. The Promised Land proved to be nothing but promises. They grew sick from the cold winters, weary of the struggle to find work, and homesick for the land, the families, and the lives they left behind. Nevertheless, few returned to the South, and each year thousands more headed north.

Cartoon from newspaper of the time

Linking to . . .
- Keep this information about the Great Migration in mind as you read the following selections.

Before You Read

Living for the City

Stevie Wonder
Born 1950

"Many of us feel we walk alone without a friend Never communicating with the one who lives within."

About Wonder

Stevland Morris was born in Saginaw, Michigan, at the beginning of a decade that would see a revolution in popular music—a revolution in which he would play a starring role. Although blind since shortly after birth, Morris soon proved to be a musical prodigy. At the age of eight, he was an accomplished musician, able to master virtually any instrument he chose. Berry Gordy Jr., the president of Motown Records, offered Morris a recording contract when he was just twelve. Gordy also renamed the young boy Little Stevie

Wonder. A year later, in 1963, Wonder had his first hit single, "Fingertips (Part 2)." The hits would flow nonstop for the next two decades.

Not only a skilled musician and an inventive singer whose voice blended jazz, blues, and soul, Wonder also proved to be a prolific composer. He wrote most of his own songs and also collaborated with other musicians. By the time he was sixteen, Wonder had already worked with the legendary Smokey Robinson, sharing composing credits on the smash hit "The Tears of a Clown." During the early 1970s, Wonder gained complete artistic control over his music from Motown, and he began to write more socially conscious songs. Despite this new musical direction, Wonder maintained his dynamic stage presence. Wonder would take his place at the center of a circle of instruments and proceed to bring down the house with his exuberant musical artistry.

Wonder continues to compose, record, and perform. As a testament to his enduring musical appeal, concertgoers not yet born when Little Stevie Wonder first took the stage flock to his performances to experience the magic that is the man and his music.

LIVING FOR THE CITY

— *Stevie Wonder*

A boy is born in hard time Mississippi
Surrounded by four walls that ain't so pretty
His parents give him love and affection
To keep him strong moving in the right direction
5   Living just enough, just enough for the city . . . ee ha!

His father works some days for fourteen hours
And you can bet he barely makes a dollar
His mother goes to scrub the floors for many
And you'd best believe she hardly gets a penny
10   Living just enough, just enough for the city . . . yeah!

His sister's black but she is sho'nuff pretty
Her skirt is short but Lord her legs are sturdy
To walk to school she's got to get up early
Her clothes are old but never are they dirty
15   Living just enough, just enough for the city . . . um hum

Her brother's smart he's got more sense than many
His patience's long but soon he won't have any
To find a job is like a haystack needle
Cause where he lives they don't use colored people
20   Living just enough, just enough for the city . . .

Living just enough . . .
For the city . . . ooh, ooh
(Repeat several times)

His hair is long, his feet are hard and gritty
He spends his life walking the streets of New York City
25   He's almost dead from breathing in air pollution
He tried to vote but to him there's no solution
Living just enough, just enough for the city . . .
yeah, yeah, yeah!

I hope you hear inside my voice of sorrow
30   And that it motivates you to make a better tomorrow
This place is cruel no where could be much colder
If we don't change the world will soon be over
Living just enough, stop giving just enough for the city!!!!

Responding to the Selection ─────────────

Questions for Discussion

1. Describe the picture Wonder paints in "Living for the City." What is the central struggle for the people in the song?

2. What do the words "Living just enough, just enough for the city" mean to you?

3. What evidence can you find in the song that the characters continue to strive to rise above their situation?

4. What "place is cruel" in the last stanza? Could it be more than one place?

Activities

Listening to Music

1. Listen to the song "Living for the City." How does listening to the song differ from just reading the lyrics? Jot down your reactions to the recording and share them with your classmates.

Social Consciousness

2. During the 1960s and 1970s, many African American composers began including socially conscious songs on their albums. Research the lyrics and recordings of some of these songs and write an **expository essay** about songs of African American social consciousness.

Before You Read

from *The Man Who Lived Underground*

Richard Wright
1908–1960

"It's strong, it's raw—but it's life as I see and lived it."

About Wright

In April 1943, thirty-four-year-old Richard Wright, already a well-known writer, gave a speech at Fisk University in Nashville, Tennessee. Of that speech, Wright said:

> I gave a clumsy, conversational kind of speech to the folks, white and black, reciting what I felt and thought about the world, what I remembered about my life, about being a Negro. There was but little applause. Indeed, the audience was terribly still, and it was not until I was halfway through my speech that it crashed upon me that I was saying things that Negroes were not supposed to say publicly.

After the speech, people inundated Wright with questions and comments. He realized that the truth he had shared about his life and about race relations had been a powerful stimulant to his audience. It was then that he decided to write his autobiography.

At the time, his novel, *Native Son,* was already a critical and commercial success and had been adapted for the stage. The play was rewritten as a movie script and filmed in Argentina, with Wright as the star. His next novel was *The Man Who Lived Underground.*

The autobiography, *Black Boy,* which details Wright's childhood in the South, was published in 1945. It depicts the deprivation, insecurity, and crushing lack of respect African Americans faced during the period in which Wright grew up.

Wright considered his childhood typical for African Americans of his time. Furthermore, he did not see social conditions in the United States changing for the better any time soon. In 1947 Wright moved his family to Paris, France, to spare them the racial and social injustices they would have had to face in the United States. Although he continued writing and speaking, Wright never again lived in the United States.

from
The Man Who Lived Underground

— *Richard Wright*

I've got to hide, he told himself. His chest heaved as he waited, crouching in a dark corner of the vestibule. He was tired of running and dodging. Either he had to find a place to hide, or he had to surrender. A police car swished by through the rain, its siren rising sharply. They're looking for me all over . . . He crept to the door and squinted through the fogged plate glass. He stiffened as the siren rose and died in the distance. Yes, he had to hide, but where? He gritted his teeth. Then a sudden movement in the street caught his attention. A throng of tiny columns of water snaked into the air from the perforations of a manhole cover. The columns stopped abruptly, as though the perforations had become clogged; a gray spout of sewer water jutted up from underground and lifted the circular metal cover, juggled it fox a moment, then let it fall with a clang.

He hatched a tentative plan: he would wait until the siren sounded far off, then he would go out. He smoked and waited, tense. At last the siren gave him his signal; it wailed, dying, going away from him. He stepped to the sidewalk, then paused and looked curiously at the open manhole, half expecting the cover to leap up again. He went to the center of the street and stooped and peered into the hole, but could see nothing. Water rustled in the black depths.

He started with terror; the siren sounded so near that he had the idea that he had been dreaming and had awakened to find the car upon him. He dropped instinctively to his knees and his hands grasped the rim of the manhole. The siren seemed to hoot directly above him and with a wild gasp of exertion he snatched the cover far enough off to admit his body. He swung his legs over the opening and lowered himself into watery darkness. He hung for an eternal moment to the rim by his finger tips, then he felt rough metal prongs and at once he knew that sewer workmen used these ridges to lower themselves into manholes. Fist over fist, he let his body sink until he could feel no more prongs. He swayed in dank space; the siren seemed to howl at the very rim of the manhole. He dropped and was washed violently into an ocean of warm, leaping water. His head was battered against a wall and he wondered if this were death. Frenziedly his fingers clawed and sank into a crevice. He steadied himself and measured the strength of the current with his own muscular tension. He stood slowly in water that dashed past his knees with fearful velocity.

He heard a prolonged scream of brakes and the siren broke off. Oh, God! They had found him! Looming above his head in the rain a white face hovered over the hole. "How did this damn thing get off?" he heard a policeman ask. He saw the steel cover move slowly until the hole looked like a quarter moon turned black. "Give me a hand here," someone called. The cover clanged into place, muffling the sights and sounds of the upper world. Knee-deep in the pulsing current, he breathed with aching chest, filling his lungs with the hot stench of yeasty rot.

From the perforations of the manhole cover, delicate lances of hazy violet sifted down and wove a mottled pattern upon the surface of the streaking current. His lips parted as a car swept past along the wet pavement overhead, its heavy rumble soon dying out, like the hum of a plane speeding through a dense cloud. He had never thought that cars could sound like that; everything seemed strange and unreal under here. He stood in darkness for a long time, knee-deep in rustling water, musing.

The odor of rot had become so general that he no longer smelled it. He got his cigarettes, but discovered that his matches were wet. He searched and found a dry folder in the pocket of his shirt and managed to strike one; it flared weirdly in the wet gloom, glowing greenishly, turning red, orange, then yellow. He lit a crumpled cigarette; then, by the flickering light of the match, he looked for support so that he would not have to keep his muscles flexed against the pouring water. His pupils narrowed and he saw to either side of him two steaming walls that rose and curved inward some six feet above his head to form a dripping, mouse-colored dome. The bottom of the sewer was a sloping V-trough. To the left, the sewer vanished in ashen fog. To the right was a steep down-curve into which water plunged.

He saw now that had he not regained his feet in time, he would have been swept to death, or had he entered any other manhole he would have probably drowned. Above the rush of the current he heard sharper juttings of water; tiny streams were spewing into the sewer from smaller conduits. The match died; he struck another and saw a mass of debris sweep past him and clog the throat of the down-curve. At once the water began rising rapidly. Could he climb out before he drowned? A long hiss sounded and the debris was sucked from sight; the current lowered. He understood now what had made the water toss the manhole cover; the downcurve had become temporarily obstructed and the perforations had become clogged.

He was in danger; he might slide into a down-curve; he might wander with a lighted match into a pocket of gas and blow himself up; or he might contract some horrible disease . . . Though he wanted to leave, an irrational impulse held him rooted. To the left, the convex ceiling swooped to a height of less than five feet. With cigarette slanting from pursed lips, he waded with taut muscles, his feet sloshing over the slimy bottom, his shoes sinking into spongy slop, the slate-colored water cracking in creamy foam against his knees. Pressing his flat left palm against the lowered ceiling, he struck another match and saw a metal pole nestling in a niche of the wall. Yes, some sewer workman had left it. He reached for it, then jerked his head away as a whisper of scurrying life whisked past and was still. He held the match close and saw a huge rat, wet with slime, blinking beady eyes and baring tiny fangs. The light blinded the rat and the frizzled head moved aimlessly. He grabbed the pole and let it fly against the rat's soft body; there was shrill piping and the grizzly body splashed into the dun-colored water and was snatched out of sight, spinning in the scuttling stream.

He swallowed and pushed on, following the curve of the misty cavern, sounding the water with the pole. By the faint light of another manhole cover he saw, amid loose wet brick, a hole with walls of damp earth leading into blackness. Gingerly he poked the pole into it; it was hollow and went beyond the length of the pole. He shoved the pole before him, hoisted himself upward, got to his hands and knees, and crawled. After a few yards he paused, struck to wonderment by the silence; it seemed that he had traveled a million miles away from the world. As he inched forward again he could sense the bottom of the dirt tunnel becoming dry and lowering slightly. Slowly he rose and to his astonishment he stood erect. He could not hear the rustling of the water now and he felt confoundingly alone, yet lured by the darkness and silence.

He crept a long way, then stopped, curious, afraid. He put his right foot forward and it dangled in space; he drew back in fear. He thrust the pole outward and it swung in emptiness. He trembled, imagining the earth crumbling and burying him alive. He scratched a match and saw that the dirt floor sheered away steeply and widened into a sort of cave some five feet below him. An old sewer, he muttered. He cocked his head, hearing a feathery cadence which he could not identify. The match ceased to burn.

Using the pole as a kind of ladder, he slid down and stood in darkness. The air was a little fresher and he could still hear vague noises. Where was he? He felt suddenly that someone was standing near him and he turned sharply, but there was only darkness. He poked cautiously and felt a brick wall; he followed it and the strange sounds grew louder. He ought to get out of here. This was crazy. He could not remain here for any length of time; there was no food and no place to sleep. But the faint sounds tantalized him; they were strange but familiar. Was it a motor? A baby crying? Music? A siren? He groped on, and the sounds came so clearly that he could feel the pitch and timbre of human voices. Yes, singing! That was it! He listened with open mouth. It was a church service. Enchanted, he groped toward the waves of melody.

> *Jesus, take me to your home above*
> *And fold me in the bosom of Thy love . . .*

The singing was on the other side of a brick wall. Excited, he wanted to watch the service without being seen. Whose church was it? He knew most of the churches in this area above ground, but the singing sounded too strange and detached for him to guess. He looked to the left, to the right, down to the black dirt, then upward and was startled to see a bright sliver of light slicing the darkness like the blade of a razor. He struck one of his two remaining matches and saw rusty pipes running along an old concrete ceiling. Photographically he located the exact position of the pipes in his mind. The match flame sank and he sprang upward; his hands clutched a pipe. He swung his legs and tossed his body onto the bed of pipes and they creaked, swaying up and down; he thought that the tier was about to crash, but nothing happened. He edged to the crevice and saw a segment of black men and women, dressed in white robes, singing, holding tattered songbooks in their black palms. His first impulse was to laugh, but he checked himself.

What was he doing? He was crushed with a sense of guilt. Would God strike him dead for that? The singing swept on and he shook his head, disagreeing in spite of himself. They oughtn't to do that, he thought. But he could think of no reason *why* they should not do it. Just singing with the air of the sewer blowing in on them . . . He felt that he was gazing upon something abysmally obscene, yet he could not bring himself to leave.

After a long time he grew numb and dropped to the dirt. Pain throbbed in his legs and a deeper pain, induced by the sight of those black people groveling and begging for something they could never get, churned in him. A vague conviction made him feel that those people should stand unrepentant and yield no quarter in singing and praying, yet *he* had run away from the police, had pleaded with them to believe in *his* innocence. He shook his head, bewildered.

How long had he been down here? He did not know. This was a new kind of living for him; the intensity of feelings he had experienced when looking at the church people sing made him certain that he had been down here a long time, but his mind told him that the time must have been short. In this darkness the only notion he had of time was when a match flared and measured time by its fleeting light. He groped back through the hole toward the sewer and the waves of song subsided and finally he could not hear them at all. He came to where the earth hole ended and he heard the noise of the current and time lived again for him, measuring the moments by the wash of water.

Responding to the Selection

Questions for Discussion

1. Who or what is the central character running from? Why?

2. What does the sewer **symbolize** in the story? Explain.

3. What role do the gospel singers play in the selection? Why does the central character find their situation "abysmally obscene"?

4. What dangers does the central character face above ground? In the sewer?

Activities

Spatial Orientation

1. Try to picture the sewer in which the central character has sought refuge. How is it laid out? What is to the left and right of the central character? Where is the old sewer cave? The pipes? Draw a **diagram** of the interior of the sewer as you imagine it.

Writing to Compare

2. In what ways is the sewer a metaphor for the central character's life or anyone's life? Write an **expository essay** in which you compare the structures and dangers of the sewer to life above ground. Use quotations from the selection to reinforce your comparison.

Before You Read

Nikki-Roasa

Nikki Giovanni
Born 1943

". . . sometimes happiness is a good enough reason to write a poem."

About Giovanni

Nikki Giovanni is one of the most respected and widely read African American poets to emerge during the 1960s, a decade of protest, violence, and radical change in the United States. In fact, Giovanni's early poems focus on the themes of change, revolution, and black pride and solidarity. In her later poems, Giovanni's focus softened somewhat as she turned increasingly to such personal subjects as family, love, and loneliness.

Giovanni was born in Knoxville, Tennessee, and raised in Cincinnati, Ohio. She earned a bachelor of arts degree from Fisk University in Nashville, Tennessee, in 1967 and has been awarded numerous honorary doctoral degrees from various colleges and universities. She was deeply involved in the Civil Rights movement and the Black Arts Movement (BAM) in the 1960s and 1970s.

Today, Giovanni is a professor of English at Virginia Polytechnic Institute and State University. She has written twelve volumes of award-winning poetry and has given readings and lectures throughout the United States and Europe, which attract large, enthusiastic audiences. In 1973 she received a commendation from the American Library Association for her book *My House*. A collection of her essays, *Sacred Cows . . . and Other Edibles,* was published in 1988.

Nikki-Roasa

— Nikki Giovanni

childhood remembrances are always a drag
if you're Black
you always remember things like living in Woodlawn
with no inside toilet
5   and if you become famous or something
they never talk about how happy you were to have your mother
all to yourself and
how good the water felt when you got your bath from one of those
big tubs that folk in chicago barbecue in
10   and somehow when you talk about home
it never gets across how much you
understood their feelings
as the whole family attended meetings about Hollydale
and even though you remember
15   your biographers never understand
your father's pain as he sells his stock
and another dream goes
and though you're poor it isn't poverty that
concerns you
20   and though they fought a lot
it isn't your father's drinking that makes any difference
but only that everybody is together and you
and your sister have happy birthdays and very good christmasses
and I really hope no white person ever has cause to write about me
25   because they never understand Black love is Black wealth and they'll
probably talk about my hard childhood and never understand that
all the while I was quite happy

Responding to the Selection

Questions for Discussion

1. Why are childhood remembrances "always a drag / if you're Black"?

2. What do the words "Black love is Black wealth" mean to you?

3. What made the speaker happy as a child?

4. Think about the meaning of this poem. What personal truth do you think Giovanni is trying to explain?

Activities

Writing About Personal Hardships

1. Most people endure some hardships in their lives; still, they find reasons to love being alive. Write a **personal narrative** about a hardship you've endured. What generalizations would an outsider have made about your life in light of that hardship? What were you really feeling? What got you through?

Defining Happiness

2. Everyone has a different definition of happiness. What's yours? Make a **list** of all the things that make you happy and then use that list to write a brief paragraph explaining your idea of happiness. Share your ideas with your classmates.

Before You Read

Jack in the Pot

Dorothy West
1907–1998

"We didn't know it was the Harlem Renaissance, because we were all young and all poor."

About West

Until her death in 1998, at the age of 91, Dorothy West was the last surviving artist of the Harlem Renaissance. The only child of a freed slave, West began writing at the age of seven. Just after graduation from the Girls' Latin School in Boston, she entered a short-story contest sponsored by the National Urban League's journal, *Opportunity.* Her story "The Typewriter" tied for second place with that of another soon-to-be Harlem luminary, Zora Neale Hurston. When West arrived in Harlem with her cousin, the poet Helene Johnson, she began socializing with other African American writers, including Hurston, Richard Wright, Countee Cullen, Wallace Thurman, and Langston Hughes, who nicknamed her "the Kid." For the next seven decades, West wrote fiction and essays. In 1948 she published her first novel, *The Living Is Easy,* to critical acclaim.

A year earlier, West had moved to Martha's Vineyard to care for an ailing older relative. There, she wrote essays and stories for the *Vineyard Gazette* newspaper. West began writing a second novel, *The Wedding,* during the 1960s, but the rise of radical African American groups such as the Black Panthers made her wonder whether she was out of touch with contemporary black culture. Convinced that the novel would be rejected by her own people, she abandoned it.

Some twenty years later, her Martha's Vineyard neighbor and Doubleday editor, Jacqueline Kennedy Onassis, encouraged West to finish the book. Nearly fifty years after her first novel was published, *The Wedding* debuted to enthusiastic praise. Doubleday then published a collection of West's short stories, *The Richer, the Poorer,* and her literary legacy was secure.

Jack in the Pot

— Dorothy West

When she walked down the aisle of the theater, clutching the money in her hand, hearing the applause and laughter, seeing, dimly, the grinning black faces, she was trembling so violently that she did not know how she could ever regain her seat.

It was unbelievable. Week after week she had come on Wednesday afternoon to this smelly, third-run neighborhood movie house, paid her dime, received her beano card, and gone inside to wait through an indifferent feature until the houselights came on and a too-jovial white man wheeled a board onto the stage and busily fished in a bowl for numbers.

Today it had happened. As the too-jovial white man called each number, she found a corresponding one on her card. When he called the seventh number and explained dramatically that whoever had punched five numbers in a row had won the jackpot of fifty-five dollars, she listened in smiling disbelief that there was that much money in his pocket. It was then that the woman beside her leaned toward her and said excitedly, "Look, lady, you got it!"

She did not remember going down the aisle. Undoubtedly her neighbor had prodded her to her feet. When it was over, she tottered dazedly to her seat and sat in a dreamy stupor, scarcely able to believe her good fortune.

The drawing continued, the last dollar was given away, the theater darkened, and the afternoon crowd filed out. The little gray woman, collecting her wits, followed them.

She revived in the sharp air. Her head cleared and happiness swelled in her throat. She had fifty-five dollars in her purse. It was wonderful to think about.

She reached her own intersection and paused before Mr. Spiro's general market. Here she regularly shopped, settling part of her bill fortnightly out of her relief check. When Mr. Spiro put in inferior stock because most of his customers were poor-paying reliefers, she had wanted to shop elsewhere. But she could never get paid up.

Excitement smote her. She would go in, settle her account, and say goodbye to Mr. Spiro forever. Resolutely she turned into the market.

Mr. Spiro, broad and unkempt, began to boom heartily, from behind the counter. "Hello, Mrs. Edmunds."

She lowered her eyes and asked diffidently, "How much is my bill, Mr. Spiro?"

He recoiled in horror. "Do I worry about your bill, Mrs. Edmunds? Don't you pay something when you get your relief check? Ain't you one of my best customers?"

"I'd like to settle," said Mrs. Edmunds breathlessly.

Mr. Spiro eyed her shrewdly. His voice was soft and insinuating. "You got cash, Mrs. Edmunds? You hit the number? Every other week you give me something on account. This week you want to settle. Am I losing your trade? Ain't I always treated you right?"

"Sure, Mr. Spiro," she answered nervously. "I was telling my husband just last night, ain't another man treats me like Mr. Spiro. And I said I wished I could settle my bill."

"Gee," he said triumphantly. "It's like I said. You're one of my best customers. Worrying about your bill when I ain't even worrying. I was telling your investigator"—he paused significantly—"when Mr. Edmunds gets a job, I know I'll get the balance. Mr. Edmunds got himself a job maybe?"

She was stiff with fright. "No, I'd have told you right off, and her too. I ain't one to cheat on relief. I was only saying how I wished I could settle. I wasn't saying that I was."

"Well, then, what you want for supper?" Mr. Spiro asked soothingly.

"Loaf of bread," she answered gratefully, "two pork chops, one kinda thick, can of spaghetti, little can of milk."

The purchases were itemized. Mrs. Edmunds said good night and left the store. She felt sick and ashamed, for she had turned tail in the moment that was to have been her triumph over tyranny.

A little boy came toward her in the familiar rags of the neighborhood children. Suddenly Mrs. Edmunds could bear no longer the intolerable weight of her mean provisions.

"Little boy," she said.

"Ma'am?" He stopped and stared at her.

"Here." She held out the bag to him. "Take it home to your mama. It's food. It's clean."

He blinked, then snatched the bag from her hands and turned and ran very fast in the direction from which he had come.

Mrs. Edmunds felt better at once. Now she could buy a really good supper. She walked ten blocks to a better neighborhood, and the cold did not bother her. Her misshapen shoes were winged.

She pushed inside a resplendent store and marched to the meat counter. A porterhouse steak caught her eye. She could not look past it. It was big and thick and beautiful.

Jack in the Pot

The clerk leaned toward her. "Steak, moddom?"

"That one."

It was glorious not to care about the cost of things. She bought mush-
rooms, fresh peas, cauliflower, tomatoes, a pound of good coffee, a pint of
real cream, a dozen dinner rolls, and a maple walnut layer cake.

The winter stars were pricking the sky when she entered the dimly lit
hallway of the old-law tenement in which she lived. The dank smell smote
her instantly after the long walk in the brisk, clear air. The Smith boy's
dog had dirtied the hall again. Mr. Johnson, the janitor, was mournfully
mopping up.

"Evenin', Mis' Edmunds, ma'am," he said plaintively.

"Evening," Mrs. Edmunds said coldly. Suddenly she hated Mr.
Johnson. He was so humble.

Five young children shared the uninhabitable basement with him.
They were always half sick, and he was always neglecting his duties to tend
to them. The tenants were continually deciding to report him to the agent
and then at the last moment deciding not to.

"I'll be up tomorrow to see 'bout them windows, Mis' Edmunds,
ma'am. My baby kep' frettin' today, and I been so busy doctorin'."

"Those children need a mother," said Mrs. Edmunds severely. "You
ought to get married again."

"My wife ain' daid," cried Mr. Johnson, shocked out of his servility. "She's
in that T.B. home. Been there two years and 'bout on the road to health."

"Well," said Mrs. Edmunds inconclusively, and then added briskly, "I
been waiting weeks and weeks for them window strips. Winter's half over.
If the place was kept warm—"

"Yes'm, Mis' Edmunds," he said hastily, his bloodshot eyes imploring.
"It's that ol' furnace. I done tol' the agent time and again, but they ain'
fixin' to fix up this house 'long as you all is relief folks."

The steak was sizzling on the stove when Mr. Edmunds' key turned in the
lock of the tiny three-room flat. His step dragged down the hall. Mrs.
Edmunds knew what that meant: "No man wanted." Two years ago Mr.
Edmunds had begun, doggedly, to canvas the city for work, leaving home
soon after breakfast and rarely returning before supper.

Once he had had a little stationery store. After losing it, he had
spent his small savings and sold or pawned every decent article of furniture
and clothing before applying for relief. Even so, there had been a long
investigation while he and his wife slowly starved. Fear had been implanted
in Mrs. Edmunds. Thereafter she was never wholly unafraid. Mr. Edmunds
had had to stand by and watch his wife starve. He never got over being
ashamed.

Mr. Edmunds stood in the kitchen doorway, holding his rain-streaked hat in his knotted hand. He was forty-nine, and he looked like an old man.

"I'm back," he said. "Cooking supper."

It was not a question. He seemed unaware of the intoxicating odors.

She smiled at him brightly. "Smell good?"

He shook suddenly with the cold that was still in him. "Smells like always to me."

Her face fell in disappointment, but she said gently, "You oughtn't to be walking 'round this kind of weather."

"I was looking for work," he said fiercely. "Work's not going to come knocking."

She did not want to quarrel with him. He was too cold, and their supper was too fine.

"Things'll pick up in the spring," she said soothingly.

"Not for me," he answered gloomily. "Look how I look. Like a bum. I wouldn't hire me myself."

"What you want me to do about it?" she asked furiously.

"Nothing," he said with wry humor, "unless you can make money, and make me just about fifty dollars."

She caught her breath and stared at his shabbiness. She had seen him look like this so long that she had forgotten that clothes would make a difference.

She nodded toward the stove. "That steak and all. Guess you think I got a fortune. Well, I won a little old measly dollar at the movies."

His face lightened, and his eyes grew soft with affection. "You shouldn't have bought a steak," he said. "Wish you'd bought yourself something you been wanting. Like gloves. Some good warm gloves. Hurts my heart when I see you with cold hands."

She was ashamed, and wished she knew how to cross the room to kiss him. "Go wash," she said gruffly. "Steak's 'most too done already."

It was a wonderful dinner. Both of them had been starved for fresh meat. Mrs. Edmunds' face was flushed, and there was color in her lips, as if the good blood of the meat had filtered through her skin. Mr. Edmunds ate a pound and a half of the two-pound steak, and his hands seemed steadier with each sharp thrust of the knife.

Over coffee and cake they talked contentedly. Mrs. Edmunds wanted to tell the truth about the money, and waited for an opening.

"We'll move out of this hole someday soon," said Mr. Edmunds. "Things won't be like this always." He was full and warm and confident.

"If I had fifty dollars," Mrs. Edmunds began cautiously, "I believe I'd move tomorrow. Pay up these people what I owe and get me a fit place to live in."

Jack in the Pot

"Fifty dollars would be a drop in the bucket. You got to have something coming in steady."

He had hurt her again. "Fifty dollars is more than you got," she said meanly.

"It's more than you got too," he said mildly. "Look at it like this. If you had fifty dollars and made a change, them relief folks would worry you like a pack of wolves. But say, f' instance, you had fifty dollars and I had a job, we could walk out of here without a howdy-do to anybody."

It would have been anticlimactic to tell him about the money. She got up. "I'll do the dishes. You sit still."

He noticed no change in her and went on earnestly, "Lord's bound to put something in my way soon. We don't live human. I never see a paper 'cept when I pick one up in the subway. I ain't had a cigarette in three years. We ain't got a radio. We don't have no company. All the pleasure you get is a ten-cent movie one day a week. I don't even get that."

Presently Mrs. Edmunds ventured, "You think the investigator would notice if we got a little radio for the bedroom?"

"Somebody got one to give away?" His face was eager.

"Maybe."

"Well, seeing how she could check with the party what give it to you, I think it would be all right."

"Well, ne' mind—" Her voice petered out.

It was his turn to try. "Want to play me a game of cards?"

He had not asked her for months. She cleared her throat.

"I'll play a hand or two."

He stretched luxuriously. "I feel so good. Feeling like this, bet I'll land something tomorrow."

She said very gently, "The investigator comes tomorrow."

He smiled quickly to hide his disappointment. "Clean forgot. It don't matter. That meal was so good it'll carry me straight through Friday."

She opened her mouth to tell him about the jackpot, to promise him as many meals as there was money. Suddenly someone upstairs pounded on the radiator for heat. In a moment someone downstairs pounded. Presently their side of the house resounded. It was maddening. Mrs. Edmunds was bitterly aware that her hands and feet were like ice.

"'Tisn't no use," she cried wildly to the walls. She burst into tears. "'Tisn't nothing no use."

Her husband crossed quickly to her. He kissed her cheek. "I'm going to make all this up to you. You'll see."

By half-past eight they were in bed. By quarter to nine Mrs. Edmunds was quietly sleeping. Mr. Edmunds lay staring at the ceiling. It kept coming closer.

Jack in the Pot 185

Jack in the Pot

Mrs. Edmunds waked first and decided to go again to the grand market. She dressed and went out into the street. An ambulance stood in front of the door. In a minute an intern emerged from the basement, carrying a bundled child. Mr. Johnson followed, his eyes more bleary and bloodshot than ever.

Mrs. Edmunds rushed up to him. "The baby?" she asked anxiously.

His face worked pitifully. "Yes, ma'am, Mis' Edmunds. Pneumonia. I heard you folks knockin' for heat last night but my hands was too full. I ain't forgot about them windows, though. I'll be up tomorrow bright and early."

Mr. Edmunds stood in the kitchen door. "I smell meat in the morning?" he asked incredulously. He sat down, and she spread the feast: kidneys and omelet, hot buttered rolls, and strawberry jam. "You mind," he said happily, "explaining this mystery? Was that dollar of yours made out of elastic?"

"It wasn't a dollar like I said. It was five. I wanted to surprise you."

She did not look at him and her voice was breathless. She had decided to wait until after the investigator's visit to tell him the whole truth about the money. Otherwise they might both be nervous and betray themselves by their guilty knowledge.

"We got chicken for dinner," she added shyly.

"Lord, I don't know when I had a piece of chicken."

They ate, and the morning passed glowingly. With Mr. Edmunds' help, Mrs. Edmunds moved the furniture and gave the flat a thorough cleaning. She liked for the investigator to find her busy. She felt less embarrassed about being on relief when it could be seen that she occupied her time.

The afternoon waned. The Edmundses sat in the living room, and there was nothing to do. They were hungry but dared not start dinner. With activity suspended, they became aware of the penetrating cold and the rattling windows.

Mr. Edmunds began to have that wild look of waiting for the investigator. Mrs. Edmunds suddenly had an idea. She would go and get a newspaper and a package of cigarettes for him.

At the corner, she ran into Mr. Johnson. Rather, he ran into her, for he turned the corner with his head down and his gait as unsteady as if he had been drinking.

"That you, Mr. Johnson?" she said sharply.

He raised his head, and she saw that he was not drunk.

"Yes, ma'am, Mis' Edmunds."

"The baby—is she worse?"

Tears welled out of his eyes. "The Lord done took her."

Tears stood in her own eyes. "God knows I'm sorry to hear that. Let me know if there's anything I can do."

"Thank you, Mis' Edmunds, ma'am. But ain't nothin' nobody can do. I been pricin' funerals. I can get one for fifty dollars. But I been to my brother, and he ain't got it. I been everywhere. Couldn't raise no more than ten dollars." He was suddenly embarrassed. "I know all you tenants is on relief. I wasn't fixin' to ask you all."

"Fifty dollars," she said strainedly, "is a lot of money."

"God'd have to pass a miracle for me to raise it. Guess the city'll have to bury her. You reckon they'll let me take flowers?"

"You being the father, I guess they would," she said weakly.

When she returned home the flat was a little warmer. She entered the living room. Her husband's face brightened.

"You bought a paper!"

She held out the cigarettes. "You smoke this kind?" she asked lifelessly.

He jumped up and crossed to her. "I declare I don't know how to thank you! Wish that investigator'd come. I sure want to taste them."

"Go ahead and smoke," she cried fiercely. "It's none of her business. We got our rights same as working people."

She turned into the bedroom. She was utterly spent. Too much had happened in the last twenty-four hours.

"Guess I'll stretch out for a bit. I'm not going to sleep. If I do drop off, listen out for the investigator. The bell needs fixing. She might have to knock."

At half-past five Mr. Edmunds put down the newspaper and tiptoed to the bedroom door. His wife was still asleep. He stood for a moment in indecision, then decided it was long past the hour when the investigator usually called and went down the hall to the kitchen. He wanted to prepare supper as a surprise. He opened the window, took the foodstuffs out of the crate that in winter served as icebox, and set them on the table.

The doorbell tinkled faintly.

He went to the door and opened it. The investigator stepped inside. She was small and young and white.

"Good evening, miss," he said.

"I'm sorry to call so late," she apologized. "I've been busy all day with an evicted family. But I knew you were expecting me, and I didn't want you to stay in tomorrow."

"You come on up front, miss," he said. "I'll wake up my wife. She wasn't feeling so well and went to lie down."

She saw the light from the kitchen, and the dark rooms beyond.

"Don't wake Mrs. Edmunds," she said kindly, "if she isn't well. I'll just sit in the kitchen for a minute with you."

He looked down at her, but her open, honest face did not disarm him. He braced himself for whatever was to follow.

"Go right on in, miss," he said.

He took the dish towel and dusted the clean chair. "Sit down, miss."

He stood facing her with a furrow between his brows, and his arms folded. There was an awkward pause. She cast about for something to say and saw the table.

"I interrupted your dinner preparations."

His voice and his face hardened for the blow.

"I was getting dinner for my wife. It's chicken."

"It looks like a nice one," she said pleasantly.

He was baffled. "We ain't had chicken once in three years."

"I understand," she said sincerely. "Sometimes I spend my whole salary on something I want very much."

"You ain't much like an investigator," he said in surprise. "One we had before you woulda raised Ned." He sat down suddenly, his defenses down. "Miss, I been wanting to ask you this for a long time. You ever have any men's clothes?"

Her voice was distressed. "Every once in a while. But with so many people needing assistance, we can only give them to our employables. But I'll keep your request in mind."

He did not answer. He just sat staring at the floor, presenting an adjustment problem. There was nothing else to say to him.

She rose. "I'll be going now, Mr. Edmunds."

"I'll tell my wife you was here, miss."

A voice called from the bedroom. "Is that you talking?"

"It's the investigator lady," he said. "She's just going."

Mrs. Edmunds came hurrying down the hall, the sleep in her face and tousled hair.

"I was just lying down, ma'am. I didn't mean to go to sleep. My husband should've called me."

"I didn't want him to wake you."

"And he kept you sitting in the kitchen."

She glanced inside to assure herself that it was sufficiently spotless for the fine clothes of the investigator. She saw the laden table and felt so ill that water welled into her mouth.

"The investigator lady knows about the chicken," Mr. Edmunds said quickly. "She—"

"It was only five dollars," his wife interrupted, wringing her hands.

"Five dollars for a chicken?" The investigator was shocked and incredulous.

"She didn't buy that chicken out of none of your relief money," Mr. Edmunds said defiantly. "It was money she won at a movie."

"It was only five dollars," Mrs. Edmunds repeated tearfully.

Jack in the Pot

"We ain't trying to conceal nothing," Mr. Edmunds snarled. He was cornered and fighting. "If you'd asked me how we come by the chicken, I'd have told you."

"For God's sake, ma'am, don't cut us off," Mrs. Edmunds moaned. "I'll never go to another movie. It was only ten cents. I didn't know I was doing wrong." She burst into tears.

The investigator stood tense. They had both been screaming at her. She was tired and so irritated that she wanted to scream back.

"Mrs. Edmunds," she said sharply, "get hold of yourself. I'm not going to cut you off. That's ridiculous. You won five dollars at a movie and you bought some food. That's fine. I wish my family could win five dollars for food."

She turned and tore out of the flat. They heard her stumbling and sobbing down the stairs.

"You feel like eating?" Mrs. Edmunds asked dully.

"I guess we're both hungry. That's why we got so upset."

"Maybe we'd better eat, then."

"Let me fix it."

"No." She entered the kitchen. "I kinda want to see you just sitting and smoking a cigarette."

He sat down and reached in his pocket with some eagerness. "I ain't had one yet." He lit a cigarette, inhaled, and felt better immediately.

"You think," she said bleakly, "she'll write that up in our case?"

"I don't know, dear."

"You think they'll close our case if she does?"

"I don't know that neither, dear."

She clutched the sink for support. "My God, what would we do?"

The smoke curled around him luxuriously. "Don't think about it till it happens."

"I got to think about it. The rent, the gas, the light, the food."

"They wouldn't hardly close our case for five dollars."

"Maybe they'd think it was more."

"You could prove it by the movie manager."

She went numb all over. Then suddenly she got mad about it.

It was nine o'clock when they sat down in the living room. The heat came up grudgingly. Mrs. Edmunds wrapped herself in her sweater and read the funnies. Mr. Edmunds was happily inhaling his second cigarette. They were both replete and in good humor.

The window rattled and Mr. Edmunds looked around at it lazily. "Been about two months since you asked Mr. Johnson for weatherstrips."

The paper shook in her hand. She did not look up. "He promised to fix it this morning, but his baby died."

"His baby! You don't say!"

She kept her eyes glued to the paper. "Pneumonia."

His voice filled with sympathy. He crushed out his cigarette. "Believe I'll go down and sit with him awhile."

"He's not there," she said hastily. "I met him when I was going to the store. He said he'd be out all evening."

"I bet the poor man's trying to raise some money."

She let the paper fall in her lap and clasped her hands to keep them from trembling. She lied again, as she had been lying steadily in the past twenty-four hours, as she had not lied before in all her life.

"He didn't say nothing to me about raising money."

"Wasn't no need to. Where would you get the first five cents to give him?"

"I guess," she cried jealously, "you want me to give him the rest of my money."

"No," he said. "I want you to spend what little's left on yourself. Me, I wish I had fifty dollars to give him."

"As poor as you are," she asked angrily, "you'd give him that much money? That's easy to say when you haven't got it."

"I look at it this way," he said simply. "I think how I'd feel in his shoes."

"You got your own troubles," she argued heatedly. "The Johnson baby is better off dead. You'd be a fool to put fifty dollars in the ground. I'd spend my fifty dollars on the living."

"Tain't no use to work yourself up," he said. "You ain't got fifty dollars, and neither have I. We'll be quarreling in a minute over make-believe money. Let's go to bed."

Mrs. Edmunds waked at seven and tried to lie quietly by her husband's side, but lying still was torture. She dressed and went into the kitchen and felt too listless to make her coffee. She sat down at the table and dropped her head on her folded arms. No tears came. There was only the burning in her throat and behind her eyes.

She sat in this manner for half an hour. Suddenly she heard a man's slow tread outside her front door. Terror gripped her. The steps moved on down the hall, but for a moment her knees were water. When she could control her trembling, she stood up and knew that she had to get out of the house. It could not contain her and Mr. Johnson.

She walked quickly away from her neighborhood. It was a raw day, and her feet and hands were beginning to grow numb. She felt sorry for herself. Other people were hurrying past in overshoes and heavy gloves. There was fifty-one dollars in her purse. It was her right to do what she pleased with it. Determinedly she turned into the subway.

Jack in the Pot

In a downtown department store she rode the escalator to the dress department. She walked up and down the rows of lovely garments, stopping to finger critically, standing back to admire.

A salesgirl came toward her, looking straight at her with soft, expectant eyes.

"Do you wish to be waited on, madam?"

Mrs. Edmunds opened her mouth to say yes, but the word would not come. She stared at the girl stupidly. "I was just looking," she said.

In the shoe department, she saw a pair of comfort shoes and sat down timidly in a fine leather chair.

A salesman lounged toward her. "Something in shoes?"

"Yes, sir. That comfort shoe."

"Size?" His voice was bored.

"I don't know," she said.

"I'll have to measure you," he said reproachfully. "Give me your foot." He sat down on a stool and held out his hand.

She dragged her eyes up to his face. "How much you say those shoes cost?"

"I didn't say. Eight dollars."

She rose with acute relief. "I ain't got that much with me."

She retreated unsteadily. Something was making her knees weak and her head light.

Her legs steadied. She went quickly to the down escalator. She reached the third floor and was briskly crossing to the next down escalator when she saw the little dresses. A banner screamed that they were selling at the sacrifice price of one dollar. She decided to examine them.

She pushed through the crowd of women and emerged triumphantly within reach of the dresses. She searched carefully. There were pinks and blues and yellows. She was looking for white. She pushed back through the crowd. In her careful hands lay a little white dress. It was spun gold and gossamer.

Boldly she beckoned a salesgirl. "I'll take this, miss," she said.

All the way home she was excited and close to tears. She was in a fever to see Mr. Johnson. She would let the regret come later. A child lay dead and waiting burial.

She turned her corner at a run. Going down the rickety basement stairs, she prayed that Mr. Johnson was on the premises.

She pounded on his door and he opened it. The agony in his face told her instantly that he had been unable to borrow the money. She tried to speak, and her tongue tripped over her eagerness.

Fear took hold of her and rattled her teeth. "Mr. Johnson, what about the funeral?"

"I give the baby to the student doctors."

"Oh, my God, Mr. Johnson! Oh, my God!"

"I bought her some flowers."

She turned and went blindly up the stairs. Drooping in the front doorway was a frost-nipped bunch of white flowers. She dragged herself up to her flat. Once she stopped to hide the package under her coat. She would never look at that little white dress again. The ten five-dollar bills were ten five-pound stones in her purse. They almost hurled her backward.

She turned the key in her lock. Mr. Edmunds stood at the door. He looked rested and confident.

"I been waiting for you. I just started to go."

"You had any breakfast?" she asked tonelessly.

"I made some coffee. It was all I wanted."

"I shoulda made some oatmeal before I went out."

"You have on the big pot time I come home. Bet I'll land something good," he boasted. "You brought good luck in this house. We ain't seen the last of it." He pecked her cheek and went out, hurrying as if he were late for work.

She plodded into the bedroom. The steam was coming up fine. She sank down on the side of the bed and unbuttoned her coat. The package fell on her lap. She took the ten five-dollar bills and pushed them between a fold of the package. It was burial money. She could never use it for anything else. She hid the package under the mattress.

Wearily she buttoned up her coat and opened her purse again. It was empty, for the few cents remaining from her last relief check had been spent indiscriminately with her prize money.

She went into the kitchen to take stock of her needs. There was nothing left from their feasts. She felt the coffeepot. It was still hot, but her throat was too constricted for her to attempt to swallow.

She took her paper shopping bag and started out to Mr. Spiro's.

Responding to the Selection

Questions for Discussion

1. How did Mrs. Edmunds come by her good fortune?

2. Why was Mrs. Edmunds unable to pay off her debt to Mr. Spiro?

3. Why does Mrs. Edmunds give the food she bought from Mr. Spiro to the young boy?

4. When the investigator from the welfare office leaves the Edmunds's apartment, she is stumbling and sobbing. What happened in the apartment? How do you think the investigator feels about her job?

5. Describe Mrs. Edmunds's shopping trip to the department store. Why doesn't she buy the things she needs?

6. The narrator say of Mrs. Edmunds, "The ten five-dollar bills were ten five-pound stones in her purse. They almost hurled her backward." What do these words mean to you?

Activity

Being Human

"Jack in the Pot" has much to say about human nature, human needs, and human dignity. What do you think the theme of this story might be? Write an **essay** in which you present your interpretation of the theme and discuss how it becomes apparent as the story unfolds.

Before You Read

The Weakness

Toi Derricotte
Born 1941

> "All my life I have passed
> invisibly into the white world,
> and all my life I have felt that
> sudden and alarming moment
> of consciousness there, of
> remembering I am black. It
> may feel like emerging too
> quickly from deep in the ocean,
> or touching an electric fence, or
> like a deer paralyzed in the
> headlights of an oncoming car."

About Derricotte

Toi Derricotte is an award-winning writer of poetry and nonfiction. She has published several collections of poetry, including *Captivity, Tender,* and *The Empress of the Death House.* In 1999 Derricotte published a literary memoir, *The Black Notebooks: An Interior Journey.*

In it she discusses how her light skin has affected the way she sees herself and the way others see her. "I believed that my unconsciousness of my blackness, my 'forgetting,' was symptomatic of some deep refusal of 'self,' a kind of death wish."

Derricotte earned a master of arts degree from New York University. She has been awarded the Folger Shakespeare Library Poetry Book Award, the Lucille Medwick Memorial Award from the Poetry Society of America, a Pushcart Prize, and the Distinguished Pioneering of the Arts Award from the United Black Artists. She teaches at the University of Pittsburgh.

The Weakness

— *Toi Derricotte*

That time my grandmother dragged me
through the perfume aisles at Saks, she held me up
by my arm, hissing, "Stand up,"
through clenched teeth, her eyes
5   bright as a dog's
cornered in the light.
She said it over and over,
as if she were Jesus,
and I were dead. She had been
10   solid as a tree,
a fur around her neck, a
light-skinned matron whose car was parked, who walked on
    swirling
marble and passed through
brass openings—in 1945.
15   There was not even a black
elevator operator at Saks.
The saleswoman had brought velvet
leggings to lace me in, and cooed,
as if in the service of all grandmothers.
20   My grandmother had smiled, but not
hungrily, not like my mother
who hated them, but wanted to please,
and they had smiled back, as if
they were wearing wooden collars.

The Weakness

25   When my legs gave out, my grandmother
       dragged me up and held me like God
       holds saints by the
       roots of the hair. I begged her
       to believe I couldn't help it. Stumbling,
30   her face white
       with sweat, she pushed me through the crowd, rushing
       away from those eyes
       that saw through
       her clothes, under
35   her skin, all the way down
       to the transparent
       genes confessing.

Responding to the Selection

Questions for Discussion

1. When and where does the incident the speaker describes take place? Why is this significant?

2. Explain the difference between the way the speaker's grandmother smiles at the sales clerks and the way her mother does.

3. Why is the speaker being dragged through the store? What does this suggest about the grandmother?

4. Describe the grandmother's state of mind at the end of the poem and what the cause might be.

Activity

Interpreting Poetry

Study the quotation that precedes the biography of Toi Derricotte. Write an **essay** in which you discuss how what happens in the poem is related to the quotation and what that suggests to you about the relationship between art and life.

Before You Read

aunt rubie goes to market

Quraysh Ali Lansana
Born 1964

"*Aunt Rubie Hooper was one of the wisest people I have ever known and perhaps the greatest storyteller I've ever heard. She didn't need costumes or props. Her long and varied list of life experiences and her extensive vocabulary were all she needed. She was an extraordinary woman, but she was not famous or wealthy. This poem celebrates her and the rest of us ordinary people who do amazing things every day that never make the evening news.*"

About Lansana

Quraysh Ali Lansana is an award-winning poet, editor, and publisher. He is the author of three poetry collections, *southside rain, The Walmart Republic* (with Christopher Stewart), and *cockroach children: corner poems and street psalms,* and serves as a poetry editor for *FYAH!,* an online literary journal. His work has been performed as theater and broadcast on National Public Radio. Lansana is the artistic director of Chicago's Guild Complex, a National Endowment for the Arts award-winning literary center. As founder and managing editor of nappy-head press, Lansana has been publishing fine poetry chapbooks since 1995. He has led literary workshops in prisons, public schools, and universities throughout the United States. He currently makes his home in New York City with his wife and two sons.

aunt rubie goes to market

— *Quraysh Ali Lansana*

she needed a few things
but, not much
pushing her wooden cane
against february's attitude

5   the tiny steps of a giant
steps which taunt forever
those beige, thick-soled shoes
bearing just over a pound per year

across seventy-ninth street
10   she sits at the busstop
unmoved by the wait
ninety years wise

when the bus arrives
she sits at the front
15   so she can see everything

she does

aunt **rubie** goes to **market**

> one hundred blocks later
> the driver helps her out
> her mouth still moving
> 20   the mall growing anxious
>
> shoppers scurry around her
> but, she is not concerned
> aunt rubie needed a few things
> but, not much.

Responding to the Selection

Questions for Discussion

1. The speaker says of Aunt Rubie, "she needed a few things / but, not much." Suggest a few different ways to interpret these lines.

2. Why do you think the speaker describes Aunt Rubie as a "giant"?

3. Why do you suppose it's important for Aunt Rubie to "see everything"?

4. What happens when Aunt Rubie gets to the mall? What does this tell you about her?

Activities

Writing a Character Sketch

1. Write a **character sketch** of Aunt Rubie. Use your imagination to describe Aunt Rubie's personal qualities. Your sketch should address questions such as the following: Who is Aunt Rubie? What is she like? What has she seen?

Writing About Your Life

2. It has been said that with age often comes wisdom. Think about the elders in your family. Choose one who has become wise and write a second **character sketch** that describes the person and how his or her wisdom has affected your life. Does this person share any character traits with Aunt Rubie?

Before You Read

New York Day Women

Edwidge Danticat
Born 1969

"[In Krik? Krak!] I wanted to raise the voice of a lot of the people that I knew growing up, and this was, for the most part, . . . poor people who had extraordinary dreams but also very amazing obstacles."

About Danticat

Born in Haiti, Edwidge Danticat was two years old when her father immigrated to New York City and four when her mother followed. They planned to work hard, save money, and then send for their children. Danticat was raised by her aunt in a poor neighborhood of the Haitian capital, Port-au-Prince. "While I was growing up, most of the writers I knew were either in hiding, missing, or dead," Danticat says. "We were living under the brutal Duvalier dictatorship in Haiti, and silence was the law of the land." Nevertheless, Danticat wrote her first story when she was nine.

She was reunited with her parents in New York when she was twelve. Teased by classmates because of her accent and dress and torn between two languages—Haitian Creole and English—Danticat stopped writing. She resumed when she was fourteen and had an essay published about her experiences as a new immigrant.

Although her parents urged her to study medicine, Danticat studied writing. In 1993 she received a master of fine arts degree from Brown University. Her first novel, *Breath, Eyes, Memory,* was published in 1994. A short story collection, *Krik? Krak!* followed the year after. Danticat often writes of her native land. "I'm writing to save my life," she says, "to honor the sacrifices made by all those who came before me."

Krik? Krak!

The title of Danticat's collection of short stories is a reference to the call-and-response tradition of Haitian storytellers. Just before the storytelling begins, the storyteller calls out "Krik?" and the listeners respond "Krak!"

New York Day Women

— Edwidge Danticat

Today, walking down the street, I see my mother. She is strolling with a happy gait, her body thrust toward the DON'T WALK sign and the yellow taxicabs that make forty-five-degree turns on the corner of Madison and Fifty-seventh Street.

I have never seen her in this kind of neighborhood, peering into Chanel and Tiffany's and gawking at the jewels glowing in the Bulgari windows. My mother never shops outside of Brooklyn. She has never seen the advertising office where I work. She is afraid to take the subway, where you may meet those young black militant street preachers who curse black women for straightening their hair.

Yet, here she is, my mother, who I left at home that morning in her bathrobe, with pieces of newspapers twisted like rollers in her hair. My mother, who accuses me of random offenses as I dash out of the house.

Would you get up and give an old lady like me your subway seat? In this state of mind, I bet you don't even give up your seat to a pregnant lady.

My mother, who is often right about that. Sometimes I get up and give my seat. Other times, I don't. It all depends on how pregnant the woman is and whether or not she is with her boyfriend or husband and whether or not *he* is sitting down.

As my mother stands in front of Carnegie Hall, one taxi driver yells to another, "What do you think this is, a dance floor?"

My mother waits patiently for this dispute to be settled before crossing the street.

In Haiti when you get hit by a car, the owner of the car gets out and kicks you for getting blood on his bumper.

My mother who laughs when she says this and shows a large gap in her mouth where she lost three more molars to the dentist last week. My mother, who at fifty-nine, says dentures are okay.

You can take them out when they bother you. I'll like them. I'll like them fine.

Will it feel empty when Papa kisses you?

Oh no, he doesn't kiss me that way anymore.

My mother, who watches the lottery drawing every night on channel 11 without ever having played the numbers.

A third of that money is all I would need. We would pay the mortgage, and your father could stop driving that taxicab all over Brooklyn.

I follow my mother, mesmerized by the many possibilities of her journey. Even in a flowered dress, she is lost in a sea of pinstripes and gray suits, high heels and elegant short skirts, Reebok sneakers, dashing from building to building.

My mother, who won't go out to dinner with anyone.

If they want to eat with me, let them come to my house, even if I boil water and give it to them.

My mother, who talks to herself when she peels the skin off poultry.

Fat, you know, and cholesterol. Fat and cholesterol killed your aunt Hermine.

My mother, who makes jam with dried grapefruit peel and then puts in cinnamon bark that I always think is cockroaches in the jam. My mother, whom I have always bought household appliances for, on her birthday. A nice rice cooker, a blender.

I trail the red orchids in her dress and the heavy faux leather bag on her shoulders. Realizing the ferocious pace of my pursuit, I stop against a wall to rest. My mother keeps on walking as though she owns the sidewalk under her feet.

As she heads toward the Plaza Hotel, a bicycle messenger swings so close to her that I want to dash forward and rescue her, but she stands dead in her tracks and lets him ride around her and then goes on.

My mother stops at a corner hot-dog stand and asks for something. The vendor hands her a can of soda that she slips into her bag. She stops by another vendor selling sundresses for seven dollars each. I can tell that she is looking at an African print dress, contemplating my size. I think to myself, Please Ma, don't buy it. It would be just another thing I would bury in the garage or give to Goodwill.

Why should we give to Goodwill when there are so many people back home who need clothes? We save our clothes for the relatives in Haiti.

Twenty years we have been saving all kinds of things for the relatives in Haiti. I need the place in the garage for an exercise bike.

You are pretty enough to be a stewardess. Only dogs like bones.

This mother of mine, she stops at another hot-dog vendor's and buys a frankfurter that she eats on the street. I never knew that she ate frank-furters. With her blood pressure, she shouldn't eat anything with sodium. She has to be careful with her heart, this day woman.

I cannot just swallow salt. Salt is heavier than a hundred bags of shame.

She is slowing her pace, and now I am too close. If she turns around, she might see me. I let her walk into the park before I start to follow again.

My mother walks toward the sandbox in the middle of the park. There a woman is waiting with a child. The woman is wearing a leotard with biker's shorts and has small weights in her hands. The woman kisses the child good-bye and surrenders him to my mother, then she bolts off, running on the cemented stretches in the park.

The child given to my mother has frizzy blond hair. His hand slips into hers easily, like he's known her for a long time. When he raises his face to look at my mother, it is as though he is looking at the sky.

My mother gives this child the soda that she bought from the vendor on the street corner. The child's face lights up as she puts in a straw in the can for him. This seems to be a conspiracy just between the two of them.

My mother and the child sit and watch the other children play in the sandbox. The child pulls out a comic book from a knapsack with Big Bird on the back. My mother peers into his comic book. My mother, who taught herself to read as a little girl in Haiti from the books that her brothers brought home from school.

My mother, who has now lost six of her seven sisters in Ville Rose and has never had the strength to return for their funerals.

Many graves to kiss when I go back. Many graves to kiss.

New York Day Women

She throws away the empty soda can when the child is done with it. I wait and watch from a corner until the woman in the leotard and biker's shorts returns, sweaty and breathless, an hour later. My mother gives the woman back her child and strolls farther into the park.

I turn around and start to walk out of the park before my mother can see me. My lunch hour is long since gone. I have to hurry back to work. I walk through a cluster of joggers, then race to a *Sweden Tours* bus. I stand behind the bus and take a peek at my mother in the park. She is standing in a circle, chatting with a group of women who are taking other people's children on an afternoon outing. They look like a Third World Parent-Teacher Association meeting.

I quickly jump into a cab heading back to the office. Would Ma have said hello had she been the one to see me first?

As the cab races away from the park, it occurs to me that perhaps one day I would chase an old woman down a street by mistake and that old woman would be somebody else's mother, who I would have mistaken for mine.

Day women come out when nobody expects them.

Tonight on the subway, I will get up and give my seat to a pregnant woman or a lady about Ma's age.

My mother, who stuffs thimbles in her mouth and then blows up her cheeks like Dizzy Gillespie while sewing yet another Raggedy Ann doll that she names Suzette after me.

I will have all these little Suzettes in case you never have any babies, which looks more and more like it is going to happen.

My mother who had me when she was thirty-three—*l'âge du Christ*—at the age that Christ died on the cross.

That's a blessing, believe you me, even if American doctors say by that time you can make retarded babies.

My mother, who sews lace collars on my company softball T-shirts when she does my laundry.

Why, you can't look like a lady playing softball?

My mother, who never went to any of my Parent-Teacher Association meetings when I was in school.

You're so good anyway. What are they going to tell me? I don't want to make you ashamed of this day woman. Shame is heavier than a hundred bags of salt.

Responding to the Selection ——————

Questions for Discussion

1. Why do you think the narrator follows her mother around New York City without revealing herself?

2. Describe the relationship between the narrator and her mother.

3. Is the mother's behavior in the city surprising to you? Why?

4. What do the italicized sections represent? How do they add meaning to the story?

5. At the end of the story, what has the narrator learned about her mother?

Activities

Writing a Review

1. Write a **critical review** of the story. Your review should address the following issues:

   a very brief summary of the plot

   what you liked or disliked about the story

   the meaning of the story to you

   how the structure of the story imparts meaning

The Oral Tradition in Haiti

2. **Research** the oral tradition in Haiti. What role do storytellers play in contemporary Haitian society? Try to discover some of the traditional stories that are still told today. Do any of these stories have a common theme? Discuss your findings in class.

Before You Read

A Walk to the Jetty

Jamaica Kincaid
Born 1949

"I didn't think of myself as an outsider because of my race because . . . where I grew up I was the same race as almost everyone else . . . It is true that I noticed things that no one else seemed to notice. And I think only people who are outsiders do this."

About Kincaid

Jamaica Kincaid (Elaine Potter Richardson) was born on the Caribbean island of Antigua. Because her parents were unable to send her to university, she moved to the United States at age seventeen in search of opportunity. Nine years later, she began submitting articles to *The New Yorker* and eventually came to the attention of William Shawn, the magazine's editor, who was amused by her comments about U.S. culture. In 1976 Shawn hired Kincaid as a staff writer and later began publishing her fiction.

Kincaid is widely praised for her poetic literary style and her insight into relationships between parents and children. Much of her work is autobiographical, and although she admits she has been "incredibly lucky" in her personal life, she refuses to write happy endings. "I think life is difficult," Kincaid has said. "I am interested in pursuing a truth, and the truth often seems to be not happiness but its opposite."

Annie John

The following selection is an excerpt from the last chapter of *Annie John,* a coming-of-age novel about a girl growing up on Antigua. In the early chapters, young Annie is with her mother constantly, helping with the housework and shopping. As Annie enters young womanhood, her mother begins to distance herself from the girl. Resentful over the loss of her intimacy, Annie begins to rebel against her mother, whom she still loves. At age seventeen, Annie decides to travel to England and study for a career in nursing.

A Walk to the Jetty

from

Annie John

— *Jamaica Kincaid*

My mother had arranged with a stevedore to take my trunk to the jetty ahead of me. At ten o'clock on the dot, I was dressed, and we set off for the jetty. An hour after that, I would board a launch that would take me out to sea, where I then would board the ship. Starting out, as if for old time's sake and without giving it a thought, we lined up in the old way: I walking between my mother and my father. I loomed way above my father and could see the top of his head. We must have made a strange sight: a grown girl all dressed up in the middle of a morning, in the middle of the week, walking in step in the middle between her two parents, for people we didn't know stared at us. It was all of half an hour's walk from our house to the jetty, but I was passing through most of the years of my life. We passed by the house where Miss Dulcie, the seamstress that I had been apprenticed to for a time, lived, and just as I was passing by, a wave of bad feeling for her came over me, because I suddenly remembered that the months I spent with her all she had me do was sweep the floor, which was always full of threads and pins and needles, and I never seemed to sweep it clean enough to please her. Then she would send me to the store to buy buttons or thread, though I was only allowed to do this if I was given a sample of the button or thread, and then she would find fault even though they were an exact match of the samples she had given me. And all the while she said to me, "A girl like you will never learn to sew properly, you know." At the time, I don't suppose I minded it, because it was customary to treat the first-year apprentice with such scorn, but now I placed on the dustheap of my life Miss Dulcie and everything that I had had to do with her.

We were soon on the road that I had taken to school, to church, to Sunday school, to choir practice, to Brownie meetings, to Girl Guide meetings, to meet a friend. I was five years old when I first walked on this road unaccompanied by someone to hold my hand. My mother had placed three pennies in my little basket, which was a duplicate of her bigger basket, and sent me to the chemist's shop to buy a pennyworth of senna leaves, a pennyworth of eucalyptus leaves, and a pennyworth of camphor. She then instructed me on what side of the road to walk, where to make a turn, where to cross, how to look carefully before I crossed, and if I met anyone that I knew to politely pass greetings and keep on my way. I was wearing a freshly ironed yellow dress that had printed on it scenes of acrobats flying through the air and swinging on a trapeze. I had just had a bath, and after it, instead of powdering me with my baby-smelling talcum powder, my mother had, as a special favor, let me use her own talcum powder, which smelled quite perfumy and came in a can that had painted on it people going out to dinner in nineteenth-century London and was called Mazie. How it pleased me to walk out the door and bend my head down to sniff at myself and see that I smelled just like my mother. I went to the chemist's shop, and he had to come from behind the counter and bend down to hear what it was that I wanted to buy, my voice was so little and timid then. I went back just the way I had come, and when I walked into the yard and presented my basket with its three packages to my mother, her eyes filled with tears and she swooped me up and held me high in the air and said that I was wonderful and good and that there would never be anybody better. If I had just conquered Persia, she couldn't have been more proud of me.

We passed by our church—the church in which I had been christened and received and had sung in the junior choir. We passed by a house in which a girl I used to like and was sure I couldn't live without had lived. Once, when she had mumps, I went to visit her against my mother's wishes, and we sat on her bed and ate the cure of roasted, buttered sweet potatoes that had been placed on her swollen jaws, held there by a piece of white cloth. I don't know how, but my mother found out about it, and I don't know how, but she put an end to our friendship. Shortly after, the girl moved with her family across the sea to somewhere else. We passed the doll store, where I would go with my mother when I was little and point out the doll I wanted that year for Christmas. We passed the store where I bought the much-fought-over shoes I wore to church to be received in. We passed the bank. On my sixth birthday, I was given, among other things, the present of a sixpence. My mother and I then went to this bank, and with the sixpence I opened my own savings account. I was given

A Walk to the Jetty

a little gray book with my name in big letters on it, and in the balance column it said "6d." Every Saturday morning after that, I was given a sixpence—later a shilling, and later a two-and-sixpence piece—and I would take it to the bank for deposit. I had never been allowed to withdraw even a farthing from my bank account until just a few weeks before I was to leave; then the whole account was closed out, and I received from the bank the sum of six pounds ten shillings and two and a half pence.

We passed the office of the doctor who told my mother three times that I did not need glasses, that if my eyes were feeling weak a glass of carrot juice a day would make them strong again. This happened when I was eight. And so every day at recess I would run to my school gate and meet my mother, who was waiting for me with a glass of juice from carrots she had just grated and then squeezed, and I would drink it and then run back to meet my chums. I knew there was nothing at all wrong with my eyes, but I had recently read a story in *The Schoolgirl's Own Annual* in which the heroine, a girl a few years older than I was then, cut such a figure to my mind with the way she was always adjusting her small, round, horn-rimmed glasses that I felt I must have a pair exactly like them. When it became clear that I didn't need glasses, I began to complain about the glare of the sun being too much for my eyes, and I walked around with my hands shielding them—especially in my mother's presence. My mother then bought for me a pair of sunglasses with the exact horn-rimmed frames I wanted, and how I enjoyed the gestures of blowing on the lenses, wiping them with the hem of my uniform, adjusting the glasses when they slipped down my nose, and just removing them from their case and putting them on. In three weeks, I grew tired of them and they found a nice resting place in a drawer, along with some other things that at one time or another I couldn't live without.

We passed the store that sold only grooming aids, all imported from England. This store had in it a large porcelain dog—white, with black spots all over and a red ribbon of satin tied around its neck. The dog sat in front of a white porcelain bowl that was always filled with fresh water, and it sat in such a way that it looked as if it had just taken a long drink. When I was a small child, I would ask my mother, if ever we were near this store, to please take me to see the dog, and I would stand in front of it, bent over slightly, my hands resting on my knees, and stare at it and stare at it. I thought this dog more beautiful and more real than any actual dog I had ever seen or any actual dog I would ever see. I must have outgrown my interest in the dog, for when it disappeared I never asked what became of it. We passed the library, and if there was anything on this walk that I might have wept over leaving, this most surely would have been the thing. My mother had been a member of the library long before I was

A Walk to the Jetty

born. And since she took me everywhere with her when I was quite little, when she went to the library she took me along there, too. I would sit in her lap very quietly as she read books that she did not want to take home with her. I could not read the words yet, but just the way they looked on the page was interesting to me. Once, a book she was reading had a large picture of a man in it, and when I asked her who he was she told me that he was Louis Pasteur and that the book was about his life. It stuck in my mind, because she said it was because of him that she boiled my milk to purify it before I was allowed to drink it, that it was his idea, and that that was why the process was called pasteurization. One of the things I had put away in my mother's old trunk in which she kept all my childhood things was my library card. At that moment, I owed sevenpence in overdue fees.

As I passed by all these places, it was as if I were in a dream, for I didn't notice the people coming and going in and out of them, I didn't feel my feet touch ground, I didn't even feel my own body—I just saw these places as if they were hanging in the air, not having top or bottom, and as if I had gone in and out of them all in the same moment. The sun was bright; the sky was blue and just above my head. We then arrived at the jetty.

My heart now beat fast, and no matter how hard I tried, I couldn't keep my mouth from falling open and my nostrils from spreading to the ends of my face. My old fear of slipping between the boards of the jetty and falling into the dark-green water where the dark-green eels lived came over me. When my father's stomach started to go bad, the doctor had recommended a walk every evening right after he ate his dinner. Sometimes he would take me with him. When he took me with him, we usually went to the jetty, and there he would sit and talk to the night watchman about cricket or some other thing that didn't interest me, because it was not personal; they didn't talk about their wives, or their children, or their parents, or about any of their likes and dislikes. They talked about things in such a strange way, and I didn't see what they found funny, but sometimes they made each other laugh so much that their guffaws would bound out to sea and send back an echo. I was always sorry when we got to the jetty and saw that the night watchman on duty was the one he enjoyed speaking to; it was like being locked up in a book filled with numbers and diagrams and what-ifs. For the thing about not being able to understand and enjoy what they were saying was I had nothing to take my mind off my fear of slipping in between the boards of the jetty.

Now, too, I had nothing to take my mind off what was happening to me. My mother and my father—I was leaving them forever. My home on an island—I was leaving it forever. What to make of everything? I felt a familiar hollow space inside. I felt I was being held down against my will.

A Walk to the Jetty

I felt I was burning up from head to toe. I felt that someone was tearing me up into little pieces and soon I would be able to see all the little pieces as they floated out into nothing in the deep blue sea. I didn't know whether to laugh or cry. I could see that it would be better not to think too clearly about any one thing. The launch was being made ready to take me, along with some other passengers, out to the ship that was anchored in the sea. My father paid our fares, and we joined a line of people waiting to board. My mother checked my bag to make sure that I had my passport, the money she had given me, and a sheet of paper placed between some pages in my Bible on which were written the names of the relatives—people I had not known existed—with whom I would live in England. Across from the jetty was a wharf, and some stevedores were loading and unloading barges. I don't know why seeing that struck me so, but suddenly a wave of strong feeling came over me, and my heart swelled with a great gladness as the words "I shall never see this again" spilled out inside me. But then, just as quickly, my heart shriveled up and the words "I shall never see this again" stabbed at me. I don't know what stopped me from falling in a heap at my parents' feet.

When we were all on board, the launch headed out to sea. Away from the jetty, the water became the customary blue, and the launch left a wide path in it that looked like a road. I passed by sounds and smells that were so familiar that I had long ago stopped paying any attention to them. But now here they were, and the ever-present "I shall never see this again" bobbed up and down inside me. There was the sound of the seagull diving down into the water and coming up with something silver-ish in its mouth. There was the smell of the sea and the sight of small pieces of rubbish floating around in it. There were boats filled with fishermen coming in early. There was the sound of their voices as they shouted greetings to each other. There was the hot sun, there was the blue sea, there was the blue sky. Not very far away, there was the white sand of the shore, with the run-down houses all crowded in next to each other, for in some places only poor people lived near the shore. I was seated in the launch between my parents, and when I realized that I was gripping their hands tightly I glanced quickly to see if they were looking at me with scorn, for I felt sure that they must have known of my never-see-this-again feelings. But instead my father kissed me on the forehead and my mother kissed me on the mouth, and they both gave over their hands to me, so that I could grip them as much as I wanted. I was on the verge of feeling that it had all been a mistake, but I remembered that I wasn't a child anymore, and that now when I made up my mind about something I had to see it through. At that moment, we came to the ship, and that was that.

212 Jamaica Kincaid

A Walk to the Jetty

The good-byes had to be quick, the captain said. My mother introduced herself to him and then introduced me. She told him to keep an eye on me, for I had never gone this far away from home on my own. She gave him a letter to pass on to the captain of the next ship that I would board in Barbados. They walked me to my cabin, a small space that I would share with someone else—a woman I did not know. I had never before slept in a room with someone I did not know. My father kissed me good-bye and told me to be good and to write home often. After he said this, he looked at me, then looked at the floor and swung his left foot, then looked at me again. I could see that he wanted to say something else, something that he had never said to me before, but then he just turned and walked away. My mother said, "Well," and then she threw her arms around me. Big tears streamed down her face, and it must have been that—for I could not bear to see my mother cry—which started me crying, too. She then tightened her arms around me and held me to her close, so that I felt that I couldn't breathe. With that, my tears dried up and I was suddenly on my guard. "What does she want now?" I said to myself. Still holding me close to her, she said, in a voice that raked across my skin, "It doesn't matter what you do or where you go, I'll always be your mother and this will always be your home."

I dragged myself away from her and backed off a little, and then I shook myself, as if to wake myself out of a stupor. We looked at each other for a long time with smiles on our faces, but I know the opposite of that was in my heart. As if responding to some invisible cue, we both said, at the very same moment, "Well." Then my mother turned around and walked out the cabin door. I stood there for I don't know how long, and then I remembered that it was customary to stand on deck and wave to your relatives who were returning to shore. From the deck, I could not see my father, but I could see my mother facing the ship, her eyes searching to pick me out. I removed from my bag a red cotton handkerchief that she had earlier given me for this purpose, and I waved it wildly in the air. Recognizing me immediately, she waved back just as wildly, and we continued to do this until she became just a dot in the matchbox-size launch swallowed up in the big blue sea.

I went back to my cabin and lay down on my berth. Everything trembled as if it had a spring at its very center. I could hear the small waves lap-lapping around the ship. They made an unexpected sound, as if a vessel filled with liquid had been placed on its side and now was slowly emptying out.

Responding to the Selection

Questions for Discussion

1. What is the literary purpose of the narrator's walk to the jetty?

2. Which event in the story suggests that the narrator and her mother were very close when the narrator was very young?

3. An **internal conflict** is a struggle that takes place within a character. Which characters experience internal conflicts? What are their internal conflicts?

4. What might the narrator's father have wanted to say to her that he had never said before? Why was he unable to get the words out?

5. What is the sound of the waves compared to as the ship heads out to sea? What does this comparison symbolize?

Activities

Reflecting on Your Childhood

1. Imagine you were to take a walk from your home to some distant part of town. What places would you pass that might have played an important role in your childhood? Which significant people would you meet? Try writing a **personal narrative** that resembles the first half of "A Walk to the Jetty." Then write a **reflective paragraph** that discusses what you have learned about yourself as a result of writing the narrative.

Reporting on Geography

2. Consult an atlas to discover where Antigua and Barbados are located and where they are in relation to England. Then search the Internet for sites about Antigua. Prepare a **report** about the island's history, its people, and its place in the modern world.

Before You Read

Letter from Foreign

Rohan B. Preston
Born 1966

"'Letter from Foreign' is an actual letter to my great grandmother, Gladys Campbell Holmes, who died in 1999 at the age of 106. I find that when I write with family as an in-mind audience, I can be honest in a loving way, truthful without hurting. It's a liberating feeling for a writer."

About Preston

Rohan B. Preston authored the poetry collection *Dreams in Soy Sauce* and coedited the multigenre anthology *Soulfires: Young Black Men on Love and Violence.* His poems have appeared in *Crab Orchard Review, Drumvoices Revue, Ploughshares,* and *Triquarterly,* and his nonfiction writing has been published in the *Chicago Tribune, The New York Times,* and the *Washington Post.* He is the lead theater critic at the *Star Tribune* in Minneapolis, where he lives with his wife and daughter.

Letter from Foreign

— Rohan B. Preston

for A.W. S.

> Dear Mum, there are so many things I have
> to tell 'bout 'Merica, the place where you said
> the streets are gold and there are many people
> with good hair (like those in the movies).
>
> 5   'Member when I use to play with the toy helicopter
> and fly away a foreign? Well, Mum, Dearest Grand Mamaa,
> I have some news for you. 'Merica is not in the sky
> like the planes but is on land, flat land, droopy corn-fields
> and choking chimneys, with latrines, and doo-doo
> 10   and frowsy ragamuffins as good as dead on sidewalks.
>
> Mum, you tell me say God bless America for the people
> here good, I have some more news for you.
> Sure, some people go to church and chapel
> and mosque and synagogue and march and pray
> 15   and some smile when they see you on the street
> (some don't say 'Morning, dog' and sometimes
> them cross the street when we pass them—
> for an healthy Black man is a dinosaur
> blowing fire at the people with pretty hair
> 20   and you know how easy it is for hair to catch fire.)

Mum, you tell me that they have scholarships galore.
And, a true. But you never say anything 'bout glass,
'bout aquarium and how buckra can encase you
in glass so that no matter how loud you scream
25   no matter how much you bark, the ceiling still there.

I don't want to bring down God on me so I must say
that education here good and that we learn all kinds
of things 'bout Greece and Rome, me speak Italian
now, some French—even Japanese. All these things
30   that you wanted me to do, Mum, but there is lots of glass about,
lenses, ceilings, bottles and they're all trained on me, you know,
reflecting, watching, waiting and laughing,
but I have to follow your lead, almost a century
and still not weary yet, I must never get weary yet.

Responding to the Selection

Questions for Discussion

1. What has Mum told the speaker about America? What is the purpose of the letter the speaker writes?

2. Explain the reference to ". . . good hair (like those in the movies)."

3. What is the speaker implying when he says ". . . an healthy Black man is a dinosaur / blowing fire at the people with pretty hair"?

4. Why does the speaker say, "I must never get weary yet"?

5. What does the glass **symbolize** to the speaker? Why?

Activity

Interpreting Poetry

At the end of the poem, the speaker says ". . . but there is lots of glass about, / lenses, ceilings, bottles and they're all trained on me, you know, / reflecting, watching, waiting and laughing. . . ." Write an **interpretive essay** in which you explore the meaning behind these images. What might the lenses be? The ceilings? The bottles? Why are they trained on the speaker and who is doing the training? Is there any escape for the speaker?

Before You Read

To Da-duh, in Memoriam

Paule Marshall
Born 1929

"Sometimes a person has to go back, really back—to have a sense, an understanding of all that's gone to make them— before they can go forward."

About Barbados

"To Da-duh, in Memoriam" takes place in Barbados in the 1930s. Barbados is a tiny Caribbean island with mostly flat terrain. Its highest point, Mount Hillaby, is shorter than New York City's Empire State Building. The island became an independent state in 1966, after being under British colonial rule for more than three centuries. Although the people of Barbados speak English, the folk culture is of African origin. In 1937–1938, the island experienced violent unrest as a result of economic depression and other stresses.

About Marshall

Paule Marshall grew up in a Barbadian community in New York City, where, she says, she learned all about writing in her mother's kitchen. In this "wordshop," her mother and her mother's friends passed on to her "the rich legacy of language and culture" that they shared after their work-days of "scrubbing floor." Marshall went on to write many award-winning novels, short stories, and articles, including her most famous work, *Praisesong for the Widow.* The story you are about to read is "the most autobiographical of the stories."

To Da-duh,
in Memoriam

— Paule Marshall

"... Oh Nana! all of you is not involved in this evil business Death,
Nor all of us in life."

— from "At My Grandmother's Grave,"
by Lebert Bethune

I did not see her at first I remember. For not only was it dark inside the
crowded disembarkation shed in spite of the daylight flooding in from outside, but standing there waiting for her with my mother and sister I was still
somewhat blinded from the sheen of tropical sunlight on the water of the
bay which we had just crossed in the landing boat, leaving behind us the
ship that had brought us from New York lying in the offing. Besides, being
only nine years of age at the time and knowing nothing of islands I was busy
attending to the alien sights and sounds of Barbados, the unfamiliar smells.

I did not see her, but I was alerted to her approach by my mother's
hand which suddenly tightened around mine, and looking up I traced her
gaze through the gloom in the shed until I finally made out the small, pur-
poseful, painfully erect figure of the old woman headed our way.

Her face was drowned in the shadow of an ugly rolled-brim brown felt
hat, but the details of her slight body and of the struggle taking place
within it were clear enough—an intense, unrelenting struggle between her
back which was beginning to bend ever so slightly under the weight of her
eighty-odd years and the rest of her which sought to deny those years and
hold that back straight, keep it in line. Moving swiftly toward us (so
swiftly it seemed she did not intend stopping when she reached us but
would sweep past us out the doorway which opened onto the sea and like
Christ walk upon the water!), she was caught between the sunlight at her
end of the building and the darkness inside—and for a moment she
appeared to contain them both: the light in the long severe old-fashioned
white dress she wore which brought the sense of a past that was still alive

into our bustling present and in the snatch of white at her eye; the darkness in her black high-top shoes and in her face which was visible now that she was closer.

It was as stark and fleshless as a death mask, that face. The maggots might have already done their work, leaving only the framework of bone beneath the ruined skin and deep wells at the temple and jaw. But her eyes were alive, unnervingly so for one so old, with a sharp light that flicked out of the dim clouded depths like a lizard's tongue to snap up all in her view. Those eyes betrayed a child's curiosity about the world, and I wondered vaguely seeing them, and seeing the way the bodice of her ancient dress had collapsed in on her flat chest (what had happened to her breasts?), whether she might not be some kind of child at the same time that she was a woman, with fourteen children, my mother included, to prove it. Perhaps she was both, both child and woman, darkness and light, past and present, life and death—all the opposites contained and reconciled in her.

"My Da-duh," my mother said formally and stepped forward. The name sounded like thunder fading softly in the distance.

"Child," Da-duh said, and her tone, her quick scrutiny of my mother, the brief embrace in which they appeared to shy from each other rather than touch, wiped out the fifteen years my mother had been away and restored the old relationship. My mother, who was such a formidable figure in my eyes, had suddenly with a word been reduced to my status.

"Yes, God is good," Da-duh said with a nod that was like a tic. "He has spared me to see my child again."

We were led forward then, apologetically because not only did Da-duh prefer boys but she also liked her grandchildren to be "white," that is, fair-skinned; and we had, I was to discover, a number of cousins, the outside children of white estate managers and the like, who qualified. We, though, were as black as she.

My sister being the oldest was presented first. "This one takes after the father," my mother said and waited to be reproved.

Frowning, Da-duh tilted my sister's face toward the light. But her frown soon gave way to a grudging smile, for my sister with her large mild eyes and little broad winged nose, with our father's high-cheeked Barbadian cast to her face, was pretty.

"She's goin' be lucky," Da-duh said and patted her once on the cheek. "Any girl child that takes after the father does be lucky."

She turned then to me. But oddly enough she did not touch me. Instead leaning close, she peered hard at me, and then quickly drew back. I thought I saw her hand start up as though to shield her eyes. It was almost as if she saw not only me, a thin truculent child who it was said took after no one but myself, but something in me which for some reason she found disturbing,

To Da-duh, in Memoriam

even threatening. We looked silently at each other for a long time there in the noisy shed, our gaze locked. She was the first to look away.

"But Adry," she said to my mother and her laugh was cracked, thin, apprehensive. "Where did you get this one here with this fierce look?"

"We don't know where she came out of, my Da-duh," my mother said, laughing also. Even I smiled to myself. After all I had won the encounter. Da-duh had recognized my small strength—and this was all I ever asked of the adults in my life then.

"Come, soul," Da-duh said and took my hand. "You must be one of those New York terrors you hear so much about."

She led us, me at her side and my sister and mother behind, out of the shed into the sunlight that was like a bright driving summer rain and over to a group of people clustered beside a decrepit lorry. They were our relatives, most of them from St. Andrews although Da-duh herself lived in St. Thomas, the women wearing bright print dresses, the colors vivid against their darkness, the men rusty black suits that encased them like strait-jackets. Da-duh, holding fast to my hand, became my anchor as they circled round us like a nervous sea, exclaiming, touching us with their calloused hands, embracing us shyly. They laughed in awed bursts: "But look Adry got big-big children!" / "And see the nice things they wearing, wristwatch and all!" / "I tell you, Adry has done all right for sheself in New York. . . ."

Da-duh, ashamed at their wonder, embarrassed for them, admonished them the while. . . . "Why you all got to get on like you never saw people from 'Away' before? You would think New York is the only place in the world to hear wunna. That's why I don't like to go anyplace with you St. Andrews people, you know. You all ain't been colonized."

We were in the back of the lorry finally, packed in among the barrels of ham, flour, cornmeal and rice and the trunks of clothes that my mother had brought as gifts. We made our way slowly through Bridgetown's clogged streets, part of a funereal procession of cars and open-sided buses, bicycles and donkey carts. The dim little limestone shops and offices along the way marched with us, at the same mournful pace, toward the same grave ceremony—as did the people, the women balancing huge baskets on top their heads as if they were no more than hats they wore to shade them from the sun. Looking over the edge of the lorry I watched as their feet slurred the dust. I listened, and their voices, raw and loud and dissonant in the heat, seemed to be grappling with each other high overhead.

Da-duh sat on a trunk in our midst, a monarch amid her court. She still held my hand, but it was different now. I had suddenly become her anchor, for I felt her fear of the lorry with its asthmatic motor (a fear and distrust, I later learned, she held of all machines) beating like a pulse in her rough palm.

To Da-duh, in Memoriam

As soon as we left Bridgetown behind though, she relaxed, and while the others around us talked she gazed at the canes standing tall on either side of the winding marl road. "C'dear," she said softly to herself after a time. "The canes this side are pretty enough."

They were too much for me. I thought of them as giant weeds that had overrun the island, leaving scarcely any room for the small tottering houses of sunbleached pine we passed or the people, dark streaks as our lorry hurtled by. I suddenly feared that we were journeying, unaware that we were, toward some dangerous place where the canes, grown as high and thick as a forest, would close in on us and run us through with their stiletto blades. I longed then for the familiar: for the street in Brooklyn where I lived, for my father who had refused to accompany us ("Blowing out good money on foolishness," he had said of the trip), for a game of tag with my friends under the chestnut tree outside our aging brownstone house.

"Yes, but wait till you see St. Thomas canes," Da-duh was saying to me. "They's canes father, bo," she gave a proud arrogant nod. "Tomorrow, God willing, I goin' take you out in the ground and show them to you."

True to her word Da-duh took me with her the following day out into the ground. It was a fairly large plot adjoining her weathered board and shingle house and consisting of a small orchard, a good-sized canepiece and behind the canes, where the land sloped abruptly down, a gully. She had purchased it with Panama money sent her by her eldest son, my uncle Joseph, who had died working on the canal. We entered the ground along a trail no wider than her body and as devious and complex as her reasons for showing me her land. Da-duh strode briskly ahead, her slight form filled out this morning by the layers of sacking petticoats she wore under her working dress to protect her against the damp. A fresh white cloth, elaborately arranged around her head, added to her height, and lent her a vain, almost roguish air.

Her pace slowed once we reached the orchard, and glancing back at me occasionally over her shoulder, she pointed out the various trees.

"This here is a breadfruit," she said. "That one yonder is a papaw. Here's a guava. This is a mango. I know you don't have anything like these in New York. Here's a sugar apple." (The fruit looked more like artichokes than apples to me.) "This one bears limes. . . ." She went on for some time, intoning the names of the trees as though they were those of her gods. Finally, turning to me, she said, "I know you don't have anything this nice where you come from." Then, as I hesitated: "I said I know you don't have anything this nice where you come from. . . ."

"No," I said and my world did seem suddenly lacking.

Da-duh nodded and passed on. The orchard ended and we were on the narrow cart road that led through the canepiece, the canes clashing like swords above my cowering head. Again she turned and her thin muscular

To Da-duh, in Memoriam

arms spread wide, her dim gaze embracing the small field of canes, she said—and her voice almost broke under the weight of her pride, "Tell me, have you got anything like these in that place where you were born?"

"No."

"I din' think so. I bet you don't even know that these canes here and the sugar you eat is one and the same thing. That they does throw the canes into some damn machine at the factory and squeeze out all the little life in them to make sugar for you all so in New York to eat. I bet you don't know that."

"I've got two cavities and I'm not allowed to eat a lot of sugar."

But Da-duh didn't hear me. She had turned with an inexplicably angry motion and was making her way rapidly out of the canes and down the slope at the edge of the field which led to the gully below. Following her apprehensively down the incline amid a stand of banana plants whose leaves flapped like elephants' ears in the wind, I found myself in the middle of a small tropical wood—a place dense and damp and gloomy and tremulous with the fitful play of light and shadow as the leaves high above moved against the sun that was almost hidden from view. It was a violent place, the tangled foliage fighting each other for a chance at the sunlight, the branches of the trees locked in what seemed an immemorial struggle, one both necessary and inevitable. But despite the violence, it was pleasant, almost peaceful in the gully, and beneath the thick undergrowth the earth smelled like spring.

This time Da-duh didn't even bother to ask her usual question, but simply turned and waited for me to speak.

"No," I said, my head bowed. "We don't have anything like this in New York."

"Ah," she cried, her triumph complete. "I din' think so. Why, I've heard that's a place where you can walk till you near drop and never see a tree."

"We've got a chestnut tree in front of our house," I said.

"Does it bear?" She waited. "I ask you, does it bear?"

"Not anymore," I muttered. "It used to, but not anymore."

She gave the nod that was like a nervous twitch. "You see," she said. "Nothing can bear there." Then, secure behind her scorn, she added, "But tell me, what's this snow like that you hear so much about?"

Looking up, I studied her closely, sensing my chance, and then I told her, describing at length and with as much drama as I could summon not only what snow in the city was like, but what it would be like here, in her perennial summer kingdom.

". . . And you see all these trees you got here," I said. "Well, they'd be bare. No leaves, no fruit, nothing. They'd be covered in snow. You see your canes. They'd be buried under tons of snow. The snow would be higher than your head, higher than your house, and you wouldn't be able to come down into this here gully because it would be snowed under. . . ."

To Da-duh, in Memoriam

She searched my face for the lie, still scornful but intrigued. "What a thing, huh?" she said finally, whispering it softly to herself.

"And when it snows you couldn't dress like you are now," I said. "Oh no, you'd freeze to death. You'd have to wear a hat and gloves and galoshes and ear muffs so your ears wouldn't freeze and drop off, and a heavy coat. I've got a Shirley Temple coat with fur on the collar. I can dance. You wanna see?"

Before she could answer I began, with a dance called the Truck which was popular back then in the 1930s. My right forefinger waving, I trucked around the nearby trees and around Da-duh's awed and rigid form. After the Truck I did the Suzy-Q, my lean hips swishing, my sneakers sidling zigzag over the ground. "I can sing," I said and did so, starting with "I'm Gonna Sit Right Down and Write Myself a Letter," then without pausing, "Tea For Two," and ending with "I Found a Million Dollar Baby in a Five and Ten Cent Store."

For long moments afterwards Da-duh stared at me as if I were a creature from Mars, an emissary from some world she did not know but which intrigued her and whose power she both felt and feared. Yet something about my performance must have pleased her, because bending down she slowly lifted her long skirt and then, one by one, the layers of petticoats until she came to a drawstring purse dangling at the end of a long strip of cloth tied round her waist. Opening the purse she handed me a penny. "Here," she said half-smiling against her will. "Take this to buy yourself a sweet at the shop up the road. There's nothing to be done with you, soul."

From then on, whenever I wasn't taken to visit relatives, I accompanied Da-duh out into the ground, and alone with her amid the canes or down in the gully I told her about New York. It always began with some slighting remark on her part: "I know they don't have anything this nice where you come from," or "Tell me, I hear those foolish people in New York does do such and such. . . ." But as I answered, recreating my towering world of steel and concrete and machines for her, building the city out of words, I would feel her give way. I came to know the signs of her surrender: the total stillness that would come over the little hard dry form, the probing gaze that like a surgeon's knife sought to cut through my skull to get at the images there, to see if I were lying; above all, her fear, a fear nameless and profound, the same one I had felt beating in the palm of her hand that day in the lorry.

Over the weeks I told her about refrigerators, radios, gas stoves, elevators, trolley cars, wringer washing machines, movies, airplanes, the cyclone at Coney Island, subways, toasters, electric lights: "At night, see, all you have to do is flip this little switch on the wall and all the lights in the house go on. Just like that. Like magic. It's like turning on the sun at night."

"But tell me," she said to me once with a faint mocking smile, "do the white people have all these things too or it's only the people looking like us?"

To Da-duh, in Memoriam

I laughed. "What d'ya mean," I said. "The white people have even better." Then: "I beat up a white girl in my class last term."

"Beating up white people!" Her tone was incredulous.

"How you mean!" I said, using an expression of hers. "She called me a name."

For some reason Da-duh could not quite get over this and repeated in the same hushed, shocked voice, "Beating up white people now! Oh, the lord, the world's changing up so I can scarce recognize it anymore."

One morning toward the end of our stay, Da-duh led me into a part of the gully that we had never visited before, an area darker and more thickly overgrown than the rest, almost impenetrable. There in a small clearing amid the dense bush, she stopped before an incredibly tall royal palm which rose cleanly out of the ground, and drawing the eye up with it, soared high above the trees around it into the sky. It appeared to be touching the blue dome of sky, to be flaunting its dark crown of fronds right in the blinding white face of the late morning sun.

Da-duh watched me a long time before she spoke, and then she said, very quietly, "All right, now, tell me if you've got anything this tall in that place you're from."

I almost wished, seeing her face, that I could have said no. "Yes," I said. "We've got buildings hundreds of times this tall in New York. There's one called the Empire State Building that's the tallest in the world. My class visited it last year and I went all the way to the top. It's got over a hundred floors. I can't describe how tall it is. Wait a minute. What's the name of that hill I went to visit the other day, where they have the police station?"

"You mean Bissex?"

"Yes, Bissex. Well, the Empire State Building is way taller than that."

"You're lying now!" she shouted, trembling with rage. Her hand lifted to strike me.

"No, I'm not," I said. "It really is, if you don't believe me I'll send you a picture postcard of it soon as I get back home so you can see for yourself. But it's way taller than Bissex."

All the fight went out of her at that. The hand poised to strike me fell limp to her side, and as she stared at me, seeing not me but the building that was taller than the highest hill she knew, the small stubborn light in her eyes (it was the same amber as the flame in the kerosene lamp she lit at dusk) began to fail. Finally, with a vague gesture that even in the midst of her defeat still tried to dismiss me and my world, she turned and started back through the gully, walking slowly, her steps groping and uncertain, as if she were suddenly no longer sure of the way, while I followed triumphant yet strangely saddened behind.

The next morning I found her dressed for our morning walk but stretched out on the Berbice chair in the tiny drawing room where she sometimes

To Da-duh, in Memoriam

napped during the afternoon heat, her face turned to the window beside her. She appeared thinner and suddenly indescribably old.

"My Da-duh," I said.

"Yes, nuh," she said. Her voice was listless and the face she slowly turned my way was, now that I think back on it, like a Benin mask, the features drawn and almost distorted by an ancient abstract sorrow.

"Don't you feel well?" I asked.

"Girl, I don't know."

"My Da-duh, I goin' boil you some bush tea," my aunt, Da-duh's youngest child, who lived with her, called from the shed roof kitchen.

"Who tell you I need bush tea?" she cried, her voice assuming for a moment its old authority. "You can't even rest nowadays without some malicious person looking for you to be dead. Come girl," she motioned me to a place beside her on the old-fashioned lounge chair, "give us a tune."

I sang for her until breakfast at eleven, all my brash irreverent Tin Pan Alley songs, and then just before noon we went out into the ground. But it was a short, dispirited walk. Da-duh didn't even notice that the mangoes were beginning to ripen and would have to be picked before the village boys got to them. And when she paused occasionally and looked out across the canes or up at her trees it wasn't as if she were seeing them but something else. Some huge, monolithic shape had imposed itself, it seemed, between her and the land, obstructing her vision. Returning to the house she slept the entire afternoon on the Berbice chair.

She remained like this until we left, languishing away the mornings on the chair at the window gazing out at the land as if it were already doomed; then, at noon, taking the brief stroll with me through the ground during which she seldom spoke, and afterwards returning home to sleep till almost dusk sometimes.

On the day of our departure she put on the austere, ankle length white dress, the black shoes and brown felt hat (her town clothes she called them), but she did not go with us to town. She saw us off on the road outside her house and in the midst of my mother's tearful protracted farewell, she leaned down and whispered in my ear, "Girl, you're not to forget now to send me the picture of that building, you hear."

By the time I mailed her the large colored picture postcard of the Empire State Building she was dead. She died during the famous '37 strike which began shortly after we left. On the day of her death England sent planes flying low over the island in a show of force—so low, according to my aunt's letter, that the downdraft from them shook the ripened mangoes from the trees in Da-duh's orchard. Frightened, everyone in the village fled into the canes. Except Da-duh. She remained in the house at the window so my aunt said, watching as the planes came swooping and screaming like monstrous birds down over the village, over her house, rattling her trees

To Da-duh, in Memoriam

and flattening the young canes in her field. It must have seemed to her lying there that they did not intend pulling out of their dive, but like the hardback beetles which hurled themselves with suicidal force against the walls of the house at night, those menacing silver shapes would hurl themselves in an ecstasy of self-immolation onto the land, destroying it utterly.

When the planes finally left and the villagers returned they found her dead on the Berbice chair at the window.

She died and I lived, but always, to this day even, within the shadow of her death. For a brief period after I was grown I went to live alone, like one doing penance, in a loft above a noisy factory in downtown New York and there painted seas of sugarcane and huge swirling Van Gogh suns and palm trees striding like brightly-plumed Tutsi warriors across a tropical landscape, while the thunderous tread of the machines downstairs jarred the floor beneath my easel, mocking my efforts.

Responding to the Selection

Questions for Discussion

1. At what point in the story do Da-duh's appearance and behavior abruptly change? Describe this change.

2. Why do you think the narrator tries to "win" the initial encounter between Da-duh and herself?

3. What conclusions can you draw about Da-duh, based on her reactions to the girl's descriptions of New York?

4. In what **setting** does the narrator later live and paint? How does this setting reflect the **conflict** between Da-duh and the narrator?

Activities

Writing to Win

1. Da-duh and her granddaughter seem to be playing a game that might be called "Can You Top This?" Write about a time when you played a game of one-upmanship. Did you win or lose?

Exploring the Unknown

2. The young girl in this story finds herself in surroundings that are new and unfamiliar. Describe a similar experience you have had. How did you cope with your new environment?

Before You Read

April Fools' Day

Yusef Komunyakaa
Born 1947

"Oral language is our first music, and the body is an amplifier."

About Komunyakaa

Yusef Komunyakaa was raised in Bogalusa, Louisiana, which he describes as "a typical Southern town: one paper mill that dominated the place, and a public library that did not admit blacks." Early in his life, Komunyakaa became interested in music, specifically the jazz and blues of such African American musical artists as Dinah Washington and Louis Armstrong. The rhythm, structure, and language of his poetry owe much to the music of his childhood.

As a young man, Komunyakaa joined the military and found himself in Vietnam, where he served as an information specialist and was awarded a Bronze Star. Back in the states, Komunyakaa pursued an education, studying creative writing, English, and sociology. He published his first collection of poetry, *Dedications and Other Dark Horses,* in 1977. In 1994, Komunyakaa was awarded the Pulitzer Prize for *Neon Vernacular: New and Selected Poems,* a collection of autobiographical poetry that focused on his childhood in Bogalusa, his experiences in Vietnam, and his identity as an African American. To date, Komunyakaa has published more than twelve collections of poetry. He lives in New York City and is a professor in the Council of Humanities and Creative Writing Program at Princeton University.

April Fools' Day

— *Yusef Komunyakaa*

They had me laid out in a white
satin casket. What the hell
went wrong, I wanted to ask.
Whose midnight-blue sedan
5   mowed me down, what unnameable fever
bloomed amber & colchicum
in my brain, which doctor's scalpel
slipped? Did it happen
on a rainy Saturday, blue
10   Monday, Vallejo's Thursday?
I think I was on a balcony
overlooking the whole thing.
My soul sat in a black chair
near the door, sullen
15   & no-mouthed. I was fifteen
in a star-riddled box,
in heaven up to my eyelids.
My skin shone like damp light,
my face was the gray of something
20   gone. They were all there.

My mother behind an opaque veil,
so young. My brothers huddled like stones,
my sister rocked her Shirley Temple
doll to sleep. Three fat ushers fanned
25   my grandmamas, used smelling salts.
All my best friends—Cowlick,
Sneaky Pete, Happy Jack, Pie Joe,
& Comedown Jones.
I could smell lavender,
30   a tinge of dust. Their mouths,
palms of their hands
stained with mulberries.
Daddy posed in his navy-blue suit
as doubting Thomas: some twisted
35   soft need in his eyes, wondering if
I was just another loss
he'd divided his days into.

Responding to the Selection

Questions for Discussion

1. What has happened to the speaker in "April Fools' Day"?

2. Describe the scene at the funeral home as the speaker sees it. How does he describe himself?

3. Why does the speaker describe his father as a "doubting Thomas"? What do you think the speaker means by the "twisted soft need" in the father's eyes?

4. How would you describe the **mood** of the poem? What words and phrases set the mood? Does the mood change?

Before You Read

Black Stone Lying on a White Stone

César Vallejo
1892–1938

"I do not feel this suffering as César Vallejo. I am not suffering now as a creative person, or as a man, nor even as a simple living being. . . . Today I am simply in pain."

About Vallejo

César Vallejo was a Peruvian poet, novelist, and short story writer who was born into a large family of mixed Spanish and Indian origins. Early in his life, he became acquainted with the poverty, hunger, and social injustice that haunted Peru's Indian population. After studying literature and law at the National University of Trujillo, Vallejo began his career as a writer. His first collection of poetry, *Los heraldos negros (The Black Heralds),* introduced readers to the themes that would dominate his life's work, especially the idea that social injustice was the principal evil that prevented oppressed people from rising above their oppression.

Vallejo's political activism on behalf of the Peruvian Indians landed him in jail. Sometime after serving a three-month sentence, Vallejo left his homeland for Paris, never to return. In Paris he barely earned a living as a translator, tutor, and writer. Eventually, his radical politics got him into trouble once again, and he was expelled from France. Vallejo settled in Madrid, Spain, during that country's civil war. He died in Spain in 1938 after a lingering illness.

Black Stone Lying on a White Stone

— *César Vallejo*
Translated by Robert Bly and John Knoepfle

I will die in Paris, on a rainy day,
on some day I can already remember.
I will die in Paris—and I don't step aside—
perhaps on a Thursday, as today is Thursday, in autumn.

5   It will be a Thursday, because today, Thursday,
        setting down
these lines, I have put my upper arm bones on
wrong, and never so much as today have I found myself
with all the road ahead of me, alone.

César Vallejo is dead. Everyone beat him,
10   although he never does anything to them;
they beat him hard with a stick and hard also

with a rope. These are the witnesses;
the Thursdays, and the bones of my arms,
the solitude, and the rain, and the roads . . .

Responding to the Selection

Questions for Discussion

1. Who or what is the black stone? The white stone?
2. Why is the speaker so certain that he will die on a Thursday?
3. How are the openings of the two poems similar?
4. In what way are the witnesses to each speaker's death different? How is this difference significant?

Activity

Writing About Connections

Given what you know about the lives of Komunyakaa and Vallejo, write an **essay** in which you explore the ways each poem reflects the history and culture of the poet. Consider subject matter, language, imagery, mood—whichever aspects of each poem that illustrate a connection.

Magic of Nigeria, 1971. Loïs Mailou Jones. Watercolor, 34 x 22 in. Collection of Dr. Tritobia Hayes Benjamin, Washington, DC.

We Wear the Mask

*Who
can be born black
and not
sing
the wonder of it
the joy
the
challenge*

— Mari Evans

Before You Read

On Being Brought from Africa to America

Phillis Wheatley
c. 1753–1784

*"When the whole human race
    by sin had fall'n,
He deigned to die that they
    might rise again,
And share with in the
    sublimest skies,
Life without death, and glory
    without end"*

About Wheatley

At a time when nearly all African Americans were enslaved, Phillis Wheatley was being celebrated in New England and Europe for her poetry. Born in Senegal in West Africa, she was kidnapped by slave traders when she was only seven and brought to New England to be sold. The young African girl was purchased by John Wheatley, a wealthy Boston merchant, to work for his family.

The Wheatleys treated her as a member of their family and encouraged her to learn to read and write. Although she never attended school, Wheatley learned Greek and Latin and developed a fondness for three English poets whose verse would influence her own poetic style: John Milton, Alexander Pope, and Thomas Gray.

Wheatley began writing poetry at age fourteen and three years later caused a sensation with her first published poem, a tribute to the recently deceased Reverend George Whitefield, who had been a highly respected evangelical preacher. Whitefield's good friend, the Countess of Huntington, brought Wheatley to England and assisted her in publishing her poems. In 1776 Wheatley won further acclaim with a poem dedicated to George Washington.

Freed when she was about twenty, Phillis Wheatley stayed with the Wheatley household until the last Wheatley died. In 1778 she married a free black man named John Peters. Poverty and the death of two infants marked their difficult marriage. In 1784 Wheatley wrote her last poem; her husband died in debtor's prison; and on December 5, she died of malnutrition.

On Being Brought from Africa to America

— *Phillis Wheatley*

Twas mercy brought me from my Pagan land,
Taught my benighted soul to understand
That there's a God, that there's a Saviour too.
Once I redemption neither sought nor knew.
Some view our sable race with scornful eye;
"Their colour is a diabolic dye."
Remember, Christians, Negroes, black as Cain,
May be refined, and join the angelic train.

Responding to the Selection

Questions for Discussion

1. Why does the speaker refer to Africa as a "Pagan land"?

2. What does the speaker mean in line 6 by "diabolic dye"?

3. What is the "angelic train" mentioned in the last line of the poem?

4. What is the speaker's message in the first four lines of the poem? In the last four lines?

Activities

Writing About Slavery

1. Wheatley gained much when she was sold into slavery, but she also lost much. In an **essay** or a **poem,** explain what Phillis Wheatley lost and gained.

Discussing the Time and Place

2. Phillis Wheatley had a unique perspective on the events of the American Revolution. Research this period of U.S. history and read Wheatley's poem and letter "To His Excellency, George Washington." Discuss how Wheatley's writing might have been influenced by living in Boston before and after the war.

Before You Read

A Knowing

Jacqueline Johnson
Born 1957

Mountain Center and the MacDowell Colony. She was also the recipient of the 1987 poetry award given by the Mid-Atlantic Writers Association of Baltimore and has been a New York Foundation for the Arts Gregory Millard Fellow in Poetry.

"In the poem 'A Knowing,' I ask the reader to consider the historical sources of our racial differences and to begin to own that as part of our cultural and intellectual wealth. To consider not only what makes us different but what unifies."

About Johnson

Jacqueline Johnson, who was born in Philadelphia, writes poetry about the African American experience. Her nonfiction work includes *Stokely Carmichael: The Story of Black Power.* She has also contributed to *UpSouth: African American Migration* and *Streetlights: Illuminating Black Urban Tales.* A graduate of New York University, Johnson has received writing fellowships from the Blue

A Knowing

— *Jacqueline Johnson*

We furthest away from our African mother
seek out everything, Mali basket,
anago bead, yam dance and
coweried half-shell shields.
5   We wear young skin of new selves,
old ancients masked in new world ways.
Sometimes we recognize how we did survive,
claiming everything, Navajo stone, Arawak corn,
Hopi rain. African and Indian becoming
10   resistant, soulminds, nimble
in their splendor.

Even if now we are Bantu,
Malian, Ethiopian, Geechee,
African people, forced blend
15   of congoblue, copper and raffia brown,
our differences are our blessings.
Even though, there was no way
to tell which of our broken limbs
belonged to whom, we have a knowing
20   about who we are. We carry
an African mother's wisdom
wealthy in our knowingness.
Our differences are our blessings.

Responding to the Selection

Questions for Discussion

1. Who are "We furthest away from our African mother"? In the first four lines of the poem, what does the speaker say "we" are seeking?

2. How do you interpret these lines: "We wear young skin of new selves, / old ancients masked in new world ways"?

3. The speaker refers to a "forced blend" of African cultures and of "no way / to tell which of our broken limbs / belonged to whom." What do you think the speaker is referring to?

4. How are the people "wealthy" in their knowingness?

Activity

Interpreting Poetry

Twice the speaker says, "our differences are our blessings." Think about what this means in the context of the poem. Write an **interpretive essay** in which you explain the phrase, including why you think the poet repeated it.

Before You Read

We Wear the Mask

Paul Laurence Dunbar
1872–1906

". . . I cannot help being overwhelmed by self-doubts. I hope there is something worthy in my writings and not merely the novelty of a black face associated with the power to rhyme that has attracted attention."

About Dunbar

One of the first African American writers to attain national recognition, Paul Laurence Dunbar was the son of formerly enslaved people from Kentucky. Their stories of pre-emancipation days would provide a wealth of material for his work.

Dunbar was the only African American student at his Dayton, Ohio, high school.

There he excelled at his studies, edited the school paper, and served as president of the literary society. Despite his success in school, however, the adult world was reluctant to give Dunbar a chance to prove himself. Because he initially could not support himself with his writing, he took a four-dollar-a-week job as an elevator operator. Between calls for the elevator, he wrote.

Dunbar took out a loan to publish his first volume of poetry, *Oak and Ivy.* A second volume, *Majors and Minors,* was published in 1895. He gained national attention when the influential writer and critic William Dean Howells favorably reviewed his work. Much to Dunbar's growing disappointment, the poems that received the most notice were not those written with serious artistic intent but rather those written in black dialect, which he called "jingles in a broken tongue." He was criticized for these poems because they did not address racial stereotyping and discrimination. However, he also produced poems in Standard English that expressed pride in African Americans and lamented their thwarted efforts to live and create freely.

We Wear the Mask

— *Paul Laurence Dunbar*

We wear the mask that grins and lies,
It hides our cheeks and shades our eyes,—
This debt we pay to human guile;
With torn and bleeding hearts we smile,
5   And mouth with myriad subtleties.

Why should the world be over-wise,
In counting all our tears and sighs?
Nay, let them only see us, while
    We wear the mask.

10   We smile, but, O great Christ, our cries
To thee from tortured souls arise.
We sing, but oh the clay is vile
Beneath our feet, and long the mile;
But let the world dream otherwise,
15   We wear the mask.

Responding to the Selection

Questions for Discussion

1. Why do people wear masks?

2. In the poem, who wears the mask? What does the mask **symbolize?**

3. Explain the meaning behind these words of the speaker: "With torn and bleeding hearts we smile" and

   > We smile, but, O great Christ, our cries
   > To thee from tortured souls arise.
   > We sing, but oh the clay is vile
   > Beneath our feet, and long the mile.

4. Why is the speaker so insistent that "We wear the mask"?

Activities

Writing a Report

1. Masks have been worn for thousands of years by people in virtually every culture. Research the use of masks by a particular culture, paying special attention to what the masks symbolize and why they are culturally important. Then create an **illustrated report** that shows the results of your research.

Writing a Reflective Essay

2. When have *you* worn a mask? Write a **reflective essay** that tells about a time you needed to appear to be someone or something you were not. Did you find it easy to wear the mask? How did it feel?

Before You Read

Telephone Conversation

Wole Soyinka
Born 1934

"*Books and all forms of writing have always been objects of terror to those who seek to suppress the truth.*"

About Soyinka

At the start of the Nigerian civil war in 1967, Wole Soyinka was falsely accused of a crime, arrested, and imprisoned for more than two years. He spent most of the time in solitary confinement in a four-by-eight foot cell. To save his sanity, he wrote on anything he could find—toilet paper, cigarette packages, and book pages. These notes were later published in *The Man Died: Prison Notes of Wole Soyinka.*

The son of teachers, Soyinka was born in Nigeria when it was under British rule. As a youth, he became inspired by the political activism of his mother, who led a revolt against a tax on women, and by the independence movement in Nigeria. These events sparked his lifelong involvement in politics.

In 1955, while attending the University of Leeds in England, Soyinka had his first play produced. After returning to Nigeria in 1960, he researched and began to incorporate into his writing the folklore of the Yoruba, his native people. While writing plays, poetry, and novels, Soyinka taught at universities and became active in Nigerian politics, often fighting against the country's dictatorial government.

In 1986 Soyinka received the Nobel Prize for Literature. He is Woodruff Professor of the Arts in African American Studies at Emory University.

TELEPHONE Conversation

ℓℓℓℓℓℓℓℓℓℓℓℓℓℓℓℓℓℓ

— *Wole Soyinka*

The price seemed reasonable, location
Indifferent. The landlady swore she lived
Off premises. Nothing remained
But self-confession. "Madam," I warned,
5   "I hate a wasted journey—I am—African."
Silence. Silenced transmission of
Pressurized good breeding. Voice, when it came,
Lipstick-coated, long gold-rolled
Cigarette-holder pipped. Caught I was, foully.
10 "HOW DARK?" . . . I had not misheard . . . "ARE YOU LIGHT
OR VERY DARK?" Button B. Button A. Stench
Of rancid breath of public hide-and-speak.
Red booth. Red pillar-box. Red double-tiered
Omnibus squelching tar. It *was* real! Shamed
15 By ill-mannered silence, surrender
Pushed dumbfoundment to beg simplification.
Considerate she was, varying the emphasis—
"ARE YOU DARK? OR VERY LIGHT?" Revelation came.
"You mean—like plain or milk chocolate?"
20 Her assent was clinical, crushing in its light
Impersonality. Rapidly, wavelength adjusted,
I chose, "West African sepia"—and as an afterthought,
"Down in my passport." Silence for spectroscopic
Flight of fancy, till truthfulness clanged her accent
25 Hard on the mouthpiece. "WHAT'S THAT?" conceding
"DON'T KNOW WHAT THAT IS." "Like brunette."
"THAT'S DARK, ISN'T IT?" "Not altogether.
Facially, I am brunette, but madam, you should see
The rest of me. Palm of my hand, soles of my feet

30   Are a peroxide blond. Friction, caused—
Foolishly madam—by sitting down, has turned
My bottom raven black—One moment madam!"—sensing
Her receiver rearing on the thunderclap
About my ears—"Madam," I pleaded, "Wouldn't you rather
35   See for yourself?"

Responding to the Selection

Questions for Discussion

1. What is the purpose of the telephone conversation? What is its result?

2. Why does the speaker make an issue of his color? What point does the land-lady's response make?

3. Dunbar writes about people's need to hide who they really are and what they really feel. How is this subject addressed in "Telephone Conversation"?

4. Discuss the tone in each poem. How do they differ? How do they reflect meaning?

Activities

Researching Prison Memoirs

1. Many prisoners, especially political prisoners, have used writing as a way to survive the torment of imprisonment. **Research** prison writings or memoirs or imprisonment, and discuss your findings as a group.

Comparing Writers' Ideas

2. Paul Laurence Dunbar's life ended twenty-eight years before Wole Soyinka's began. Dunbar was an African American, whereas Soyinka is a Yoruba from Nigeria. Imagine a conversation the two might have had about their poems—about openness and honesty versus hiding and secrecy. How do you think Soyinka would react to wearing the mask? In turn, how might Dunbar view Soyinka's declaration?

Before You Read

Florence

Alice Childress
1916–1994

"The black writer explains
pain to those who inflict it."

About Childress

Although born in Charleston, South
Carolina, Alice Childress grew up in
Harlem, New York City. In the 1940s, she
joined the American Negro Theater and
began a literary career that would span
four decades. As a playwright, Childress
became known for her sharply drawn
characters, straightforward language, and
realistic portrayals of the struggles and triumphs of African Americans.

Childress was the first African American
woman to have a play produced profes-
sionally. In 1956 she received an Obie
award when her play *Trouble in Mind* was
honored as the best original off-Broadway
production of the season.

Childress also wrote novels for young
adults. Her best-known work, *A Hero Ain't
Nothing but a Sandwich,* was cited by the
American Library Association as one of
the best young-adult novels of 1975.

About Black Theater

Although the first known plays by African
Americans date back to the early nineteenth century, it was not until the early
twentieth century that black theater began
to thrive. Black theater companies were
formed in major cities throughout the
United States during the Harlem
Renaissance. In 1940 in Harlem, the
American Negro Theatre was founded, as
the original eighteen members proclaimed, "to break down the barriers of
Black participation in the theater; to por-
tray Negro life as they honestly saw it;
[and] to fill in the gap of a Black theater
which did not exist."

It was not until 1959 that the first drama
by an African American woman appeared
on Broadway. Lorraine Hansberry's *A
Raisin in the Sun,* considered one of the
one hundred most significant works of the
twentieth century by a National Theatre
poll, won the New York Drama Critics'
Circle Award for best play.

Florence

— *Alice Childress*

CHARACTERS

MARGE

MAMA

PORTER

MRS. CARTER

PLACE: A very small town in the South.

TIME: The present.

SCENE: *A railway station waiting room. The room is divided in two sections by a low railing. Upstage center is a double door which serves as an entrance to both sides of the room. Over the doorway stage right is a sign "Colored," over the doorway stage left is another sign "White." Stage right are two doors . . . one marked "Colored Men" . . . the other "Colored Women." Stage left two other doorways are "White Ladies" and "White Gentlemen." There are two benches, one on each side. The room is drab and empty looking. Through the double doors upstage center can be seen a gray lighting which gives the effect of an early evening and open platform.*

At rise of curtain the stage remains empty for about twenty seconds . . . A middle aged Negro woman enters, looks offstage . . . then crosses to the "Colored" side and sits on the bench. A moment later she is followed by a young Negro woman about twenty-one years old. She is carrying a large new cardboard suitcase and a wrapped shoebox. She is wearing a shoulder strap bag and a newspaper protrudes from the flap. She crosses to the "Colored" side and rests the suitcase at her feet as she looks at her mother with mild annoyance.

Florence

MARGE.   You didn't have to get here so early, mama. Now you got to wait!

MAMA.   If I'm goin' someplace . . . I like to get there in plenty time. You don't have to stay.

MARGE.   You shouldn't wait 'round here alone.

MAMA.   I ain't scared. Ain't a soul going to bother me.

MARGE.   I got to get back to Ted. He don't like to be in the house by himself. [*She picks up the bag and places it on the bench by* MAMA.]

MAMA.   You'd best go back. [*Smiles.*] You know I think he misses Florence.

MARGE.   He's just a little fellow. He needs his mother. You make her come home! She shouldn't be way up there in Harlem. She ain't got nobody there.

MAMA.   You know Florence don't like the South.

MARGE.   It ain't what we like in this world! You tell her that.

MAMA.   If Mr. Jack ask about the rent, you tell him we gonna be a little late on account of the trip.

MARGE.   I'll talk with him. Don't worry so about everything. [*Places suitcase on floor.*] What you carryin', mama . . . bricks?

MAMA.   If Mr. Jack won't wait . . . write to Rudley. He oughta send a little somethin'.

MARGE.   Mama . . . Rudley ain't got nothin' to himself. I hate to ask him to give us.

MAMA.   That's your brother! If push come to shove, we got to ask.

MARGE.   [*Places box on bench.*] Don't forget to eat your lunch . . . and try to get a seat near the window so you can lean on your elbow and get a little rest.

MAMA.   Hmmmm . . . mmmph. Yes.

MARGE.   Buy yourself some coffee when the man comes through. You'll need something hot and you can't go to the diner.

MAMA.   I know that. You talk like I'm a northern greenhorn.

MARGE.   You got handkerchiefs?

MAMA.   I got everything, Marge.

MARGE.   [*Wanders upstage to the railing division line.*] I know Florence is real bad off or she wouldn't call on us for money. Make her come home. She ain't gonna get rich up there and we can't afford to do for her.

MAMA.   We talked all of that before.

MARGE.   [*Touches rail.*] Well, you got to be strict on her. She got notions a Negro woman don't need.

Florence

MAMA. But she was in a real play. Didn't she send us twenty-five dollars a week?

MARGE. For two weeks.

MAMA. Well the play was over.

MARGE. [Crosses to MAMA and sits beside her.] It's not money, Mama. Sarah wrote us about it. You know what she said Florence was doin'. Sweepin' the stage!

MAMA. She was *in* the play!

MARGE. Sure she was in it! Sweepin'! Them folks ain't gonna let her be no actress. You tell her to wake up.

MAMA. I . . . I . . . think.

MARGE. Listen, Mama . . . She won't wanna come. We know that . . . but she gotta!

MAMA. Maybe we shoulda told her to expect me. It's kind of mean to just walk in like this.

MARGE. I bet she's livin' terrible. What's the matter with her? Don't she know we're keepin' her son?

MAMA. Florence don't feel right 'bout down here since Jim got killed.

MARGE. Who does? I should be the one goin' to get her. You tell her she ain't gonna feel right in no place. Mama, honestly! She must think she's white!

MAMA. Florence is brownskin.

MARGE. I don't mean that. I'm talkin' about her attitude. Didn't she go to Strumley's down here and ask to be a salesgirl? [Rises.] Now ain't that somethin'? They don't hire no Colored folks.

MAMA. Others besides Florence been talkin' about their rights.

MARGE. I know it . . . but there's things we can't do cause they ain't gonna let us. [She wanders over to the "White" side of the stage.] Don't feel a damn bit different over here than it does on our side. [Silence.]

MAMA. Maybe we shoulda just sent her the money this time. This one time.

MARGE. [Coming back to the "Colored" side.] Mama! Don't you let her cash that check for nothin' but to bring her back home.

MAMA. I know.

MARGE. [Restless . . . fidgets with her hair . . . patting it in place.] I oughta go now.

MAMA. You best get back to Ted. He might play with the lamp.

MARGE. He better not let me catch him! If you got to go to the ladies' room take your grip.

MAMA.   I'll be alright. Make Ted get up on time for school.

MARGE.   [Kisses her quickly and gives her the newspaper.] Here's something to read. So long, Mama.

MAMA.   G'bye, Margie baby.

MARGE.   [Goes to door . . . stops and turns to her mother.] You got your smelling salts?

MAMA.   In my pocketbook.

MARGE.   [Wistfully.] Tell Florence I love her and miss her too.

   [PORTER can be heard singing in the distance.]

MAMA.   Sure.

MARGE.   [Reluctant to leave.] Pin that check in your bosom, Mama. You might fall asleep and somebody'll rob you.

MAMA.   I got it pinned to me. [Feels for the check which is in her blouse.]

MARGE.   [Almost pathetic.] Bye, Ma.

   [MAMA sits for a moment looking at her surroundings. She opens the paper and begins to read.]

PORTER.   [Offstage.] Hello, Marge. What you doin' down here?

MARGE.   I came to see Mama off.

PORTER.   Where's she going?

MARGE.   She's in there; she'll tell you. I got to get back to Ted.

PORTER.   Bye now . . . Say, wait a minute, Marge.

MARGE.   Yes?

PORTER.   I told Ted he could have some of my peaches and he brought all them Brandford boys and they picked 'em all. I wouldn't lay a hand on him but I told him I was gonna tell you.

MARGE.   I'm gonna give it to him!

PORTER.   [Enters and crosses to "White" side of waiting room. He carries a pail of water and a mop. He is about fifty years old. He is obviously tired but not lazy.] Every peach off my tree!

MAMA.   There wasn't but six peaches on that tree.

PORTER.   [Smiles . . . glances at MAMA as he crosses to the "White" side and begins to mop.] How d'ye do, Mrs. Whitney . . . you going on a trip?

MAMA.   Fine, I thank you. I'm going to New York.

PORTER.   Wish it was me. You gonna stay?

Florence

MAMA. No, Mr. Brown. I'm bringing Florence . . . I'm visiting Florence.

PORTER. Tell her I said hello. She's a fine girl.

MAMA. Thank you.

PORTER. My brother Bynum's in Georgia now.

MAMA. Well now, that's nice.

PORTER. Atlanta.

MAMA. He goin' to school?

PORTER. Yes'm. He saw Florence in a Colored picture. A moving picture.

MAMA. Do tell! She didn't say a word about it.

PORTER. They got Colored moving picture theaters in Atlanta.

MAMA. Yes. Your brother going to be a doctor?

PORTER. [*With pride.*] No. He writes things.

MAMA. Oh.

PORTER. My son is goin' back to Howard next year.

MAMA. Takes an awful lot of goin' to school to be anything. Lot of money leastways.

PORTER. [*Thoughtfully.*] Yes'm, it sure do.

MAMA. That sure was a nice church sociable the other night.

PORTER. Yes'm. We raised 87 dollars.

MAMA. That's real nice.

PORTER. I won your cake at the bazaar.

MAMA. The chocolate one?

PORTER. [*As he wrings mop.*] Yes'm . . . was light as a feather. That old train is gonna be late this evenin'. It's number 42.

MAMA. I don't mind waitin'.

PORTER. [*Lifts pail, tucks mop handle under his arm. He looks about in order to make certain no one is around and leans over and addresses* MAMA *in a confidential tone.*] Did you buy your ticket from that Mr. Daly?

MAMA. [*In a low tone.*] No. Marge bought it yesterday.

PORTER. [*Leaning against railing.*] That's good. That man is real mean. Especially if he thinks you're goin' north. [*He starts to leave . . . then turns back to* MAMA.] If you go to the rest room, use the Colored men's . . . the other one is out of order.

MAMA. Thank you, sir.

Florence

MRS. CARTER. [*A white woman . . . well dressed, wearing furs and carrying a small, expensive overnight bag breezes in . . . breathless . . . flustered and smiling. She addresses the PORTER as she almost collides with him.*] Boy! My bags are out there. The taxi driver just dropped them. Will they be safe?

PORTER. Yes, mam. I'll see after them.

MRS. CARTER. I thought I'd missed the train.

PORTER. It's late, mam.

MRS. CARTER. [*Crosses to bench on the "White" side and rests her bag.*] Fine! You come back here and get me when it comes. There'll be a tip in it for you.

PORTER. Thank you, mam. I'll be here. [*As he leaves.*] Miss Whitney, I'll take care of your bag too.

MAMA. Thank you, sir.

MRS. CARTER. [*Wheels around . . . notices MAMA.*] Oh . . . Hello there . . .

MAMA. Howdy, mam. [*She opens her newspaper and begins to read.*]

MRS. CARTER. [*Paces up and down rather nervously. She takes a cigarette from her purse, lights it and takes a deep draw. She looks at her watch and then speaks to MAMA across the railing.*] Have you any idea how late the train will be?

MAMA. No, mam. [*Starts to read again.*]

MRS. CARTER. I can't leave this place fast enough. Two days of it and I'm bored to tears. Do you live here?

MAMA. [*Rests paper on her lap.*] Yes, mam.

MRS. CARTER. Where are you going?

MAMA. New York City, mam.

MRS. CARTER. Good for you! You can stop "maming" me. My name is Mrs. Carter. I'm not a southerner really. [*Takes handkerchief from her purse and covers her nose for a moment.*] My God! Disinfectant! This is a frightful place. My brother's here writing a book. Wants atmosphere. Well, he's got it. I'll never come back here ever.

MAMA. That's too bad, mam . . . Mrs. Carter.

MRS. CARTER. That's good. I'd die in this place. Really die. Jeff . . . Mr. Wiley . . . my brother . . . He's tied in knots, a bundle of problems . . . positively in knots.

MAMA. [*Amazed.*] That so, mam?

MRS. CARTER. You don't have to call me mam. It's so southern. Mrs. Carter! These people are still fighting the Civil War. I'm really a New Yorker now. Of course, I was born here . . . in the South I mean. Memphis. Listen . . . am I annoying you? I've simply got to talk to someone.

Florence

MAMA. [*Places her newspaper on the bench.*] No, Mrs. Carter. It's perfectly alright.

MRS. CARTER. Fine! You see Jeff has ceased writing. Stopped! Just like that! [*Snaps fingers.*]

MAMA. [*Turns to her.*] That so?

MRS. CARTER. Yes. The reviews came out on his last book. Poor fellow.

MAMA. I'm sorry, mam . . . Mrs. Carter. They didn't like his book?

MRS. CARTER. Well enough . . . but Jeff's . . . well, Mr. Wiley is a genius. He says they missed the point! Lost the whole message! Did you read . . . do you . . . have you heard of *Lost My Lonely Way*?

MAMA. No, mam. I can't say I have.

MRS. CARTER. Well, it doesn't matter. It's profound. Real . . . you know. [*Stands at the railing upstage.*] It's about your people.

MAMA. That's nice.

MRS. CARTER. Jeff poured his complete self into it. Really delved into the heart of the problem, pulled no punches! He hardly stopped for his meals . . . And of course I wasn't here to see that he didn't overdo. He suffers so with his characters.

MAMA. I guess he wants to do his best.

MRS. CARTER. Zelma! . . . That's his heroine . . . Zelma! A perfect character.

MAMA. [*Interested . . . coming out of her shell eagerly.*] She was colored, mam?

MRS. CARTER. Oh yes! . . . But of course you don't know what it's about do you?

MAMA. No, miss . . . Would you tell me?

MRS. CARTER. [*Leaning on the railing.*] Well . . . she's almost white, see? Really you can't tell except in small ways. She wants to be a lawyer . . . and . . . and . . . well, there she is full of complexes and this deep shame you know.

MAMA. [*Excitedly but with curiosity.*] Do tell! What shame has she got?

MRS. CARTER. [*Takes off her fur neckpiece and places it on bench with overnight bag.*] It's obvious! This lovely creature . . . intelligent, ambitious, and well . . . she's a Negro!

MAMA. [*Waiting eagerly.*] Yes'm, you said that . . .

MRS. CARTER. Surely you understand? She's constantly hating herself. Just before she dies she says it! . . . Right on the bridge . . .

MAMA. [*Genuinely moved.*] How sad. Ain't it a shame she had to die?

MRS. CARTER. It was inevitable . . . couldn't be any other way!

MAMA. What did she say on the bridge?

Florence

MRS. CARTER. Well . . . just before she jumped . . .

MAMA. [*Slowly straightening.*] You mean she killed *herself?*

MRS. CARTER. Of course. Close your eyes and picture it!

MAMA. [*Turns front and closes her eyes tightly with enthusiasm.*] Yes'm.

MRS. CARTER. [*Center stage on "White" side.*] Now . . . ! She's standing on the bridge in the moonlight . . . Out of her shabby purse she takes a mirror . . . and by the light of the moon she looks at her reflection in the glass.

MAMA. [*Clasps her hands together gently.*] I can see her just as plain.

MRS. CARTER. [*Sincerely.*] Tears roll down her cheeks as she says . . . almost! almost white . . . but I'm black! I'm a Negro! and then . . . [*Turns to MAMA.*] she jumps and drowns herself!

MAMA. [*Opens her eyes and speaks quietly.*] Why?

MRS. CARTER. She can't face it! Living in a world where she almost belongs but not quite. [*Drifts upstage.*] Oh it's so . . . so . . . tragic.

MAMA. [*Carried away by her convictions . . . not anger . . . she feels challenged. She rises.*] That ain't so! Not one bit it ain't!

MRS. CARTER. [*Surprised.*] But it is!

MAMA. [*During the following she works her way around the railing until she crosses over about one foot to the "White" side and is face to face with MRS. CARTER.*] I know it ain't! Don't my friend Essie Kitredge daughter look just like a German or somethin'? She didn't kill herself! She's teachin' the third grade in the colored school right here. Even the bus drivers ask her to sit in the front seats cause they think she's white! . . . an' . . . an' . . . she just says as clear as you please . . . "I'm sittin' where my people got to sit by law. I'm a Negro woman!"

MRS. CARTER. [*Uncomfortable and not knowing why.*] . . . But there you have it. The exception makes the rule. That's proof!

MAMA. No such thing! My cousin Hemsly's as white as you! . . . an' . . . an' he never . . .

MRS. CARTER. [*Flushed with anger . . . yet lost . . . because she doesn't know why.*] Are you losing your temper? [*Weakly.*] Are you angry with me?

MAMA. [*Stands silently trembling as she looks down and notices she is on the wrong side of the railing. She looks up at the "White Ladies Room" sign and slowly works her way back to the "Colored" side. She feels completely lost.*] No, mam. Excuse me please. [*With bitterness.*] I just meant Hemsly works in the colored section of the shoe store . . . He never once wanted to kill his self! [*She sits down on the bench and fumbles for her newspaper. Silence.*]

Florence

MRS. CARTER. [*Caught between anger and reason . . . she laughs nervously.*] Well! Let's not be upset by this. It's entirely my fault you know. This whole thing is a completely controversial subject. [*Silence.*] If it's too much for Jeff . . . well naturally I shouldn't discuss it with you. [*Approaching railing.*] I'm sorry. Let *me* apologize.

MAMA. [*Keeps her eyes on the paper.*] No need for that, mam. [*Silence.*]

MRS. CARTER. [*Painfully uncomfortable.*] I've drifted away from . . . What started all of this?

MAMA. [*No comedy intended or allowed on this line.*] Your brother, mam.

MRS. CARTER. [*Trying valiantly to brush away the tension.*] Yes . . . Well, I had to come down and sort of hold his hand over the reviews. He just thinks too much . . . and studies. He knows the Negro so well that sometimes our friends tease him and say he almost *seems* like . . . well you know . . .

MAMA. [*Tightly.*] Yes'm.

MRS. CARTER. [*Slowly walks over to the "Colored" side near the top of the rail.*] You know I try but it's really difficult to understand you people. However . . . I keep trying.

MAMA. [*Still tight.*] Thank you, mam.

MRS. CARTER. [*Retreats back to "White" side and begins to prove herself.*] Last week . . . Why do you know what I did? I sent a thousand dollars to a Negro college for scholarships.

MAMA. That was right kind of you.

MRS. CARTER. [*Almost pleading.*] I know what's going on in your mind . . . and what you're thinking is wrong. I've . . . I've . . . eaten with Negroes.

MAMA. Yes, mam.

MRS. CARTER. [*Trying to find a straw.*] . . . And there's Malcom! If it weren't for the guidance of Jeff he'd never written his poems. Malcom is a Negro.

MAMA. [*Freezing.*] Yes, mam.

MRS. CARTER. [*Gives up, crosses to her bench, opens her overnight bag and takes out a book and begins to read. She glances at MAMA from time to time. MAMA is deeply absorbed in her newspaper. MRS. CARTER closes her book with a bang . . . determined to penetrate the wall MAMA has built around her.*] Why are you going to New York?

MAMA. [*Almost accusingly.*] I got a daughter there.

MRS. CARTER. I lost my son in the war. [*Silence . . . MAMA is ill at ease.*] Your daughter . . . what is she doing . . . studying?

MAMA. No'm, she's trying to get on stage.

Florence

MRS. CARTER. [*Pleasantly.*] Oh . . . a singer?

MAMA. No, mam. She's . . .

MRS. CARTER. [*Warmly.*] You people have such a gift. I love spirituals . . . "Steal Away," "Swing Low, Sweet Chariot."

MAMA. They are right nice. But Florence wants to act. Just say things in plays.

MRS. CARTER. A dramatic actress?

MAMA. Yes, that's what it is. She been in a colored moving picture, and a big show for two weeks on Broadway.

MRS. CARTER. The dear, precious child! . . . But this is funny . . . no! it's pathetic. She must be bitter . . . *really* bitter. Do you know what I do?

MAMA. I can't rightly say.

MRS. CARTER. I'm an actress! A dramatic actress . . . And I haven't really worked in six months . . . And I'm pretty well-known . . . And everyone knows Jeff. I'd like to work. Of course, there are my committees, but you see, they don't need me. Not really . . . not even Jeff.

MAMA. Now that's a shame.

MRS. CARTER. Now your daughter . . . you must make her stop before she's completely unhappy. Make her stop!

MAMA. Yes'm . . . why?

MRS. CARTER. I have the best of contacts and *I've* only done a few *broadcasts* lately. Of course, I'm not counting the things I just wouldn't do. Your daughter . . . make her stop.

MAMA. A drama teacher told her she has real talent.

MRS. CARTER. A drama teacher! My dear woman, there are loads of unscrupulous whites up there that just hand out opinions for . . .

MAMA. This was a colored gentleman down here.

MRS. CARTER. Oh well! . . . And she went up there on the strength of that? This makes me very unhappy. [*Puts book away in case, and snaps lock. Silence.*]

MAMA. [*Getting an idea.*] Do you really, truly feel that way, mam?

MRS. CARTER. I do. Please . . . I want you to believe me.

MAMA. Could I ask you something?

MRS. CARTER. Anything.

MAMA. You won't be angry, mam?

MRS. CARTER. [*Remembering.*] I won't. I promise you.

Florence

MAMA. [*Gathering courage.*] Florence is proud . . . but she's having it hard.

MRS. CARTER. I'm sure she is.

MAMA. Could you help her out some, mam? Knowing all the folks you do . . . maybe . . .

MRS. CARTER. [*Rubs the outside of the case.*] Well . . . it isn't that simple . . . but . . . you're very sweet. If only I could . . .

MAMA. Anything you did, I feel grateful. I don't like to tell it, but she can't even pay her rent and things. And she's used to my cooking for her . . . I believe my girl goes hungry sometime up there . . . and yet she'd like to stay so bad.

MRS. CARTER. [*Looks up, resting case on her knees.*] How can I refuse? You seem like a good woman.

MAMA. Always lived as best I knew how and raised my children up right. We got a fine family, mam.

MRS. CARTER. And I've no family at all. I've got to! It's clearly my duty. Jeff's books . . . guiding Malcom's poetry . . . It isn't enough . . . oh I know it isn't. Have you ever hear of Melba Rugby?

MAMA. No, mam. I don't know anybody much . . . except right here.

MRS. CARTER. [*Brightening.*] She's in California, but she's moving East again . . . hates California.

MAMA. Yes'm.

MRS. CARTER. A most versatile woman. Writes, directs, acts . . . everything!

MAMA. That's nice, mam.

MRS. CARTER. Well, she's uprooting herself and coming back to her first home . . . New York . . . to direct "Love Flowers" . . . it's a musical.

MAMA. Yes'm.

MRS. CARTER. She's grand . . . helped so many people . . . and I'm sure she'll help your . . . what's her name.

MAMA. Florence.

MRS. CARTER. [*Turns back to bench, opens bag, takes out a pencil and an address book.*] Yes, Florence. She'll have to *make* a place for her.

MAMA. Bless you, mam.

MRS. CARTER. [*Holds handbag steady on rail as she uses it to write on.*] Now let's see . . . the best thing to do would be to give you the telephone number . . . since you're going there.

MAMA. Yes'm.

Florence

MRS. CARTER. [*Writing address on paper.*] Your daughter will love her . . . and if she's a deserving girl . . .

MAMA. [*Looking down as* MRS. CARTER *writes.*] She's a good child. Never a bit of trouble. Except about her husband, and neither one of them could help that.

MRS. CARTER. [*Stops writing, raises her head questioning.*] Oh?

MAMA. He got killed at voting time. He was a good man.

MRS. CARTER. [*Embarrassed.*] I guess that's worse than losing him in the war.

MAMA. We all got our troubles passing through here.

MRS. CARTER. [*Gives her the address.*] Tell your dear girl to call this number about a week from now.

MAMA. Yes, mam.

MRS. CARTER. Her experience won't matter with Melba. I know she'll understand. I'll call her too.

MAMA. Thank you, mam.

MRS. CARTER. I'll just tell her . . . no heavy washing or ironing . . . just light cleaning and a little cooking . . . does she cook?

MAMA. Mam? [*Slowly backs away from* MRS. CARTER *and sits down on bench.*]

MRS. CARTER. Don't worry, that won't matter to Melba. [*Silence. Moves around the rail to "Colored" side, leans over* MAMA.] I'd take your daughter myself, but I've got Binnie. She's been with me for years, and I just can't let her go . . . can I?

MAMA. [*Looks at* MRS. CARTER *closely.*] No, mam.

MRS. CARTER. Of course she must be steady. I couldn't ask Melba to take a fly-by-night. [*Touches* MAMA's *arm.*] But she'll have her own room and bath, and above all . . . security.

MAMA. [*Reaches out, clutches* MRS. CARTER's *wrist almost pulling her off balance.*] Child!

MRS. CARTER. [*Frightened.*] You're hurting my wrist.

MAMA. [*Looks down, realizes how tight she's clutching her, and releases her wrist.*] I mustn't hurt you, must I.

MRS. CARTER. [*Backing away rubbing her wrist.*] It's all right.

MAMA. [*Rises.*] You better get over on the other side of that rail. It's against the law for you to be over here with me.

MRS. CARTER. [*Frightened and uncomfortable.*] If you think so.

MAMA. I don't want to break the law.

Florence

MRS. CARTER. [*Keeps her eye on* MAMA *as she drifts around railing to bench on her side. Gathers overnight bag.*] I know I must look like a fright. The train should be along soon. When it comes, I won't see you until New York. These silly laws. [*Silence.*] I'm going to powder my nose. [*Exits into "White Ladies" room.*]

PORTER [*Singing offstage.*]

[MAMA *sits quietly, staring in front of her . . . then looks at the address for a moment . . . tears the paper into little bits and lets them flutter to the floor. She opens the suitcase, takes out notebook, an envelope and a pencil. She writes a few words on the paper.*]

PORTER. [*Enters with broom and dust pan.*] Number 42 will be coming along in nine minutes. [*When* MAMA *doesn't answer him, he looks up and watches her. She reaches in her bosom, unpins the check, smooths it out, places it in the envelope with the letter. She closes the suitcase.*] I said the train's coming. Where's the lady?

MAMA. She's in the *ladies'* room. You got a stamp?

PORTER. No. But I can get one out of the machine. Three for a dime.

MAMA. [*Hands him the letter.*] Put one on here and mail it for me.

PORTER. [*Looks at it.*] Gee . . . you writing Florence when you're going to see her?

MAMA. [*Picks up the shoebox and puts it back on the bench.*] You want a good lunch? It's chicken and fruit.

PORTER. Sure . . . thank you . . . but you won't . . .

MAMA. [*Rises, paces up and down.*] I ain't gonna see Florence for a long time. Might be never.

PORTER. How's that, Mrs. Whitney?

MAMA. She can be anything in the world she wants to be! That's her right. Marge can't make her turn back, Mrs. Carter can't make her turn back. *Lost My Lonely Way!* That's a book! People killing themselves 'cause they look white but be black. They just don't know do they, Mr. Brown?

PORTER. Whatever happened don't you fret none. Life is too short.

MAMA. Oh, I'm gonna fret plenty! You know what I wrote Florence?

PORTER. No, mam. But you don't have to tell me.

MAMA. I said "Keep trying." . . . Oh, I'm going home.

PORTER. I'll take your bag. [*Picks up bag and starts out.*] Come on, Mrs. Whitney. [PORTER *exits.*]

Florence

[MAMA *moves around to "White" side, stares at sign over door. She starts to knock on "White Ladies" door, but changes her mind. As she turns to leave, her eye catches the railing; she approaches it gently, touches it, turns, exits. Stage is empty for about six or seven seconds. Sound of train whistle is heard in the distance. Slow curtain.*]

CURTAIN

Responding to the Selection ─────────

Questions for Discussion

1. Why is Mama going to New York City? What does her daughter Marge expect her to do while she's there? Why?

2. Marge and Florence are sisters, but they have very different attitudes toward life. Discuss the ways in which the two sisters differ.

3. Summarize the **plot** and **theme** of Mrs. Carter's brother's most recent novel. Describe how Mama's demeanor changes as she listens to the story.

4. Describe the **climax** of the play, the critical and decisive moment that changes everything. What decision does Mama make after this moment passes? Why?

Activities

Writing a Character Study

1. Mrs. Carter is a complex character. She tries very hard, but fails spectacularly, to play the role of the liberal white American who befriends African Americans. Write a **character study** of Mrs. Carter, one that shows all sides of her character. Use incidents and dialogue from the play to support your characterization.

Researching and Discussing

2. Research the Jim Crow Laws that dictated the social and political lives of black and white Southerners during the first half of the twentieth century. Discuss with your classmates the nature of these laws, their effects on both whites and blacks, and how and why they were brought to an end.

Before You Read

Back to Baton Rouge

Michael Warr
Born 1955

"I inhaled my first breath at the Our Lady of the Lake Hospital in Baton Rouge, Louisiana. Living in San Francisco by the age of three, I never had time to pick up Creole or a Southern accent. Thirty-five years later I returned 'home' to the South like a foreigner recovering ties to a lost tribe. The poem 'Back to Baton Rouge' was conceived at a grocery store as I passed a shelf lined with jars of pickled pigs' lips."

About Warr

Michael Warr is founder and former executive director of the Guild Complex, an award-winning cross-cultural literary arts center in Chicago. He is also an editor at Tia Chucha Press, the complex's publishing house. Warr's awards in cultural arts and education include an Illinois Alliance for Arts Education Service Recognition Award and the Entrepreneur of the Year in the Arts Award from Columbia College. He is also the recipient of a National Endowment for the Arts Creative Writing Fellowship.

Warr is the author of the poetry collection *We Are All the Black Boy* and co-editor of *Power Lines: A Decade of Poetry from Chicago's Guild Complex*. His poetry has been widely anthologized, and some was selected to appear on the World Literary Map at the World Expo 2000 in Hanover, Germany.

Back to Baton Rouge

— *Michael Warr*

A jar of pickled pig lips
reminds me where I come from.
Where gumbo ain't nouveau cuisine.
And folks on every corner
5   affectionately call me cuz,
breaking the Baptist/'hovah schism
that blocked our childhood dance.
I am prodigal returning to root
with Powerbook in tow.
10   Out of place. Embraced.
My Frisco/Chitown/Addis
twang mixing with their twang.
They curl "yes mams,"
to my west-coasted mother,
15   our lips won't form the sound.
The Louisiana in us too far gone.

Last time I crushed
this blackened soil
Roy Rogers was my hero.
20   I squatted and painted
rocks red with polish,
the green ice from a Dixie Cup
dripping down my face.
My Grandfather
25   black as an eclipse,
his Choctaw hair shining,
his rusty carpenter hands
twisting chicken necks at breakfast.
My Great Aunt's farm

30   smothered in shade and Magnolias.
       My Father's sky-blue Continental,
       its imperialistic grinning grill
       splattered with the state of Texas.
       My baby sister peeing
35   beside the car.
       That was Louisiana.

       Now Uncle Alton,
       not seen since seven, asks
       "is poetry making money."
40   They say this is a Creole thing.
       It doesn't matter.
       I envy my uncle's name.
       I covet all their names.
       Names worthy of phat novels.
45   My Father Alcide.
       My Mother Gaynell.
       My Willie Mae and Bessie aunts.
       Our roots so thick and gritsy.
       Now our names are circumcized,
50   missing something extra.
       Our assimilation so
       invisible, only the
       Lee's and Elwood's
       thrust between them
55   cling to the southern soil.
       I am of this place, but lost.
       An immigrant in
       old country.
       Only the gumbo
60   feels like home.

Responding to the Selection

Questions for Discussion

1. What part of the story of the speaker's return to Baton Rouge does each stanza tell?
2. Describe what the speaker remembers about childhood in Louisiana.
3. The speaker says that he covets his Louisiana family's names. Why are their names so important to him?
4. Why does the speaker describe himself as "An immigrant in / old country"?

Activities

Writing an Essay

1. How does the speaker express his sense of being out of place? Search the poem for language that expresses this feeling in different ways and then write an **essay** in which you explain what that language suggests to you about the speaker's state of mind.

Researching and Presenting

2. Find Louisiana and Baton Rouge on a map. Then read about the history of the state. How did it become part of the United States? Who were the people that settled this part of the country? Discuss with your classmates how the history and settlers of Louisiana are present in the poem.

Before You Read

Lineage

Margaret Walker
1915–1998

*"Let a second generation
full of courage issue forth;
let a people loving freedom
come to growth."*

About Walker

Margaret Walker, whose prolific writing career spanned the Harlem Renaissance to the Black Arts Movement and well beyond, was born in Birmingham, Alabama. As a child, she was encouraged by her parents, both professors, to read and write poetry. After earning a B.A. from Northwestern University in 1935, she joined the Federal Writers' Project in Chicago, where she met and began a literary collaboration with Richard Wright.

Walker earned her M.A. in creative writing from the University of Iowa in 1940, and in 1942, published her master's thesis,

For My People, a collection of poetry celebrating African American culture, for which she won the Yale Series of Younger Poets award. She was the first African American to win this award.

Walker taught English at Jackson State College (now Jackson State University) from 1949 to 1979. During that time, she returned to the University of Iowa and earned a Ph.D. in 1965. She founded Jackson State's Institute for the Study of the History, Life and Culture of Black People in 1968 and served as its director until her retirement.

Besides a biography of Richard Wright and other critical writing, Walker published numerous volumes of poetry, including her last, *This Is My Century: New and Collected Poems,* in 1989. She wrote her best-selling novel, *Jubilee* (1966), based on the life of her enslaved great-grandmother, as her doctoral dissertation. *On Being Female, Black and Free: Essays, 1932–1992,* her final collection of essays, was published in 1997.

Of Walker, Nikki Giovanni wrote, "Margaret Walker single-handedly turned poetry upside down with her declaration of love and her challenge to the future of her people."

Lineage

— *Margaret Walker*

My grandmothers were strong.
They followed plows and bent to toil.
They moved through fields sowing seed.
They touched earth and grain grew.
5   They were full of sturdiness and singing.
My grandmothers were strong.

My grandmothers are full of memories
Smelling of soap and onions and wet clay
With veins rolling roughly over quick hands
10   They have many clean words to say.
My grandmothers were strong.
Why am I not as they?

Responding to the Selection

Questions for Discussion

1. In your opinion, who are the grandmothers? How would you describe the speaker's attitude toward them? What details from the poem reveal this attitude?

2. What might the speaker mean by "They have many clean words to say"?

3. In your opinion, why might the speaker describe herself as being different from her grandmothers? In what ways might she be different?

4. Do you think the speaker values her grandmothers only for their physical strength? Give evidence from the poem to support your opinion.

Activities

Interviewing an Elder

1. Choose an elder from your family or neighborhood to **interview** about his or her life. Ask questions about what it was like growing up so long ago. Prepare your findings to present to your class.

Teaching a Lesson

2. Our parents and other adults often share wisdom and stories to help us grow. Select an adult and write a **poem** using words of wisdom he or she has shared with you. When writing, think of the poem as a lesson you might share with a younger student.

Before You Read

And Ain't I a Woman?

Sojourner Truth
1797–1883

*"I am glad to see that men are
getting their rights, but
I want women to get theirs,
and while the water is stirring
I will step into the pool."*

About Truth

Armed with a sharp wit and common sense, Sojourner Truth went to battle against slavery and in support of women's rights. Nearly six feet tall, Truth had a deep and powerful voice that quieted rowdy crowds and won devoted supporters.

Truth was born into slavery and endured cruel slave owners, backbreaking work, and harsh beatings. When she escaped from slavery at age twenty-nine, she was taken in by a Quaker couple, Isaac and Maria Van Wagener, and she took the name Isabella Van Wagener.

For many years, Isabella believed she heard messages from God. At age forty-six, she renamed herself Sojourner Truth, indicating that she would travel across the land preaching God's word. Truth preached throughout the northeastern United States. Before long, she began to weave anti-slavery messages into her preaching.

Truth also adopted the cause of women's rights, especially the right to vote. She delivered her famous speech, "And Ain't I a Woman?" in Akron at the Ohio Women's Rights Convention in 1851.

During the Civil War, Truth helped gather supplies and money for the black volunteer regiments. Toward the end of the war, Truth accepted a job counseling formerly enslaved people for the National Freedmen's Relief Association in Washington, D.C.

The Spirit of Truth

"And Ain't I a Woman?" was not a written speech, and many versions have survived, some in Southern black dialect. In fact, Truth spoke Standard English, so the words you are about to read may not be the exact words spoken in Akron, but they nevertheless clearly reflect the spirit of Sojourner Truth.

And Ain't I a Woman?

Address to the Ohio Women's Rights Convention, 1851

— *Sojourner Truth*

Well, children, where there is so much racket there must be something out of kilter. I think that 'twixt the Negroes of the South and the women at the North, all talking about rights, the white men will be in a fix pretty soon. But what's all this here talking about? That man over there says that women need to be helped into carriages, and lifted over ditches, and to have the best place everywhere. Nobody ever helps me into carriages, or over mud-puddles, or gives me any best place! And ain't I a woman? Look at me! Look at my arm. I have ploughed and planted, and gathered into barns, and no man could head me! And ain't I a woman? I could work as much and eat as much as a man—when I could get it—and bear the lash as well! And ain't I a woman? I have borne thirteen children, and seen them most all sold off to slavery, and when I cried out with my mother's grief, none but Jesus heard me! And ain't I a woman?

Then they talk about this thing in the head; what's this they call it? [Intellect, someone whispers.] That's it, honey. What's that got to do with women's rights or Negro's rights? If my cup won't hold but a pint, and yours holds a quart, wouldn't you be mean not to let me have my little half-measure full?

Then that little man in black there, he says women can't have as much rights as men, 'cause Christ wasn't a woman! Where did your Christ come from? Where did your Christ come from? From God and a woman! Man had nothing to do with Him.

If the first woman God ever made was strong enough to turn the world upside down all alone, these women together ought to be able to turn it back, and get it right side up again! And now they is asking to do it, the men better let them.

Obliged to you for hearing me, and now old Sojourner ain't got nothing more to say.

Responding to the Selection ───────────

Questions for Discussion

1. What is Truth saying in the first two sentences of her speech?

2. Describe the **rhetorical devices** that add emphasis to Truth's arguments.

3. Why do you suppose the issue of women's rights was so important to Truth?

4. What is the purpose and meaning of Truth's reference to "the first woman God ever made"?

Activities

Listing

1. In a persuasive speech, the speaker presents arguments to make his or her case. Make a **list** of the arguments Truth presents for women's rights.

Writing a Speech

2. Try your own hand at writing a **speech** about women's rights. Argue either that the battle has been won or that the battle is still being fought. Use concrete examples, as Truth does, to bolster your argument.

Before You Read

from *The Bluest Eye*

Toni Morrison
Born 1931

"If there's a book you really want to read but it hasn't been written yet, then you must write it."

About Morrison

Highly acclaimed as a novelist, essayist, and literary critic, Toni Morrison was awarded the Nobel Prize for Literature in 1993. Morrison said of the honor, "I am outrageously happy. But what is most wonderful for me, personally, is to know that the prize at last has been awarded to an African American. Winning as an American is very special—but winning as a black American is a knockout."

Born Chloe Anthony Wofford, Morrison grew up in northern Ohio, a setting that figures prominently in many of her novels. She graduated from Howard University and received an M.A. degree from Cornell University. Throughout her career, Morrison has also held prestigious teaching positions at various colleges and universities.

When she was thirty-eight, Morrison published *The Bluest Eye,* her first of seven novels. Her novel *Beloved* won the 1988 Pulitzer Prize for Fiction.

Morrison has always emphasized both her African American heritage and her experiences as a woman as influences that have shaped her storytelling talents. When asked whether she considered herself a black writer or a female writer, Morrison responded, "I've just insisted—insisted!—upon being called a black woman novelist."

from The Bluest Eye

— *Toni Morrison*

We had fun in those few days Pecola was with us. Frieda and I stopped fighting each other and concentrated on our guest, trying hard to keep her from feeling outdoors.

When we discovered that she clearly did not want to dominate us, we liked her. She laughed when I clowned for her, and smiled and accepted gracefully the food gifts my sister gave her.

"Would you like some graham crackers?"

"I don't care."

Frieda brought her four graham crackers on a saucer and some milk in a blue-and-white Shirley Temple cup. She was a long time with the milk, and gazed fondly at the silhouette of Shirley Temple's dimpled face. Frieda and she had a loving conversation about how cu-ute Shirley Temple was. I couldn't join them in their adoration because I hated Shirley. Not because she was cute, but because she danced with Bojangles, who was *my* friend, *my* uncle, *my* daddy, and who ought to have been soft-shoeing it and chuckling with me. Instead he was enjoying, sharing, giving a lovely dance thing with one of those little white girls whose socks never slid down under their heels. So I said, "I like Jane Withers."

They gave me a puzzled look, decided I was incomprehensible, and continued their reminiscing about old squint-eyed Shirley.

Younger than both Frieda and Pecola, I had not yet arrived at the turning point in the development of my psyche which would allow me to love her. What I felt at that time was unsullied hatred. But before that I had felt a stranger, more frightening thing than hatred for all the Shirley Temples of the world.

It had begun with Christmas and the gift of dolls. The big, the special, the loving gift was always a big, blue-eyed Baby Doll. From the clucking sounds of adults I knew that the doll represented what they thought was my fondest wish. I was bemused with the thing itself, and the way it looked. What was I supposed to do with it? Pretend I was its mother? I had no interest in babies or the concept of motherhood. I was interested only in humans my own age and size, and could not generate any enthusiasm at the prospect of being a mother. Motherhood was old age, and other remote

from The Bluest Eye 277

possibilities. I learned quickly, however, what I was expected to do with the doll: rock it, fabricate storied situations around it, even sleep with it. Picture books were full of little girls sleeping with their dolls. Raggedy Ann dolls usually, but they were out of the question. I was physically revolted by and secretly frightened of those round moronic eyes, the pancake face, and orangeworms hair.

The other dolls, which were supposed to bring me great pleasure, succeeded in doing quite the opposite. When I took it to bed, its hard unyielding limbs resisted my flesh—the tapered fingertips on those dimpled hands scratched. If, in sleep, I turned, the bone-cold head collided with my own. It was a most uncomfortable, patently aggressive sleeping companion. To hold it was no more rewarding. The starched gauze or lace on the cotton dress irritated any embrace. I had only one desire: to dismember it. To see of what it was made, to discover the dearness, to find the beauty, the desirability that had escaped me, but apparently only me. Adults, older girls, shops, magazines, newspapers, window signs—all the world had agreed that a blue-eyed, yellow-haired, pink-skinned doll was what every girl child treasured. "Here," they said, "this is beautiful, and if you are on this day 'worthy' you may have it." I fingered the face, wondering at the single-stroke eyebrows; picked at the pearly teeth stuck like two piano keys between red bowline lips. Traced the turned-up nose, poked the glassy blue eyeballs, twisted the yellow hair. I could not love it. But I could examine it to see what it was that all the world said was lovable. Break off the tiny fingers, bend the flat feet, loosen the hair, twist the head around, and the thing made one sound—a sound they said was the sweet and plaintive cry "Mama," but which sounded to me like the bleat of a dying lamb, or, more precisely, our icebox door opening on rusty hinges in July. Remove the cold and stupid eyeball, it would bleat still, "Ahhhhhh," take off the head, shake out the sawdust, crack the back against the brass bed rail, it would bleat still. The gauze back would split, and I could see the disk with six holes, the secret of the sound. A mere metal roundness.

Grown people frowned and fussed: "You-don't-know-how-to-take-care-of-nothing. I-never-had-a-baby-doll-in-my-whole-life-and-used-to-cry-my-eyes-out-for-them. Now-you-got-one-a-beautiful-one-and-you-tear-it-up-what's-the-matter-with-you?"

How strong was their outrage. Tears threatened to erase the aloofness of their authority. The emotion of years of unfulfilled longing preened in their voices. I did not know why I destroyed those dolls. But I did know that nobody ever asked me what I wanted for Christmas. Had any adult with the power to fulfill my desires taken me seriously and asked me what I wanted, they would have known that I did not want to have anything to own, or to possess any object. I wanted rather to feel something on Christmas day. The real question would have been, "Dear Claudia, what experience would you like on Christmas?" I could have spoken up, "I want to sit on the low stool in Big Mama's kitchen with my lap full of lilacs and listen to Big Papa play his violin for me alone." The lowness of the stool made for my body, the security and warmth of Big Mama's kitchen, the smell of the lilacs, the sound of the music, and, since it would be good to have all of my senses engaged, the taste of a peach, perhaps, afterward.

Instead I tasted and smelled the acridness of tin plates and cups designed for tea parties that bored me. Instead I looked with loathing on new dresses that required a hateful bath in a galvanized zinc tub before wearing. Slipping around on the zinc, no time to play or soak, for the water chilled too fast, no time to enjoy one's nakedness, only time to make curtains of soapy water careen down between the legs. Then the scratchy towels and the dreadful and humiliating absence of dirt. The irritable, unimaginative cleanliness. Gone the ink marks from legs and face, all my creations and accumulations of the day gone, and replaced by goose pimples.

Responding to the Selection

Questions for Discussion

1. Describe the character and temperament of the **narrator.**

2. Why does the narrator hate Shirley Temple so much?

3. What is the "stranger, more frightening thing than hatred for all the Shirley Temples of the world" that the narrator feels? Would the narrator have felt differently if the dolls had been black?

4. What does the narrator wish for on Christmas? What is significant about her wish?

5. What feelings might the narrator be experiencing, perhaps for the first time? Does she understand those feelings?

Activities

Writing an Essay

1. Think about the implications of giving a young black girl a white, blue-eyed doll. Make a **list** of what you think those implications might be and use the list to write an **essay** that explains your ideas.

Searching the Internet

2. Search the Internet for contemporary dolls. What do dolls look like today? Discuss with your classmates the differences between the doll given to the narrator and these contemporary dolls.

Before You Read

Purchase

Naomi Long Madgett
Born 1923

"I had no clothing of my own, only depressive hand-me-downs, frayed remnants of someone else's outgrown legacy."

About Madgett

When Naomi Long Madgett had trouble getting a poetry manuscript published, she "was determined to keep writing in my voice." She founded Lotus Press in 1972 to promote African American writers, and her *Pink Ladies in the Afternoon* was its first publication.

Born in Norfolk, Virginia, Madgett was raised in many parts of the United States. Her parents' encouragement to overcome her childhood loneliness fostered her love of literature and writing. She had written more than one hundred poems by the time she turned twelve. Her years at Charles Sumner High School in St. Louis, Missouri, saw her first published writing—in yearbooks, newspapers, and the *Missouri School Journal.*

Having earned both a teaching certificate and a master's degree from what is now Wayne State University, in Detroit, Michigan, she began teaching English in secondary school in 1955. Over the next decade, she not only included African American poetry in her American literature classes, but she also fought to establish African American literature as part of the Detroit public school curriculum, achieving her goal at last in 1966.

Madgett's postsecondary teaching career at Eastern Michigan University (1968–1984) coincided with much of her publishing career. Her invaluable publishing and editorial contributions were recognized in 1993 when she was presented with an American Book Award. Her own titles include *Octavia and Other Poems, A Student's Guide to Creative Writing,* and *Adam of Ife: Black Women in Praise of Black Men,* an anthology she edited.

Purchase

— Naomi Long Madgett

I like the smell of new clothes,
The novel aroma of challenge.
This dress has no past
Linked with regretful memories
5   To taint it,
Only a future as hopeful
As my own.
I can say of an old garment
Laid away in a trunk:
10   "This lace I wore on that day when. . . ."
But I prefer the new scent
Of a garment unworn,
Untainted like the new self
That I become
15   When I first wear it.

Responding to the Selection

Questions for Discussion

1. Why does the speaker like new clothes? Explain what they mean to her.

2. What might the speaker mean by "the novel aroma of challenge"?

3. What effect does an old garment have on the speaker? Explain, using details from the poem in your answer.

4. Would you say the speaker prefers to think about the past or to anticipate the future? What details from the poem support your answer?

Activities

Sensory Writing

1. The speaker emphasizes the "smell," "aroma," and "scent" of new clothes. This appeal to the sense of smell adds to the experience of the poem. Write a **short story** about a similar experience with something new.

Writing About the Past

2. We often associate memories and emotions with our personal possessions. Choose an item from your bedroom and write a brief **essay** about its history.

Before You Read

fury

Lucille Clifton
Born 1936

"children
when they ask you
why your mama so funny
say
she is a poet
she don't have no sense."

About Clifton

Lucille Clifton has said, "In the bigger scheme of things the universe is not asking us to *do* something, the universe is asking us to *be* something." Clifton has chosen to be many things in her life— among them a writer, a teacher, and a mother to six children.

Clifton has written nine books of poetry, an autobiographical work, *Generations: A Memoir,* and more than sixteen children's books. Her work has been nominated for the National Book Award and twice for the Pulitzer Prize, and she has received an Emmy Award from the American Academy of Television Arts and Sciences. In 1999 she was elected chancellor of the Academy of American Poets. She is currently distinguished professor of humanities at St. Mary's College of Maryland.

Pride is a theme that runs through Clifton's work—pride in being African American, a woman, and a poet. Clifton's dedication to her literary craft is clear. "Poetry," she has said, "is a matter of life, not just a matter of language."

— Lucille Clifton

for mama
     remember this.
     she is standing by
     the furnace.
     the coals
5   glisten like rubies.
     her hand is crying.
     her hand is clutching
     a sheaf of papers.
     poems.
10   she gives them up.
     they burn
     jewels into jewels.
     her eyes are animals.
     each hank of her hair
15   is a serpent's obedient
     wife.
     she will never recover.
     remember. there is nothing
     you will not bear
20   for this woman's sake.

Responding to the Selection

Questions for Discussion

1. Explain what happens in this poem.

2. What does the speaker mean when she says "her hand is crying"? What are the tears?

3. Explain the **narrator's** description of the poems burning: "jewels into jewels."

4. What is the emotional state of the woman burning the poems? What makes you think so?

5. What do you think the last four lines of the poem mean?

6. Who is feeling the "fury" of the title?

Activity

Writing About Your Feelings

Have you ever intentionally destroyed something that was extremely important to you—perhaps a gift from a friend or some other valued possession? Why did you do it? What emotions were you feeling? Write a **personal narrative** that describes the incident, the reasons for it, and how you feel about it now.

Before You Read

The Power of Names

Irma McClaurin
Born 1952

> "Because I carry the same middle name as my mother (Pearl), I have often wondered to what extent I also have inherited her dreams and aspirations."

About McClaurin

Irma McClaurin is both a poet and an anthropologist—one who studies the physical, social, and cultural development of a people. At first, this blending of science and literature may seem odd, but in fact it affords McClaurin the opportunity to use her scientific expertise to study people and her poetic expressiveness to write about what she has discovered.

McClaurin has published three books of poetry, which have been translated into both Spanish and Swedish. In addition, her work has appeared in numerous literary magazines and poetry anthologies. She is also the author of *Women of Belize: Gender and Change in Central America* and the editor of *Black Feminist Anthropology: Theory, Politics, Praxis, and Poetics.* She is currently an associate professor of anthropology at the University of Florida.

The **Power** *of* *Names*

— *Irma McClaurin*

I slip my mother's name on like a glove
and wonder if I will become like her
absolutely.
Years number the times I have worn her pain
5   as a child, as a teenager, as a woman—my second skin—
or screamed her screams
as she sat, silver head bowed
silent
hedging the storm.

10   Her name, at times, does not fit me.
I take it, turn it over on my tongue—
a key.
Shape my lips around its vowels
hoping to unlock elusive doors,
15   understand the instincts
my body follows.
The family named her Pearl,
a first among them;
yet others have owned this name.
20   They haunt me.
I follow their destiny.

Each year I return home,
a salmon caught in an act of survival.
I search my mother's face
25 neatly carved in obsidian
and wonder
how much of myself I owe this woman
whose name I have swallowed like a worm.
Her inner soul transferred through the eating.

30 I slip my mother's name on
with wonder
and become like her
absolutely.

Responding to the Selection

Questions for Discussion

1. What is the speaker describing in the first stanza? What do you make of the **simile** "I slip my mother's name on like a glove"?
2. What has the "glove" become in the second stanza? How does the speaker hope this will help her better understand her relationship to her mother?
3. Who haunts the speaker? Why?
4. What is the speaker referring to when she describes herself as "a salmon caught in an act of survival"?

Activity
Naming Yourself
Make some notes about your own name and how it affects you. Whom were you named after? Was it a relative, a family friend, a character from literature, a celebrity? Do you feel connected to this person? Do you feel any obligation to measure up to him or her? What power does your name possess? Write an **essay** that explores your name and its power over you.

Focus on . . .
The Black Arts Movement

Negro es Bello 2, 1969. Elizabeth Catlett. Lithograph, 30 x 23⅓ in.

While the Civil Rights struggle raged during the 1960s, another move-ment quietly took shape. African American artists began thinking and writing about a radically different context for black art and artists, a con-text that not only would profoundly influence African American artistic expression but also challenge many of America's assumptions about its black citizens. That movement was the Black Arts Movement (BAM).

Two philosophies energized the BAM: cultural nationalism and Black Power. Cultural nationalism was born of the belief that the United States was made up of two distinct societies, one black and the other white, each with its own history, values, lifestyles, and intellectual traditions. Cultural nationalists, such as Ron Karenga, urged African Americans to incorporate their African roots into all aspects of their lives, from their clothing to their religious practices and, of course, in their art:

> Let our art remind us of our distaste for the enemy, our love for each other, and our commitment to the revolutionary struggle that will be fought with the rhythmic reality of a permanent revolution.

Black Power was less a cultural movement than a political one. Surely it promoted racial pride, dignity, and self-esteem, but it also encouraged the creation of African American institutions meant to nurture black self-reliance and economic freedom. Groups such as the Black Panther Party for Self-Defense may have acted and dressed the part of militant revolutionaries, but in fact they provided services within their communities that both met the physical needs of the poor, the hungry, and the homeless and fostered feelings of racial empowerment. Black Power also inspired black artists, as Larry Neal, one of the intellectual voices of the BAM, explained:

> The political values inherent in the Black Power Concept are now finding concrete expression in the aesthetics of Afro-American dramatists, poets, choreographers, musicians, and novelists.

The BAM came to life through its artists and the institutions they created and nourished. The movement's leaders included Amiri Baraka, Larry Neal, Harold Cruse, and Ron Karenga. Such writers as Gwendolyn Brooks, Haki Madhubuti, Sonia Sanchez, Ed Bullins, and Nikki Giovanni enlivened and challenged the movement with their plays, essays, and poetry. The BAM also spawned black cultural institutions. Among the most influential were Baraka's Black Arts Repertory Theatre/School, Robert MacBeth's New Lafayette Theatre, and Barbara Ann Teer's Sun People's Theatre.

Although the BAM was relatively short-lived, its influences live on in the artistic expression of succeeding generations of African Americans. Like the Harlem Renaissance of the 1920s, the BAM offered black artists not only a forum for their work but also a philosophy through which they could shape their art, express their pride, and add yet another chapter to the cultural history of Africans in America.

Black Panther-sponsored breakfast

Linking to . . .
- Consider the impact of the BAM as you read the following selections.

Before You Read

Poet: What Ever Happened to Luther?

Haki R. Madhubuti
Born 1942

"Those who humble themselves before knowledge of any kind generally end up the wiser and as voices with something meaningful to say."

About Madhubuti

When Haki Madhubuti, then known as Don Luther Lee, was just sixteen, his mother died from a drug overdose. His mother, Madhubuti has said, was the spark that fired his creativity and his interest in black culture. After her death and a brief stint in the army, Madhubuti began writing poetry and essays that championed black pride, black strength, and black self-determination for African Americans.

Madhubuti was a major force in the Black Arts Movement (BAM) of the 1960s and 1970s. His first six volumes of poetry, including *Don't Cry, Scream,* were published during the 1960s. Written in black dialect and slang, the poems extol the beauty and dignity of African American culture and angrily condemn political, social, and economic injustice.

Madhubuti founded Third World Press as an outlet for not only his own writing but also that of emerging African American artists.

Madhubuti has continued to write and publish the work of African American writers in the decades following the BAM. Currently, he is director of the Gwendolyn Brooks Center at Chicago State University.

Poet: What Ever Happened to Luther?

— *Haki R. Madhubuti*

he was strange weather, this luther. he read books, mainly
poetry and sometimes long books about people in foreign
places. for a young man he was too serious, he never did smile,
and the family still don't know if he had good teeth. he liked
5   music too, even tried to play the trumpet until he heard the
young miles davis. he then said that he'd try writing. the family
didn't believe him because there ain't never been no writers in
this family, and everybody knows that whatever you end up
doing, it's gotta be in your blood. it's like loving women, it's in
10 the blood, arteries and brains. this family don't even write letters,
they call everybody. thats why the phone is off 6 months
out of a year. then again, his brother willie t. use to write long,
long letters from prison about the books he was reading by
malcolm x, frantz fanon, george jackson, richard wright and others.
15 luther, unlike his brother, didn't smoke or drink and he'd
always be doing odd jobs to get money. even his closest friends
clyde and t. bone didn't fully understand him. while they be partying
all weekend, luther would be traveling. he would take his
little money with a bag full of food, mainly fruit, and a change of

20   underwear and get on the greyhound bus and go. he said he be
visiting cities. yet, the real funny thing about luther was his
ideas. he was always talking about afrika and black people. He
was into that black stuff and he was as light skinned as a piece
of golden corn on the cob. he'd be calling himself black and
25   afrikan and upsetting everybody, especially white people. they
be calling him crazy but not to his face. anyway the family,
mainly the educated side, just left him alone. they would just be
polite to him, and every child of god knows that when family
members act polite, that means that they don't want to be
30   around you. It didn't matter much because after his mother died
he left the city and went into the army. the last time we heard
from him was in 1963. he got put out the army for rioting. he
disappeared somewhere between mississippi and chicago. a
third cousin, who family was also polite to, appeared one day
35   and said that luther had grown a beard, changed his name and
stopped eating meat. she said that he had been to afrika and
now lived in chicago doing what he wanted to do, writing books,
she also said that he smiles a lot and kinda got good teeth.

Responding to the Selection

Questions for Discussion

1. "Poet: What Ever Happened to Luther?" is a story told in **verse.** Summarize the story the speaker is telling.

2. What do you think the speaker means when he says that Luther was "strange weather"?

3. The speaker notes that Luther spent weekends traveling while his friends were partying. What happens when you travel that doesn't happen when you party?

4. What does the last line of the poem tell you about Luther and the choices he made in his life?

Activity

Writing an Essay

The poem tells the story of a journey. Write an **essay** in which you discuss Luther's journey; descibe where he comes from and where he goes.

MEDIA
connection

Journal Interview

Twenty-five years after the Black Arts Movement, Haki Madhubuti continues to be a presence in American letters.

Conversation with Haki Madhubuti

from *River Oak Review,* Spring 1999 — *Quraysh Ali Lansana*

Quraysh Ali Lansana: Third World Press is over thirty years old. You have been writing and publishing for over three decades now. What, in your opinion, is the current state of Black poetry?

Haki Madhubuti: The state of Black poetry is pretty much in the state it has always been. It is peripheral to our culture, it is not a driving force. It's akin to our great Black music, jazz. Poetry is essentially our classical language. There has always been a strong current within the culture.

Now, I do feel that the Black poetry scene has made significant inroads into the culture. The fact that you have all these Black publishing companies now, as well as the Black bookstores, illustrates that. And now you have a significant association of Black librarians, so much so that they have their own conference every other year. As a result of that, poetry will at least get a fair hearing and a share of readers. So the poetry, most certainly for the established poets—I'm talking about Gwendolyn Brooks, Amiri Baraka, Sonia Sanchez, Mari Evans—will always sell.

What has happened is a new crop, yourself included—you all are doing what we had to do too, which is buy our authors. And I think that will always be the case, as long as we don't have publishing companies who are able to really do the kind of marketing, the guerilla sales. We're [Third World Press] trying to go there, but we're not there yet.

So with that said, it must be made very clear that I think poetry is highly significant. In terms of language usage, poetry is at the foundation of

our culture, which is the same way I feel about great Black music—I think these are the two key sources of creation for all Black people, regardless of education and economics. I'm what you'd call a realistic optimist when it comes to poetry, because it's been a part of my life for so long. I consider myself primarily a poet, but there's no way in the world I feel that I could stay alive or maintain a sense of presence in this literary community by dealing just in poetry. Not a great majority, or even a minor majority, of people in our culture read poetry, Black or White.

QAL: Do you think the poets of the Black Arts Movement are now a part of the canon?

HM: Well, most certainly they are a part of the African American literary canon. I think, in a limited way, they are a part of the national literary canon, as well. The only problem is this: when we look at the bulk of accessible information, the divide is still very extreme.

QAL: Do you think we have a responsibility to write almost exclusively about our situation of being Black in this country?

HM: I think that Black writers have the right to write about anything they want. I've traveled around much of the world, and even though much of this material hasn't been published, I've written extensively about my travels. My reading is very eclectic. I mean, it's across the board. Writers who are very serious about their work read across cultures. That's the only way you can grow. I think it's our responsibility as citizens of the United States to write about anything that bothers us about our citizenship, whether it's lack of voting or the lack of presence in the economic sphere. I think that the only restriction that should be put on writers is basically the restriction of their own talent. I'm not only a product of Sterling Brown, Langston Hughes, and Gwendolyn Brooks, but also of Pablo Neruda, Nicolas Guillen, Ayi Kwei Armah, N. Scott Momaday, Octavio Paz, Aime Césaire, and thousands of other poets, writers, visual artists, musicians, and dancers.

Questions for Discussion

1. The interview opens with a question about "the current state of Black poetry." Does Madhubuti think this state is positive or negative? Summarize his thoughts.

2. Madhubuti says serious writers read work from authors of other cultures. Why do you think this is important?

Before You Read

Preface to a Twenty Volume Suicide Note

Amiri Baraka
Born 1934

> *"A Man is either free or he is not. There cannot be any apprenticeship for freedom."*

About Baraka

Born Everett Leroy (later LeRoi) Jones, Amiri Baraka moved to Greenwich Village in New York City when he was twenty-three and began a literary career that would be as prolific as it is varied. Baraka has written poetry, drama, novels, jazz operas, and nonfiction, including two important critical histories of African American music: *Blues People: Negro Music in White America* and *Black Music.*

After graduating from Howard University in 1954, Baraka joined the U.S. Air Force. During this period, he became seriously interested in literature. In 1961 he published his first collection of poetry, the critically acclaimed *Preface to a Twenty Volume Suicide Note.* At the same time, Baraka, his wife, Hettie Jones, and poet Diane Di Prima were editing two literary journals, *Yugen* and *Floating Bear.* In 1964 Baraka's first play, *Dutchman,* debuted off-Broadway and was an immediate success. A year later he founded the Black Arts Repertory Theatre/School in Harlem and in 1968, the Black Community Development and Defense Organization, a Nation of Islam group committed to celebrating African American culture and gaining political power for blacks.

Among Baraka's notable achievements is his role in helping to establish and sustain the Black Arts Movement in the late 1960s and early 1970s. Baraka's writing turned increasingly militant and nationalist, advocating the Afrocentric doctrines of separatism, self-determination, and communal African American cultural and economic self-development. Baraka went on to figure prominently in African American political events but later abandoned his separatist views.

In addition to his political work, Baraka has taught at several U.S. universities, and he continues to write.

Preface to a Twenty Volume Suicide Note

— Amiri Baraka

(For Kellie Jones, born 16 May 1959)

Lately, I've become accustomed to the way
The ground opens up and envelopes me
Each time I go out to walk the dog.
Or the broad edged silly music the wind
5   Makes when I run for a bus . . .

Things have come to that.

And now, each night I count the stars,
And each night I get the same number.
And when they will not come to be counted,
10   I count the holes they leave.

Nobody sings anymore.

And then last night, I tiptoed up
To my daughter's room and heard her
Talking to someone, and when I opened
15   The door, there was no one there . . .
Only she on her knees, peeking into

Her own clasped hands.

Responding to the Selection

Questions for Discussion

1. What feeling do you get from the first two stanzas? In what state of mind does the speaker seem to be?

2. Why does the speaker count the stars and, when there are no stars, "the holes they leave"?

3. What do you make of the lines "Things have come to that" and "Nobody sings anymore"? How do these lines function structurally in the poem?

4. What changes for the speaker in the third stanza? What does his daughter possess that the speaker seems to have lost?

Activity

Writing a Poem

Think about a time when you felt sad or despairing and then some small event occurred that gave you hope again. Write a **poem** describing this transformation in your outlook.

Before You Read

My Dungeon Shook

James Baldwin
1924–1987

"The world is before you and you need not take it or leave it as it was when you came in."

About Baldwin

James Baldwin was a writer of unparalleled grace and fierce conviction. In his work, he explored, among other things, the forces that shaped American racial identity and issues of African American identity.

During high school, Baldwin worked as a junior minister, and after graduating from high school in 1942, he took a series of jobs—handyman, dishwasher, office worker, and waiter—to help support his family.

In 1953 Baldwin published his first novel, *Go Tell It on the Mountain,* a story that reflected his search for his roots. More and more, he eloquently voiced his outrage at racial inequality and social injustice. With uncompromising realism, he exposed his readers to some basic truths about the society in which they lived.

Besides achieving fame as a writer, Baldwin was in great demand as a speaker during the Civil Rights movement. His insights, his ear for the spoken language, and his early experience as a minister made him a powerful force at the podium. As the years went by, however, Baldwin became disillusioned about the prospects for social change. In 1969 he moved to Europe, living primarily in France for the rest of his life.

In many respects, France proved friendlier to Baldwin than his own country, where he had been put under FBI surveillance. Despite his critical and popular success, he never won any major American literary prizes. He was, however, awarded one of France's most prestigious honors—Commander of the Legion of Honor.

Death brought Baldwin back to Harlem. His funeral was held near the house where he had been born. More than five thousand mourners paid their respects to the man whom the writer E. L. Doctorow credited with the ability "not to make you question but to make you see."

My Dungeon Shook

— *James Baldwin*

Letter to My Nephew
on the One Hundredth Anniversary

of the Emancipation

Dear James:

I have begun this letter five times and torn it up five times. I keep seeing your face, which is also the face of your father and my brother. Like him, you are tough, dark, vulnerable, moody—with a very definite tendency to sound truculent because you want no one to think you are soft. You may be like your grandfather in this, I don't know, but certainly both you and your father resemble him very much physically. Well, he is dead, he never saw you, and he had a terrible life; he was defeated long before he died because, at the bottom of his heart, he really believed what white people said about him. This is one of the reasons that he became so holy. I am sure that your father has told you something about all that. Neither you nor your father exhibit any tendency towards holiness: you really *are* of another era, part of what happened when the Negro left the land and came into what the late E. Franklin Frazier called "the cities of destruction." You can only be destroyed by believing that you really are what the white world calls a *nigger*. I tell you this because I love you, and please don't you ever forget it.

I have known both of you all your lives, have carried your Daddy in my arms and on my shoulders, kissed and spanked him and watched him learn to walk. I don't know if you've known anybody from that far back; if you've loved anybody that long, first as an infant, then as a child, then as a man, you gain a strange perspective on time and human pain and effort. Other people cannot see what I see whenever I look into your father's face, for behind your father's face as it is today are all those other faces which were his. Let him laugh and I see a cellar your father does not remember and a house he does not remember and I hear in his present laughter his laughter as a child. Let him curse and I remember him falling down the cellar steps, and howling, and I remember, with pain, his tears, which my hand or your grandmother's so easily wiped away. But no one's hand can wipe away those tears he sheds invisibly today, which one hears in his laughter and in his speech and in his songs. I know what the world has done to my brother and how narrowly he has survived it. And I know, which is much worse, and this is the crime of which I accuse my country and my countrymen, and for which neither I nor time nor history will ever forgive them, that they have destroyed and are destroying hundreds of thousands of lives and do not know it and do not want to know it. One can be, indeed one must strive to become, tough and philosophical concerning destruction and death, for this is what most of mankind has been best at since we have heard of man. (But remember: *most* of mankind is not *all* of mankind.) But it is not permissible that the authors of devastation should also be innocent. It is the innocence which constitutes the crime.

Now, my dear namesake, these innocent and well-meaning people, your countrymen, have caused you to be born under conditions not very far removed from those described for us by Charles Dickens in the London of more than a hundred years ago. (I hear the chorus of the innocents screaming, "No! This is not true! How *bitter* you are!"—but I am writing this letter to *you*, to try to tell you something about how to handle *them*, for most of them do not yet really know that you exist. I *know* the conditions under which you were born, for I was there. Your countrymen were *not* there, and haven't made it yet. Your grandmother was also there, and no one has ever accused her of being bitter. I suggest that the innocents check with her. She isn't hard to find. Your countrymen don't know that *she* exists, either, though she has been working for them all their lives.)

Well, you were born, here you came, something like fifteen years ago; and though your father and mother and grandmother, looking about the streets through which they were carrying you, staring at the walls into which they brought you, had every reason to be heavyhearted, yet they were not. For here you were, Big James, named for me—you were a big baby, I was not—here you were: to be loved. To be loved, baby, hard, at once, and forever, to strengthen you against the loveless world. Remember that: I know how black it looks today, for you. It looked bad that day, too, yes, we were trembling. We have not stopped trembling yet, but if we had not loved each other none of us would have survived. And now you must survive because we love you, and for the sake of your children and your children's children.

This innocent country set you down in a ghetto in which, in fact, it intended that you should perish. Let me spell out precisely what I mean by that, for the heart of the matter is here, and the root of my dispute with my country. You were born where you were born and faced the future that you faced because you were black and *for no other reason*. The limits of your ambition were, thus, expected to be set forever. You were born into a

My Dungeon Shook

society which spelled out with brutal clarity, and in as many ways as possible, that you were a worthless human being. You were not expected to aspire to excellence: you were expected to make peace with mediocrity. Wherever you have turned, James, in your short time on this earth, you have been told where you could go and what you could do (and *how* you could do it) and where you could live and whom you could marry. I know your countrymen do not agree with me about this, and I hear them saying, "You exaggerate." They do not know Harlem, and I do. So do you. Take no one's word for anything, including mine—but trust your experience. Know whence you came. If you know whence you came, there is really no limit to where you can go. The details and symbols of your life have been deliberately constructed to make you believe what white people say about you. Please try to remember that what they believe, as well as what they do and cause you to endure, does not testify to your inferiority but to their inhumanity and fear. Please try to be clear, dear James, through the storm which rages about your youthful head today, about the reality which lies behind the words *acceptance* and *integration*. There is no reason for you to try to become like white people and there is no basis whatever for their impertinent assumption that *they* must accept *you*. The really terrible thing, old buddy, is that *you* must accept *them*. And I mean that very seriously. You must accept them and accept them with love. For these innocent people have no other hope. They are, in effect, still trapped in a history which they do not understand; and until they understand it, they cannot be released from it. They have had to believe for many years, and for innumerable reasons, that black men are inferior to white men. Many of them, indeed, know better, but, as you will discover, people find it very difficult to act on what they know. To act is to be committed, and to be committed is to be in danger. In this case, the danger, in the minds of most white Americans, is the loss of their identity. Try to imagine how you would feel if you woke up one morning to find the sun shining and all the stars aflame. You would be frightened because it is out of the order of nature. Any upheaval in the universe is terrifying because it so profoundly attacks one's sense of one's own reality. Well, the black man has functioned in the white man's world as a fixed star, as an immovable pillar: and as he moves out of his place, heaven and earth are shaken to their foundations. You, don't be afraid. I said that it was intended that you should perish in the ghetto, perish by never being allowed to go behind the white man's definitions, by never being allowed to spell your proper name. You have, and many of us have, defeated this intention; and, by a terrible law, a terrible paradox, those innocents who believed that your imprisonment made them safe are losing their grasp of reality. But these men are your brothers—your lost, younger brothers. And if the word *integration* means anything, this is what it means: that we, with love, shall force our brothers to see themselves as they are, to cease fleeing from reality and begin to change it. For this is your home, my friend, do not be driven from it; great men have done great things here, and will again, and we can make America what America must become. It will be hard, James, but you come from sturdy, peasant stock, men who picked cotton and dammed rivers and built railroads, and, in the teeth of the most terrifying odds, achieved an unassailable and monumental dignity. You come from a long line of great poets, some of the greatest poets since Homer. One of them said, *The very time I thought I was lost, My dungeon shook and my chains fell off.*

You know, and I know, that the country is celebrating one hundred years of freedom one hundred years too soon. We cannot be free until they are free. God bless you, James, and Godspeed.

Your uncle,
James

Responding to the Selection

Questions for Discussion

1. How would you describe the purpose of Baldwin's letter to his nephew?

2. What is the crime of which Baldwin accuses his country?

3. Explain what you think Baldwin means when he says, "The details and symbols of your life have been deliberately constructed to make you believe what white people say about you." What are some of the details and symbols to which Baldwin refers?

4. What do these words mean to you: "To act is to be committed, and to be committed is to be in danger"?

5. Is Baldwin's letter one of hope or despair? Why do you think so?

Activities

Writing an Essay

1. Baldwin concludes his letter by writing, "We cannot be free until they are free." Write an **essay** that explores the meaning behind these words. How are white Americans not free in Baldwin's estimation? How does he say they can become free? How long does Baldwin think this process will take?

Writing a Letter

2. If you were going to write a letter to a younger relative about what the world is really like and how to deal with it successfully, what would you say? Think about what the world is like for racial, ethnic, and other minorities, or what the world is like for people with disabilities. Write a **letter** based on your experiences and offer explanations and advice for someone you hope will have an easier time with the world than you did.

Before You Read

Lament for Brothers

Glenis Redmond
Born 1963

> **"Quite simply poetry is a medium that will heal the world."**

About Redmond

Glenis Redmond is a poet, educator, and performer who has traveled the United States and Europe proclaiming her message that "poetry is a medium that will heal the world. . . . Poetry is rhythm." Redmond began writing poems at the age of twelve, and she returned to the craft after seven years as a family counselor. The artists who inspire her include Lucille Clifton, Marvin Gaye, Alice Walker, and Bob Marley.

Redmond has published two poetry chapbooks: *Naming It* and *If I Ain't African.* She is the recipient of the Carrie McCray Literary Award in Poetry and has been awarded study fellowships from the Vermont Writing Center.

Lament for Brothers

— *Glenis Redmond*

```
        too soon                    heavy air
        too soon            20      carried
        death comes around          held
        too soon                    in tight fisted
  5     like winter's night         scowls.
        snuffing out
        the brightness              We
        of spring shining   25      know
        in your eyes.               black men leave
                                    this world
 10     The dull ache               too soon.
        of mourning
        attaches to us              We are
        like tree limbs     30      empty wells
        that won't shake            filled with grief
 15     words that will not         with the memory
        be written                  the music
        music never                 of you.
        played
```

Responding to the Selection

Questions for Discussion

1. A **lament** is a poem expressing profound grief for a loss. Why does the speaker grieve?

2. To what does the speaker compare dying too soon? What is the "dull ache / of mourning"?

3. How does the speaker describe the survivors?

Activity

Writing a Report

During the 1980s and early 1990s, the subject of black-on-black violence made headlines across the country. Research newspaper and magazine articles that deal with this subject and write a **report** on what you discover. What were the causes of such violence? Is the situation any different today?

Before You Read

This Is Not a Small Voice

Sonia Sanchez
Born 1934

*". . . it is important to
leave a legacy . . . of
not being afraid
to tell the truth . . . we
must pass this on
to our children rather
than a legacy of fear
and victimization."*

About Sanchez

Sonia Sanchez is a writer and an activist. She writes poetry and drama, and she says she has a "need to put work out that will help people want to hold on and survive."

After graduating from Hunter College in 1955, Sanchez continued her studies at New York University. She embraced the social and political ferment of the 1960s, becoming an activist and publishing her first poems. The year 1969 saw the publication of *Homecoming,* her first collection of poems. In 1972 Sanchez joined the Nation of Islam, but the Nation's teaching on the roles of women were at odds with her convictions, and she left three years later.

Sanchez has played an active role in bringing black studies programs into the classroom. She also supports a variety of international causes, including rights for African countries. Today, Sanchez is a professor of black American poetry and creative writing at Temple University.

This Is Not a Small Voice

— *Sonia Sanchez*

This is not a small voice
you hear   this is a large
voice coming out of these cities.
This is the voice of LaTanya.
5   Kadesha. Shaniqua. This
is the voice of Antoine.
Darryl. Shaquille.
Running over waters
navigating the hallways
10   of our schools spilling out
on the corners of our cities and
no epitaphs spill out of their river mouths.

This is not a small love
you hear   this is a large
15   love, a passion for kissing learning
on its face.
This is a love that crowns the feet with hands
that nourishes, conceives, feels the water sails
mends the children,

20   folds them inside our history where they
toast more than the flesh
where they suck the bones of the alphabet
and spit out closed vowels.
This is a love colored with iron and lace.
25   This is a love initialed Black Genius.

This is not a small voice
you hear.

Responding to the Selection ——————

Questions for Discussion

1. Whose voice is coming out of the cities? What do you imagine the voice is saying?

2. An **epitaph** is a brief poem or inscription composed in memory of someone who has died, which sums up the person's life. What do these words mean to you: "no epitaphs spill out of their river mouths"?

3. What are the characteristics of a love "colored with iron and lace"? What does the speaker imply with this **paradox?**

4. Why do you think the voice is "not a small voice"?

Activity

Writing an Interpretive Essay

The poem speaks of love and concludes, "This is a love initialed Black Genius." Write an **interpretive essay** in which you explore the kinds of love that the poem addresses and how and why it is initialed "Black Genius."

Before You Read

What's American About America?

Ishmael Reed
Born 1938

"No one says a novel has to be one thing. It can be anything it wants to be, a vaudeville show, the six o'clock news, the mumblings of wild men saddled by demons."

About Reed

Ishmael Reed quickly earned a reputation as one of America's most inventive and provocative authors when he published his first novel, *The Free-Lance Pallbearers,* in 1967. Subsequent novels, such as *Mumbo Jumbo* and *The Last Days of Louisiana Red,* are known for a playful and experimental use of language and imaginative allegories. Reed employs a wide variety of writing styles and often satirizes literary conventions as a means of challenging traditional ideas of cultural superiority.

Reed was born in Chattanooga, Tennessee, but was raised in Buffalo, New York. After finishing college, he moved to New York City to pursue a literary career. There he wrote for various publications and helped to establish the influential alternative newspaper the *East Village Other.* Reed organized the American Festival of Negro Art in 1965. It was at this early point in his career that he began to seek out authors with similar interests—young black, hispanic, and Asian American writers and poets who created innovative and dynamic literature.

Throughout his career, Reed has gone to great lengths to encourage and promote the work of other, often lesser-known, authors. He has published numerous literary journals and edited several acclaimed anthologies of poetry, fiction, and essays.

What's American About America?

— *Ishmael Reed*

An item from the *New York Times,* June 23, 1983: "At the annual Lower East Side Jewish Festival yesterday, a Chinese woman ate a pizza slice in front of Ty Thuan Duc's Vietnamese grocery store. Beside her a Spanish-speaking family patronized a cart with two signs: 'Italian Ices' and 'Kosher by Rabbi Alper.' And after the pastrami ran out, everybody ate knishes."

On the day before Memorial Day, 1983, a poet called me to describe a city he had just visited. He said that one section included mosques, built by the Islamic people who dwelled there. Attending his reading, he said, were large numbers of Hispanic people, 40,000 of whom lived in the same city. He was not talking about a fabled city located in some mysterious region of the world. The city he'd visited was Detroit.

A few months before, as I was visiting Texas, I heard the taped voice used to guide passengers to their connections at the Dallas Airport announcing items in both Spanish and English. This trend is likely to continue; after all, for some southwestern states like Texas, where the largest minority is now Mexican-American, Spanish was the first written language and the Spanish style lives on in the western way of life.

Shortly after my Texas trip, I sat in a campus auditorium at the University of Wisconsin at Milwaukee as a Yale professor—whose original work on the influence of African cultures upon those of the Americas has led to his ostracism from some intellectual circles—walked up and down the aisle like an old-time Southern evangelist, dancing and drumming the top of the lectern, illustrating his points before some Afro-American intellectuals and artists who cheered and applauded his performance. The professor was "white." After his lecture, he conversed with a group of Milwaukeeans—all who spoke Yoruban, though only the professor had ever traveled to Africa.

One of the artists there told me that his paintings, which included African and Afro-American mythological symbols and imagery, were hanging in the local McDonald's restaurant. The next day I went to McDonald's and snapped pictures of smiling youngsters eating hamburgers below paintings that could grace the walls of any of the country's leading museums. The manager of the local McDonald's said, "I don't know what you boys are doing, but I like it," as he commissioned the local painters to exhibit in his restaurant.

Such blurring of cultural styles occurs in everyday life in the United States to a greater extent than anyone can imagine. The result is what the above-mentioned Yale professor, Robert Thompson, referred to as a cultural bouillabaisse. Yet members of the nation's present educational and cultural elect still cling to the notion that the United States belongs to some vaguely defined entity they refer to as "Western civilization," by which they mean, presumably, a civilization created by people of Europe, as if Europe can even be viewed in monolithic terms. Is Beethoven's Ninth Symphony, which includes Turkish marches, a part of Western civilization? Or the late-nineteenth- and twentieth-century French paintings, whose creators were influenced by Japanese art? And what of the cubists, through whom the influence of African art changed modern painting? Or the sur-realists, who were so impressed with the art of the Pacific Northwest Indians that, in their map of North America, Alaska dwarfs the lower forty-eight states in size?

Are the Russians, who are often criticized for their adoption of "Western" ways by Tsarist dissidents in exile, members of Western civi-lization? And what of the millions of Europeans who have black African and Asian ancestry, black Africans having occupied several European countries for hundreds of years? Are these "Europeans" a part of Western civilization? Or the Hungarians, who originated across the Urals in a place called Greater Hungary? Or the Irish, who came from the Iberian Peninsula?

Even the notion that North America is part of Western civilization because our "system of government" is derived from Europe is being chal-lenged by Native American historians who say that the founding fathers, Benjamin Franklin especially, were actually influenced by the system of government that had been adopted by the Iroquois hundreds of years prior to the arrival of Europeans.

Western civilization, then, becomes another confusing category—like Third World, or Judeo-Christian culture—as humanity attempts to impose its small-screen view of political and cultural reality upon a complex world. Our most publicized novelist recently said that Western

What's American About America?

civilization was the greatest achievement of mankind—an attitude that flourishes on the street level as scribbles in public restrooms: "White Power" or "Hitler was a prophet." Where did such an attitude, which has caused so much misery and depression in our national life, which has tainted even our noblest achievements, begin? An attitude that caused the incarceration of Japanese-American citizens during World War II, the persecution of Chicanos and Chinese Americans, the near-extermination of the Indians, and the murder and lynchings of thousands of Afro-Americans.

The Puritans of New England are idealized in our schoolbooks as the first Americans, "a hardy band" of no-nonsense patriarchs whose discipline razed the forest and brought order to the New World (a term that annoys Native American historians). Industrious, responsible, it was their "Yankee ingenuity" and practicality that created the work ethic.

The Puritans, however, had a mean streak. They hated the theater and banned Christmas. They punished people in a cruel and inhuman manner. They killed children who disobeyed their parents. They exterminated the Indians, who had taught them how to survive in a world unknown to them. And their encounter with calypso culture, in the form of a servant from Barbados working in a Salem minister's household, resulted in the witchcraft hysteria.

The Puritan legacy of hard work and meticulous accounting led to the establishment of a great industrial society, but there was the other side— the strange and paranoid attitudes of that society toward those different from the elect.

The cultural attitudes of that early elect continue to be voiced in everyday life in the United States; the president of a distinguished university, writing a letter to the *Times*, belittling the study of African civilizations; the television network that promoted its show on the Vatican art with the boast that this art represented "the finest achievements of the human spirit."

When I heard a schoolteacher warn the other night about the invasion of the American educational system by foreign curricula, I wanted to yell at the television set, "Lady, they're already here." It has already begun because the world is here. The world has been arriving at these shores for at least 10,000 years from Europe, Africa, and Asia. In the late nineteenth and early twentieth centuries, large numbers of Europeans arrived, adding their cultures to those of the European, African, and Asian settlers who were already here, and recently millions have been entering the country from South America and the Caribbean, making Robert Thompson's bouillabaisse richer and thicker.

What's American About America?

North America deserves a more exciting destiny than as a repository of "Western civilization." We can become a place where the cultures of the world crisscross. This is possible because the United States and Canada are unique in the world: The world is here.

Responding to the Selection ———

Questions for Discussion

1. What is the purpose of the first five paragraphs of the essay?

2. Explain Robert Thompson's assertion that America is a "cultural bouillabaisse."

3. According to Reed, what is the generally accepted definition of Western civilization? What examples does he provide to support his belief that it is difficult to define the term *Western civilization*?

4. What evidence does Reed offer that Western civilization is anything but "the greatest achievement of mankind"?

5. What does Reed mean when he says of the United States and Canada, "the world is here"?

Activities

Forming an Opinion

1. Reed makes several assertions about the Puritans that may or may not be accurate. Make a list of those assertions and then research Puritan life. Write a **report** in which you either support or refute each of Reed's assertions.

Exploring the Iroquois Confederacy

2. Research the Iroquois Confederacy. How did the confederacy operate? On what principles was it based? How were the founders of the United States influenced by the the Iroquois Confederacy? Write an **expository essay** that explains the structure of the Iroquois government and the influence it had on early U.S. government.

Bal Jeunesse, c. 1927 (detail). Palmer Hayden. Watercolor on paper, 17 x 14 in. Collection
Dr. Meredith F. Sirmans, New York.

Theme Five

Tree of Life

the real people loves one another
the rest bees shamin, bees walkin
backwards under the sun.

— Rob Penny

Before You Read

Preaching Blues

Robert Johnson
1911–1938

"*I got to keep movin'*
 I got to keep movin'
 blues fallin' down like hail
 blues fallin' down like hail
Umm mmm mmm mmm . . .
And the days keeps on
  worryin' me
  there's a hellhound on
  my trail"

About Johnson

Although he spent just twenty-seven years on this earth, Robert Johnson's impact on the blues was substantial. He was born in Hazlehurst, Mississippi, and spent his youth avoiding the cotton fields. After his first wife died in childbirth, Johnson returned to playing the blues. He had tried the harmonica but is best known for his unusual slide guitar style. He remarried in 1931 and began traveling throughout the Delta.

Johnson would play wherever he could find work—in juke joints, on street corners, at house parties, and in lumber camps. Although he played mostly in the South, he did travel as far north as Chicago and New York. Two years before his death, Johnson made a series of recordings, playing his own compositions. He died after drinking whiskey laced with the poison strychnine.

Johnson was inducted into the Blues Foundation Hall of Fame in 1980, into the Rock and Roll Hall of Fame in 1986, and into the Mississippi Delta Blues Hall of Fame in 1999.

Preaching BLUES

— *Robert Johnson*

Mmmmmm mmmm
Got up this morning
The blues, walking like a man
Got up this morning
5   The blues walking like a man
Worried blues:
Give me your right hand

And the blues grabbed mama's child
   And tore it all upside down
10   Blues grabbed mama's child
   And they tore me all upside down
Travel on, poor Bob,
   Just can't turn you 'round

The blu-u-ues
15   Is a low down shaking chill
   (yes)(I'm preaching 'em now)
Mmmm-mmmm
Is a low down shaking chill
You ain't never had 'em, I
20   Hope you never will

Preaching BLUES

Well the blues
Is a aching old heart disease
              (Do it now.
              You gonna do it?
25   Tell me all about it.)

The blues
Is a low down aching heart disease
And like consumption
Killing me by degrees

30   Now if it starts to raining
Gonna drive,
              gonna drive my blues
Now if it's startin' a-raining
I'm gonna drive my blues away
35   Going to the steel rig
Stay
     out
          there
              all
40   day

❖

Responding to the Selection

Questions for Discussion

1. To what does Robert Johnson compare the blues? What does this comparison tell you about the blues?

2. Why do you think some of the lyrics are in parentheses? Do these parenthetical remarks remind you of another African American oral tradition?

3. Most blues lyrics have a standard structure. Can you figure out that structure from reading "Preaching Blues"?

4. How does Robert Johnson plan on escaping his blues?

Activity

Preparing a Multimedia Presentation

The blues continues to be a popular musical genre today. Research contemporary blues singers in the United States and other countries. How is this music similar to and different from the blues of Robert Johnson's time? Create a **multimedia presentation** that showcases the blues then and now. Use time lines, illustrations, text, and recorded music to introduce others to the blues.

Before You Read

The Blues Don't Change

Al Young
Born 1939

"Music is the sigh of the spirit longing to express itself beyond the range of bodily confinement."

About Young

Al Young is an award-winning poet, novelist, essayist, and screenwriter. Born in Mississippi, Young moved with his family to Michigan where he graduated from high school and enrolled at the University of Michigan as a Spanish major. In 1961 Young succumbed to the allure of the West Coast, settling in San Francisco and pursuing a career in music. He received his B.A. from the University of California at Berkeley in 1969, the same year he published his first collection of poems, *Dancing.*

Young expressed his literary gifts in a variety of genres. In addition to writing poetry, he has authored five novels and written essays that appeared in such magazines as *Rolling Stone,* the *New York Times,* and *Harpers*. He spent several years in Los Angeles writing screenplays, and in the 1970s and 1980s, cofounded two multicultural journals with Ishmael Reed.

For his efforts, Young has been awarded numerous fellowships and literary prizes, including the Pushcart Prize and the American Book Award. He has served as distinguished visiting writer at a number of U.S. colleges and universities. Young's more than twenty books include *Who Is Angelina?* (1997) and *Heaven: Collected Poems 1956–1990* (1992), as well as *Drowning in the Sea of Love: Musical Memoirs* (1995), in which he writes about his association with the blues and blues musicians.

The Blues Don't Change

— *Al Young*

"Now I'll tell you about the Blues. All Negroes like Blues. Why? Because they was born with the Blues. And now everybody have the Blues. Sometimes they don't know what it is."

—Leadbelly

And I was born with you, wasn't I, Blues?
Wombed with you, wounded, reared and forwarded
from address to address, stamped, stomped
and returned to sender by nobody else but you,
5   Blue Rider, writing me off every chance you
got, you mean old grudgeful-hearted, table-
turning demon, you, you sexy soul-sucking gem.

Blue diamond in the rough, you *are* forever.
You can't be outfoxed don't care how they cut
10   and smuggle and shine you on, you're like a
shadow, too dumb and stubborn and necessary
to let them turn you into what you ain't
with color or theory or powder or paint.

The Blues Don't Change

That's how you can stay in style without sticking
15   and not getting stuck. You know how to sting
where I can't scratch, and you move from frying
pan to skillet the same way you move people
to go to wiggling their bodies, juggling their
limbs, loosening that goose, upping their voices,
20   opening their pores, rolling their hips and lips.

They can shake their boodies but they can't shake *you*.

Responding to the Selection

Questions for Discussion

1. What is the speaker saying about the blues in the first stanza?

2. Identify the **extended metaphor** in the second stanza. What does this metaphor imply about the blues?

3. What phrase in the third stanza seems to sum up the hurtful power of the blues?

4. How does blues music move people? What is **ironic** about this movement?

Activities

Sharing Your Blues

1. Have you ever had the blues? What did it feel like or sound like? What did the blues say to you? How did the blues become part of your soul? Were you able to shake the blues? Write a **personal narrative** about your encounter with the blues.

Researching Leadbelly

2. Who was Leadbelly? Research his life and write a brief **biography** that explains his connection to the blues.

Before You Read

Juke Box Love Song

Langston Hughes
1902–1967

"An artist must be free to choose what he does, certainly, but he must also never be afraid to do what he might choose."

About Hughes

One evening in Washington, D.C., the poet Vachel Lindsay was dining in a restaurant. A young African American busboy left three poems alongside Lindsay's plate. Later that night, at a reading of his poetry, Lindsay recounted the story and read the poems. Newspapers throughout the country reported that Lindsay had discovered a busboy poet. What Lindsay didn't know was that the busboy, Langston Hughes, had already been "discovered" by the editors of a prominent black magazine, *The Crisis,* who had published "The Negro Speaks of Rivers," a poem which Hughes had written the summer after he graduated from high school. Before Hughes received his college degree in 1929, he had already published his first two books of poetry.

During the 1920s, Hughes traveled extensively in Africa and Europe. When he returned to the United States, he settled in Manhattan's Harlem neighborhood, which he called "the greatest Negro city in the world." At the time, Harlem was experiencing an extraordinary explosion of art, music, and literature that would revolutionize African American culture, and Hughes was part of that explosion. He infused his poetry and prose with the rhythms of jazz and blues music as he gave voice to the fears, the anger, and the aspirations of black Americans. A fierce social critic, his writing often irritated both white and black Americans who preferred less "confrontational" literature.

When Hughes died in 1967, his body of work included poetry, novels, nonfiction, young adult literature, drama, songs, and the lyrics to an opera.

Juke Box Love Song

— *Langston Hughes*

I could take the Harlem night
and wrap around you,
Take the neon lights and make a crown,
Take the Lenox Avenue busses,
5   Taxis, subways,
And for your love song tone their rumble down.
Take Harlem's heartbeat,
Make a drumbeat,
Put it on a record, let it whirl,
10   And while we listen to it play,
Dance with you till day—
Dance with you, my sweet brown Harlem girl.

Responding to the Selection

1. How do the opening lines of the poem express the depth of the speaker's love?
2. How does the speaker create the music for the dance with his "sweet brown Harlem girl"?
3. What do you think "Harlem's heartbeat" is?
4. Is the speaker in love with anything or anyone else? Explain your answer.

Activity

Creating a Time Line

What is a "juke box"? How did it get its name? When did juke boxes first appear? What role did they play in popularizing music? Research the history and importance of the juke box, and create an **illustrated time line** that tells about this important musical machine.

Focus on . . .
The Harlem Renaissance

The 1920s and early 1930s was an extraordinary period of artistic activity for African Americans. It became known as the Harlem Renaissance because most of the key figures lived in Harlem, a section of New York City that one writer proclaimed "the Negro capital of the world." Never before had so many African Americans received broad recognition for their cultural achievements.

Black writers and artists flocked to New York for several reasons. It was home to the publishing industry and prominent art galleries. The National Association for the Advancement of Colored People (NAACP) and other important organizations were also based there. Harlem itself was a big attraction. Originally built for middle-class whites, the neighborhood had beautiful avenues and finely constructed apartment buildings.

W. E. B. DuBois

As editor of the NAACP's journal *The Crisis*, W. E. B. DuBois played a significant role in the Harlem Renaissance. He urged writers to create works that would promote racial equality. African American poets and novelists responded to this challenge by casting aside old stereotypes and by drawing upon their cultural heritage. DuBois believed it was important to present African Americans in a positive light only. However, many younger writers preferred to offer more complex and realistic portrayals of black life in America.

The Crisis, an important journal of the Harlem Renaissance.

W. E. B. DuBois

Members of the Movement

The writers of the Harlem Renaissance were a diverse group. For example, Countee Cullen followed conventional verse forms. Langston Hughes, on the other hand, found inspiration in blues and jazz. They were united by their desire to produce literature that was distinctly African American. James Weldon Johnson, Claude McKay, and Jean Toomer were other prominent writers. Zora Neale Hurston also emerged from the Harlem Renaissance, but she published her major works in the mid-1930s, after the movement had faded.

Langston Hughes

Linking to . . .

- Why do you think the Harlem Renaissance happened when it did? Think about the major historical events that affected African Americans prior to the Renaissance.

Before You Read

Sonnet to a Negro in Harlem

Helene Johnson
1907–1995

"[Johnson's] poetry is marked by an often lovely lyricism in which genteel sensuality and a usually muted expression of racial pride are blended."

— *The Norton Anthology of African American Literature*

ers of the Harlem Renaissance, a woman who was very proud of her cultural heritage and exhibited strong concern for life in Harlem.

About Johnson

When she was nineteen, Helene Johnson traveled from her hometown of Boston to New York City to accept her first poetry award. She had received an honorable mention in the annual poetry contest of the popular African American magazine *Opportunity.* Once Johnson saw and experienced New York City at the height of the Harlem Renaissance, she decided to stay.

When Johnson first came to New York City, she moved into one of the few apartment buildings outside Harlem that rented to African Americans. She quickly became friends with the only other African American woman in the building, famed Harlem Renaissance writer Zora Neale Hurston. Before long, Johnson was socializing with Harlem's literary elite.

Today, Johnson is remembered as one of the youngest and most promising writ-

Sonnet to A Negro in Harlem

— *Helene Johnson*

You are disdainful and magnificent—
Your perfect body and your pompous gait,

Your dark eyes flashing solemnly with hate,
Small wonder that you are incompetent
5   To imitate those whom you so despise—
Your shoulders towering high above the throng,
Your head thrown back in rich, barbaric song,
Palm trees and mangoes stretched before your eyes.
Let others toil and sweat for labor's sake
10   And wring from grasping hands their meed of gold.
Why urge ahead your supercilious feet?
Scorn will efface each footprint that you make.
I love your laughter arrogant and bold.
You are too splendid for this city street.

Responding to the Selection ───────────

Questions for Discussion

1. With what adjectives does the speaker describe her subject in the first few lines of the poem? Why might she describe her subject with contrasting adjectives?

2. In your opinion, is the subject of Johnson's poem a specific person or a representative for a group of people? Explain.

3. What is the speaker's **tone,** or attitude, toward her subject? Support your answer with details from the poem.

4. **Connotation** is the associations or suggestions that carry beyond a word's literal meaning. What is the connotation of "Palm trees and mangoes"? What might Johnson be suggesting with these words?

Activities

Writing About Literature

1. Write a two- or three-paragraph analysis of Johnson's **diction,** or word choice, in this poem. What does her diction suggest to you about the poem's setting, subject, and theme? How does her diction affect the way you read and understand the poem?

Writing Your Song

2. Johnson creates a powerful image when she writes of her subject's "rich, barbaric song." What song would best describe you? Compose a **song,** with or without lyrics, that reveals a quality that defines your personality. You might perform your song for classmates or record and play it.

Before You Read

My Mother, If She Had Won Free Dance Lessons

Cornelius Eady
Born 1954

Foundation, and the Guggenheim Foundation. Eady has also won a Lila Wallace–Reader's Digest Writer's Award and the Prairie Schooner Strousse Award. Eady is currently associate professor of English and director of the Poetry Center at the State University of New York at Stony Brook.

> *" 'this Dance you Do,' drawls the Cop,*
> *'what do you call it?'*
> *We call it scalding the air—*
> *We call it dying with your shoes on."*

About Eady

Cornelius Eady is a Rochester, New York–born poet who has written six collections of poetry: *The Autobiography of a Jukebox, You Don't Miss Your Water, The Gathering of My Name* (which was nominated for the 1992 Pulitzer Prize for Poetry), *BOOM BOOM BOOM, Victims of the Latest Dance Craze,* and *Kartunes.*

Eady has been the recipient of many honors for his work. He has been awarded fellowships from the National Endowment for the Arts, the Rockefeller

My Mother, If She Had Won Free Dance Lessons

— *Cornelius Eady*

Would she have been a person
With a completely different outlook on life?
There are times when I visit
And find her settled on a chair
5   In our dilapidated house,
The neighborhood crazy lady
Doing what the neighborhood crazy lady is
    supposed to do,
Which is absolutely nothing

And I wonder as we talk our sympathetic talk,
10   Abandoned in easy dialogue,
I, the son of the crazy lady,
Who crosses easily into her point of view
As if yawning
Or taking off an overcoat.
15   Each time I visit
I walk back into our lives

And I wonder, like any child who wakes up one day
    to find themself
Abandoned in a world larger than their
    Bad dreams,
I wonder as I see my mother sitting there,
20   Landed to the right-hand window in the living room,
Pausing from time to time in the endless loop
    of our dialogue
To peek for rascals through the
Venetian blinds,

I wonder a small thought.
25   I walk back into our lives.
Given the opportunity,
How would she have danced?
Would it have been as easily
As we talk to each other now,
30   The crazy lady
And the crazy lady's son,
As if we were old friends from opposite coasts
Picking up the thread of a long conversation,

Or two ballroom dancers
35   Who only know
One step?

What would have changed
If the phone had rung like a suitor,
If the invitation had arrived in the mail
40   Like Jesus, extending a hand?

Responding to the Selection

Questions for Discussion

1. Describe the portrait the speaker paints of his mother.

2. What do you think the speaker is referring to when he talks about how he was "like any child who wakes up one day / to find themself / Abandoned in a world larger than their / Bad dreams"?

3. What do free dance lessons **symbolize** in the poem? What makes you think so?

4. What questions is the speaker thinking about at the end of the poem? Do you think he finds answers to these questions? Why?

5. What possibility is suggested by "Jesus, extending a hand"?

Activities

Interpreting Poetry

1. Write an **interpretive essay** in which you discuss the theme, or main message, of the poem. Describe the story Eady is telling and what you believe is its intended meaning.

Writing Poetry

2. It seems every neighborhood has its own "crazy" person, someone whose peculiarities often annoy and anger adults while scaring and fascinating children. Write a poem about such a neighbor but write it from the point of view of the neighbor. What makes this person peculiar? How did he or she get that way? Could anything have changed the life this person lives?

Before You Read

from *The Importance of Pot Liquor*

Jackie Torrence
Born 1944

> "When you create or pick a
> story to tell, remember
> the universal truths,
> the truths that everyone
> knows, like love, hate, and
> fear. . . . Visualize the story
> as if you are living it,
> not just talking about it."

About Torrence

Jackie Torrence had a speech impairment as a child, which prevented her from talking clearly out loud. Thanks to the intervention of her ninth-grade teacher, she overcame this difficulty to become one of the most successful oral storytellers in the United States.

Torrence was fired once for telling stories. She was working as a librarian, telling stories to children. Word soon got around that her storytelling was something special, and she started appearing at children's parties. When the library discovered that she was moonlighting, she lost her job.

Times were hard for Torrence until the *Charlotte Observer* printed an article about her. The National Storytelling Association invited her to its convention in Memphis, Tennessee, and by the time the convention ended, she had fifty bookings.

Torrence has told her stories throughout the United States and Europe, including at the Kennedy Center in Washington, D.C., and at Lincoln Center in New York City. She has even told stories to the creative teams at the Disney and DreamWorks studios in an effort to help them create more engaging stories. She performed her 1992 play *Bluestory* in London.

Today, Torrence lives in Salisbury, North Carolina, the town where she grew up, the town that gave birth to her stories and to her career.

"Pot liquor," in the title of the following selection, refers to the liquid that is left when simmering meat or vegetables. It is a staple in traditional southern cooking.

from The Importance of Pot Liquor

— *Jackie Torrence*

My grandfather, James Carson, was the son of a slave named Samuel Mitchell Carson. Grandpa was quite proud of the family history, and he never forgot to tell me about it. He talked to me of his father's many exploits and adventures as a slave, and of the trials that his family endured as free men.

The struggle must have been a difficult one, because Pa often looked sad as he remembered the details of his stories. I would look in the same direction that he was looking in, hoping to see what he seemed to see as he talked and stared off in the distance. There was never anything there that was visible to me. I remember water welling up in his eyes as he told some long-lost tale of a journey that was predestined to end in tragedy. Other times the corners of his lips would give him away, turning up into a smile before it was even time for him to deliver the main punch line of the story. He was a very meticulous storyteller. His thoughts were always ahead of his actual words; he anticipated the actions of the tale, and his face would always give him away.

As I came to know my grandfather as a friend, I realized that he was different from the other men in the family. He never worked, but he gardened and helped in the kitchen, sharpening my grandmother's knives. He spent a lot of time at the house of his sister, my Aunt Sally. He often took long walks.

He rarely went into town. I would sometimes go to Salisbury with whoever was designated to run errands, and whenever I left, I would always say, "What do you want from town, Pa?"

And he would always reply: "Well now, I believe I could use a stack of fifty-dollar bills."

He spent time with me, but there were times when he preferred being alone. These were the times when I couldn't walk with him or be with him in the garden. These were the times when I couldn't understand what was wrong and why he couldn't take me along with him. My grandmother seemed to understand and would not let me bother him.

Why was he like this? I would wonder in confusion. What was wrong with my grandfather when these times occurred? As a child I really never understood, but many years and many stories later—stories from my uncles, aunts, and mother—I was able to put together the story of my grandfather.

Back in the days when my grandparents had only six children—Lawrence, William, Mildred, Ceola, Leonard, and James—they had a prosperous farm, with chickens in the yard, cows, a goat, and a garden that provided vegetables for eating, canning, and preserving. Just behind the house there was an area dug into the ground, six feet deep and six feet wide, and lined with shelves filled with jars of beans, beets, corn, tomatoes, squash, cucumber pickles, watermelon rind pickles, apples, peaches, jams, jellies, and preserves of all description.

Inside the house, the dresser drawers were filled with handmade linens and spreads and quilts of many colors and patterns. The children dressed in good handmade clothes that were warm in the winter and cool in the hot summer.

The family owned a wagon and two good stout mules. My grandfather worked as a yardman in Salisbury for several white people. My grandmother washed and ironed for whites who brought their laundry to her in Carson Town. These jobs did not produce a lot of money, but they allowed the family to enjoy a "fair-to-middling" kind of existence.

One year in May, my grandmother realized that Ceola was not feeling well. My grandmother was known as a healer in the community, and for one week, she used all of her expertise to try to heal her. She used every herb tea, root salve, and medicine that she knew about, to no avail. By the end of the week, Ceola, who was about twelve years old, was too sick to move, and a doctor was summoned to Carson Town. Everyone in the family was at home when the doctor arrived, except Grandpa, who got home as quickly as he could and arrived shortly before the doctor left. Ceola seemed to be his favorite child, though he tried not to show it.

As he entered the house, the doctor removed quarantine signs from his bag and nailed them to the front door. This meant that everyone in stayed in and everyone out stayed out, until the quarantine was lifted. Ceola had diphtheria.

As the disease progressed, the family turned inward. Groceries had to be obtained by sending a note, pinned to a mule named Dexter, to Aunt Sally. She would then place the flour, sugar, canned milk, coffee, and other necessities on the mule's back and point him home. The doctor visited once every two weeks. First he would examine Ceola, and then the other members of the family. No one else was ever infected by the disease, but the doctor left the quarantine signs up because Ceola was still quite ill.

from The Importance of Pot Liquor

After each visit, the doctor demanded payment. The small amount of money in savings was quickly gone. Soon my grandparents were paying the doctor with eggs and butter, then whole chickens, goat's milk, fresh garden produce, and canned produce. After a while, the family had no stores of food left, not in the root cellar under the house, not in the milk pit. The garden was empty, and there were very few people in the community who could afford to help.

My Aunt Mildred, who tells that she was thirteen years old at the time, remembers watching her brothers set traps for birds. My grandmother would sometimes cry when five or six birds were all they had to cook. Although wintertime was hard, they were able to hunt rabbit, raccoon, and possum in order to put meat on the table. When spring arrived at last, Ceola's health began to improve. She was able to eat and sit up longer. She read her Bible to my grandpa, to his delight, and sometimes she would even sing for him. He was so happy when she began to improve, and he visited her bedside frequently.

Signs of spring were evident throughout the countryside. My grandmother made several trips to the woods to gather young herbs for teas, roots for poultices, and pine and cedar for the air in the house.

One day, Pa had just finished burning the dried weed from the place he would plow for his garden when he came in to get a hot cup of tea to drink. When Grandma told him Ceola had asked for him, he drank the tea and went directly to her bed. She told him she had learned a new passage in the Bible and read it to him.

Then she sang for him. I've heard that her choice of songs was "Jacob's Ladder," but some say it was "Swing Low, Sweet Chariot." Whatever it was, she sang it then as sweetly as any angel. That day, she was well again and everyone was happy. Grandma cautioned Pa not to tire her out, and he agreed. He took her Bible, placed it on the table beside her bed, kissed her forehead, and tucked the covers around her neck. She smiled and closed her eyes to sleep.

Over in the night, my Grandmother stopped to check Ceola, and found, sadly, that she had died.

My grandpa never quite got over that.

I believe he suffered depression from then on. The pain of losing a child, coupled with losing all that they had accumulated, caused him so much confusion that he became mentally ill for a long period of time. The mental illness must have soon developed into physical pain, and by the time I came onto the scene, the suffering had taken its toll.

My grandpa thought I was the cutest, smartest, sweetest child that had ever lived. At least, that's the impression I got. I remember being given a

from The Importance of Pot Liquor

recitation for a Sunday school Christmas program. I must have been about four years old. It was a simple speech: "Today is Christmas Day, Merry Christmas to you!"

My grandma and grandpa helped me learn it and say it just right. We'd sit down to supper and after the prayer, as Grandma tied my napkin around my neck, Grandpa would ask me to say my speech and I would speak right up. "Today is Christmas Day, Merry Christmas to you!" My grandpa would grin and say with a giggle, "That girl's gonna be president!" My grandma would grunt and shrug her shoulders.

Then the day for the recitation came. When I stood in the front of the church, the grown-ups were listening intently and admiring all the children in their new clothes. I stood in front of that congregation scared to death! My grandparents sat smiling and admiring their wonderful grandchild and my Aunt Sally, who was in charge of the program, said, "Speak up, go on now . . . talk."

I started to say, "Today is Christmas Day. . . ." But then someone sneezed, distracting me, and I forgot my speech and said: "Happy Easter!"

Grandpa turned to Grandma and said, "Are you sure that gal's got good sense?"

And he was the one who said I'd be president!

Even though I may have disappointed him, he still invited me to accompany him on his long walks. In the summer, we would check on his garden. Sometimes we'd work in the garden. He would pull weeds and I'd pull vegetable plants. He would always stop me before too much damage was done.

Grandpa walked with a cane. When I was quite small, he would put the cane to rest as he was sitting and I would pick it up and run away with it. I own that cane now. I guess it was merely a prop for him because it was just a piece of lightweight bamboo. It couldn't have supported him very much or been much help in walking. I remember him using it as a pointer, to give directions to people. He even used it to knock on doors.

Sometimes we'd walk up the path to my great-aunt Sally's house. He would tire by the time we mounted the short hill and would sit down on the floor of the back porch, turn, and use the cane to knock on the floor of the porch, calling Aunt Sally at the same time.

I liked Aunt Sally a lot. She was a large woman, with shiny black hair that she kept in a ball at the nape of her neck. When she smiled, she showed a glimmer of gold on her front teeth. She always smelled sweet to me, like a freshly baked cake. I found out later that she used vanilla flavoring as a perfume.

Aunt Sally was multi-talented—a cook, a quilter, a singer, and a piano player. I also remember her as a practical joker. Most of the jokes were directed toward my grandma, who was afraid of her own shadow at times.

from The Importance of Pot Liquor

On the hottest day of one summer—I would have been three or four—Pa had gone to town with one of my uncles. Grandma and I were left at home. I was playing on the porch, and my grandma was sweeping the yard. (Grass never stood a chance with Grandma. She hated chicken droppings in the yard, so she'd often sweep three or four times a day.)

All of a sudden we heard Aunt Sally's call: "Whooo—whoa, Ola!"

My grandma stopped sweeping and looked up toward the hill at Aunt Sally's house and answered her call, "Whoo, Sally! Whatcha want?"

"Oh Lord, Ola, ain't you heard? They say a convict's done got loose from the chain gang. He might be headed this way," yelled Aunt Sally.

"Oh Lord, Sally, what we gonna do?" said my grandma, fear welling up in her voice.

"Lock your doors, Ola, lock your doors!" The way her voice trailed off, we knew she was locking up, too.

My grandma went to work. She dragged me in from the porch, closed all the windows and locked all the doors, and pulled down every shade in the house. We sat in the far corner of the bedroom in the dark for what seemed like hours. With every noise we heard, I could hear her whispering a prayer. "Oh, Lord Jesus, help us, help us, Father, help us." Eventually the combination of darkness and heat caused me to fall asleep.

I was finally awakened by my grandpa's voice at the front door. "Ola, unlock the door! What in the name of God is wrong?"

Grandma rushed to the door to open it, and when she did, the feel of fresh, cool air swept over me. I felt rather sick. It must have had the same effect on Grandma because Uncle Will rushed in and caught her before she fell and helped her to the porch. She was soaking wet with sweat.

As Uncle Will ran in the house and got her smelling salts, Grandpa stood there looking at both of us, shaking his head from side to side. "Ola," he said, "what was you doin' all locked up in the house as blame hot as it is?"

"Lord, Jim, right after you left, Sally told me there was a convict on the loose from the chain gang out here and I thought we'd better lock up."

"Jesus Christ, Ola, that convict was way on the other side of Lexington, sixteen miles away. I wish you'd quit listening to Sally; you know she's full of fool and folly all the time."

That was just one of many times that Aunt Sally had a good laugh off my grandma. It bothered Pa when Aunt Sally played such tricks, but he never got too upset. Sometimes he even laughed.

When we walked together he walked very slowly, so I never had any trouble keeping up. He'd point out things of interest and importance, things he thought I should know. "You see this chimney? I put every one of these bricks here myself. Made 'em with my own two hands. Bum'bees nest in

from **The Importance of Pot Liquor**

here so you be careful not to get too close." His voice dropped to a whisper: "You may get stung." Now the thing that was going through my mind was, *What's a bum'bee?*

We'd walk past Aunt Sally's and up the road. There was a slight hill, which would slow him down even more. I'd hear a grunt now and then, but he never complained. Once, as he stopped to rest, he took his cane and dug around in the dried leaves in the ditch. He found something and lifted it from the ground on the edge of his cane so that I could see it.

"Hey," he said loudly, "look what I found."

Well, hanging there on the end of his cane was a wiggling, squirming, long black snake.

"Grandpa, look! Look, Grandpa, look, it's a snake!" I yelled. "Throw it down, throw it down!"

"Oh, he's not gonna hurt you. This is a king snake," replied Grandpa. "They don't like to bite people. They like rats and things that get into the barn and eat the corn and grain. We try not to kill them. We'd rather just throw them back so they can help us some more."

As he turned and threw it into the woods, Pa's explanation didn't help me much. I was still shaking from being so close to that snake. He put his hand on my back and patted me rather hard and said as he chuckled and squeezed me toward his leg, "Don't worry my girl, that ol' snake would rather suck on you than bite you."

I remember those walks because we were always exploring. Sometimes when the conversation seemed at a loss, I took over. I liked to ask questions.

"What's that, Pa?"

"That's a pine tree," he'd explain.

"And that right there, what's that?"

"That's a rock," he'd say.

But those questions, I think, sometimes got on his nerves, and I could always tell when he was tired of answering because the answers turned into grunts and groans—"un huh, uh huh"—and then he'd yawn and say, "Wait, hush, did you hear something?"

Well, of course I heard nothing, but I stopped to listen just the same. As we stood perfectly still in the middle of the road, out of the woods, running just as fast as he could, was a little brown rabbit. Startled by it, I moved closer to Pa. But he assured me there was nothing that would hurt me.

"What was that, Pa?" I'd say.

"It was ol' Br'er Rabbit himself."

I knew that, but you could not get a story by being too smart.

Our walk would usually turn back to Aunt Sally's porch or to the apple tree in her front yard where the stump of another tree made a good

from **The Importance of Pot Liquor**

seat for Pa. He would then tell me of some special adventure of Br'er
Rabbit or some of Br'er Rabbit's associates who were frequent visitors to
the Big Road.

Some of Pa's tales I easily remember. I never know what may trigger them
in my memory: the cool shade of a tree like my Aunt Sally's apple tree, or
the scent of coffee brewing, bread baking, or some long-lost texture of fab-
ric that reminds me of my baby quilt or a coat or dress I once wore that
Grandma made.

    The tales that he recounted to me about his father's slave days were
sometimes puzzling. I could hear a tightening in his throat as he told of his
father's problems and triumphs as a slave in Rowan County. If we were at
Aunt Sally's house, she would help him tell about ol' Massa and the slave
named Mitchell, who never knew how old he was, who never knew his
mother or father, and who had no last name until his master asked if he
wanted one. His master gave him his first and last names: Samuel Mitchell
Carson.

    Mitchell was the one who slept at the master's feet because of his master's
painful struggle with gout. He was unable to move about easily, so Mitchell
helped him in and out of bed, on and off wagons, and onto his horse.

    Since the master's wife was unable to read or write, the master was the
only one able to conduct business. Not being a well man, this was sometimes difficult. So during these times, in the privacy of the "big house," the
master taught Samuel Mitchell Carson how to read and write—against the
law, mind you! Without anyone knowing, the slave signed papers and conducted a lot of the master's business.

    My great-grandfather was freed in 1869 and given fifty acres of land,
where he started his family, began a school for children in that settlement,
and became the preacher of what became known as Carson Town.

    As I listened to the tales of my great-grandfather, the pride Pa had for
his family was passed on to me. It grew and grew, and has helped mold me.
No matter what happens to me now, I remember that I came from proud
people, people who made a difference in the world a long time ago. My
ancestors would not be pleased if I were satisfied with not being all that I
can be.

One night, when I was close to five, I heard a lot of noise and movement
downstairs. I slipped quietly down the stairs and saw Grandma, Aunt
Mildred, and my mother rushing in and out of Grandpa's room with sheets,
blankets, and wash pans of water. I could hear him coughing as I crept
closer. As I peered in his room, I saw blood on the bed sheets and on the
floor beside his bed. My mother and Aunt Mildred were wiping his face and

cleaning up around him, rushing from place to place. My grandma was holding him, her arms wrapped around his shoulders. I didn't know exactly what was going on, but I watched until I fell asleep on the stairs.

The next day, my mother dressed me and told me that we were going to town for a few days. I went in to tell Grandpa goodbye and that I'd be back soon.

"What do you want from town, Pa?"

I waited for him to ask for his stack of fifty-dollar bills. But he didn't say anything this time.

Just as I turned to remind him of his usual response, I noticed a faint smile cross his face. He waved his hand slowly.

I didn't think this was the time to say anymore. When I returned three or four days later, my Pa was no longer in bed.

"Where's Pa?" I asked.

My grandma said, "He's gone to heaven. And no," she said quietly before I could ask, "when you go to heaven you don't come back."

I never saw my grandpa again. I wasn't so sure if I liked this place called heaven.

Responding to the Selection

Questions for Discussion

1. How did the narrator learn the story of her grandfather's sometimes strange behavior? What was causing him to behave this way?

2. What does the incident with the king snake and the story about ol' Massa and Mitchell tell you about the power of storytelling?

3. What triggers stories in the narrator's mind?

4. In what way might the "pot liquor" of the title be a **metaphor?**

Activity

Sharing Your Story

Practice telling a story of your own. The story may be about you, your family, or a friend, or it may be a story you've read or heard about. To learn more about how to tell stories effectively, check out Jackie Torrence's book *Jackie Tales: The Magic of Creating Stories and the Art of Telling Them.* Follow her suggestions as you rehearse and fine-tune your story. Share your performance with the class.

Before You Read

Battle Report

Bob Kaufman
1925–1986

> "*A quintessential subcultural poet, Kaufman is at once multiply marginal and properly paradigmatic; embodying the mainstream trends and stereotypes of his era, his work is at once high-cultural and streetwise.*"
> — Maria Damon

About Kaufman

To say that Bob Kaufman lived an unconventional life is an understatement. Born in New Orleans, Louisiana, to a German Jewish father and an African American Catholic mother, Kaufman ran away from home when he was thirteen to join the U.S. Merchant Marines. For the next twenty years, he traveled the world, reading literature and absorbing life.

Kaufman is said to have coined the word *beatnik* after arriving in San Francisco in 1958 and joining Jack Kerouac, Allen Ginsberg, Gregory Corso, and other Beat Generation writers. Kaufman himself was called "the original bebop man," perhaps because of his spontaneous, improvised, and jazzy poetic style. So committed was he to the oral tradition that he rarely wrote down his poetry. He would often recite his poems from memory in San Francisco coffeehouses. He was one of the most widely read U.S. poets in Europe in the early 1960s.

In 1963, after the assassination of President Kennedy, Kaufman took a vow of silence to protest the growing conflict in Vietnam. For the next ten years, he neither spoke nor wrote anything. It is said that on the day the war ended, in 1975, Kaufman ended his silence by walking into a coffeehouse and spontaneously reciting a new poem, "All Those Ships That Never Sailed."

Kaufman cofounded the poetry magazine *Beatitude* in 1965. His published works include *Solitudes Crowded with Loneliness* (1965), *The Ancient Rain: Poems, 1956–1978* (1981), and *Cranial Guitar: Selected Poems* (1996).

BATTLE REPORT

— Bob Kaufman

One thousand saxophones infiltrate the city,
Each with a man inside,
Hidden in ordinary cases,
Labeled FRAGILE.

5   A fleet of trumpets drops their hooks,
Inside at the outside.

Ten waves of trombones approach the city
Under blue cover
Of late autumn's neo-classical clouds.

10   Five hundred bassmen, all string feet tall,
Beating it back to the bass.

One hundred drummers, each a stick in each hand,
The delicate rumble of pianos, moving in.

The secret agent, an innocent bystander,
15   Drops a note in the wail box.

Five generals, gathered in the gallery,
Blowing plans.

At last, the secret code is flashed:
Now is the time, now is the time.

20   Attack: The sound of jazz.

The city falls.

Responding to the Selection

Questions for Discussion

1. What is the **metaphor** that runs through the poem? Which words signal the metaphor?
2. What do you suppose the "city" symbolizes?
3. The speaker says that a secret agent drops a note in the "wail box." What do you imagine a wail box might be?
4. What happens at the end of the poem? How would you interpret the last line?

Activity

Listening to Jazz

Some of Bob Kaufman's favorite jazz artists were Charlie Parker, Thelonius Monk, and Charles Mingus. Perform "Battle Report" for your class as Kaufman might have, incorporating music by one of these artists as background.

Before You Read

A Poem for "Magic"

Quincy Troupe
Born 1943

> "The African American church was a great place to hear language from the minister on down through the deacons. . . . And what a joy it was listening to the choir and the organ music. . . . although I didn't know I was going to be a writer at the time, I was still being shaped for what I do now, then—by listening to the music and the language of the church."

About Troupe

When Quincy Troupe was fifteen, he stopped going to church so he could concentrate on his passion, basketball. Growing up in St. Louis, Missouri, Troupe thought he was going to be a professional basketball player, not a writer. While playing on the All-Army Basketball Team in Paris, France, he injured a knee and, without his favorite sport to keep him occupied, turned to writing.

Troupe has published many books, including six volumes of poetry. In 1980 *Snake-Back Solos* won the American Book Award, and ten years later, *Miles: The Autobiography*, which he coauthored with jazz legend Miles Davis, did the same. He wrote and coproduced *The Miles Davis Radio Project,* for which he won a Peabody Award, and coedited the acclaimed *Giant Talk: An Anthology of Third World Writing.*

Troupe's work was beautifully described in an article in the *Los Angeles Times:* "With an uncanny ear for the language, he combines mere words into phrases and paragraphs that sing the range of life's raw emotions, from the elation of a Magic Johnson slam-dunk to the melancholy of a Miles Davis trumpet solo."

A professor of creative writing and American and Caribbean literature at the University of California, San Diego, Troupe is currently working on a novel, *The Footman Chronicles,* and a memoir, *The Accordion Years: 1965 to 1998.*

A Poem for "Magic"

— *Quincy Troupe*

for Earvin "Magic" Johnson, Donnell Reid & Richard Franklin

take it to the hoop, "magic" johnson
take the ball dazzling down the open lane
herk & jerk & raise your six feet nine inch
frame into air sweating screams of your neon name
5   "magic" johnson, nicknamed "windex" way back in high school
cause you wiped glass backboards so clean
where you first juked & shook
wiled your way to glory
a new style fusion of shake & bake energy
10   using everything possible, you created your own space
to fly through—any moment now, we expect your wings
to spread feathers for that spooky take off of yours—
then shake & glide, till you hammer home
a clotheslining deuce off glass
15   now, come back down with a reverse hoodoo gem
off the spin, & stick it in sweet, popping nets, clean
from twenty feet, right-side

put the ball on the floor, "magic"
slide the dribble behind your back, ease it deftly
20   between your bony, stork legs, head bobbing everwhichaway
up & down, you see everything on the court
off the high, yoyo patter, stop & go dribble, you shoot
a threading needle rope pass, sweet home to kareem
cutting through the lane, his skyhook pops cords

A Poem for "Magic"

25   now lead the fastbreak, hit worthy on the fly
          now, blindside a behind the back pinpointpass for two more
          off the fake, looking the other way
          you raise off balance into space
          sweating chants of your name, turn, 180 degrees
30   off the move, your legs scissoring space, like a swimmer's
          yoyoing motion, in deep water, stretching out now toward free
          flight, you double pump through human trees, hang in place
          slip the ball into your left hand
          then deal it like a las vegas card dealer
35   off squared glass, into nets, living up to your singular nickname
          so "bad," you cartwheel the crowd towards frenzy
          wearing now your electric smile, neon as your name
          in victory, we suddenly sense your glorious uplift
          your urgent need to be champion
40   & so we cheer, rejoicing with you, for this quicksilver, quicksilver
                                          quicksilver
          moment of fame, so put the ball on the floor again, "magic"
          juke & dazzle, shake & bake down the lane
          take the sucker to the hoop, "magic" johnson,
          recreate reverse hoodoo gems off the spin,
45   deal alley-oop-dunk-a-thon-magician passes
          now, double-pump, scissor, vamp through space
          hang in place & put it all up in the sucker's face, "magic"
          johnson, & deal the roundball, like the juju man that you am
          like the sho-nuff shaman man that you am
50   "magic," like the sho-nuff spaceman, you am

Responding to the Selection

Questions for Discussion

1. Although the poem has plenty of commas and dashes, it does not contain a single period. What does this absence add to the poem?

2. Which words in the poem suggest the speed and movement of a basketball game?

3. The poem includes several West African terms. Identify these terms and explain what they imply about Magic Johnson's style of play.

Activity

Comparing Poetry

Compare "A Poem for 'Magic'" to "Being There" (page 357). Write a **compare-and-contrast essay** in which you discuss how the poems are similar and different. Be sure to note such elements as language, tone, purpose, and imagery.

Before You Read

Being There

Thomas Sayers Ellis
Born 1963

" 'Being There' recalls my teenage encounter with a Hollywood film crew while playing basketball on a famous and fenced-in playground in an all-black neighborhood in Washington, D.C.
The director, Hal Ashby, hoped that something visually amazing would happen as the film's star, Peter Sellers, walked by and looked in on us.
The poem also recalls our desire to perform, at an early age, under such a gaze.
Structurally, I wanted to expand, length-wise, from half court to full court, the way in which Gwendolyn Brooks uses the pronoun we in her famous poem, 'We Real Cool.' "

About Ellis

Thomas Sayers Ellis was raised in Washington, D.C. He studied at Harvard University and earned a master's degree in fine arts at Brown University.

Ellis cofounded the influential Dark Room Collective and Dark Room reading series and was a fellow at the Fine Arts Work Center in Provincetown, Massachusetts. His poems have appeared in numerous literary journals, including *Ploughshares* and the *Harvard Review,* and such anthologies as the *Best American Poetry: 1997* and *The Garden Thrives: Twentieth Century African-American Poetry.* He is the author of two poetry collections, *The Good Junk* and *The Genuine Negro Hero.* Ellis teaches English at Case Western Reserve University and in the Bennington Writing Seminars.

Being There

In addition to being the title of Ellis's poem, *Being There* is also the title of the movie that was being shot the day Ellis and his friends were filmed playing basketball.

BEING THERE

— Thomas Sayers Ellis

Kennedy Playground
Washington, D.C.

We forced our faces
into the circular frame
a stringless hoop made,
hoping more than silence & light

5   would fall through.
We fought for position.
We fouled & shoved.
We high-fived God.

Our Converse All-Stars
10   burned enough rubber
to rival the devil and his mama.
Hoop, horseshoe, noose.

We aimed at a halo
hung at an angle we couldn't fit,
15   waiting for the camera
to record our unfocused

need to score.
We left earth.
We lost weight.
20   We disobeyed bone.

BEING THERE

> Our finger rolls
> & reverse layups
> were rejected by angels
> guarding the rim,
>
> 25   same as prayers
> returned to sinners.

Responding to the Selection ———

Questions for Discussion

1. What are *hoop, horseshoe,* and *noose*?

2. What does the speaker mean when he says, "We left earth. / We lost weight. / We disobeyed bone"?

3. Sports coaches and managers often talk about players who have "elevated their game, taking it to the next level." What does this phrase mean? What evidence can you find that the players at the Kennedy Playground have done the same? Why have they done so?

4. Find the **simile** in the poem. What comparison is being made?

Activity

Analyzing Poetry

The language of the poem includes many Christian religious references. In a brief **essay,** describe each reference and explain how, collectively, they shape the central idea of the poem.

Before You Read

To Satch

Samuel Allen (Paul Vesey)
Born 1917

"No matter how humdrum one's life may be, there is meaning and poetry if one has the sight to see it."

About Allen

Born in Columbus, Ohio, Samuel Allen belongs to a group of expatriate African Americans who lived and wrote in postwar France. While he was studying at the Sorbonne in Paris, Allen's first poems were published in the French magazine *Présence Africaine,* thanks to help from the African American novelist Richard Wright.

His first collection of poems, *Elfebein Zahne (Ivory Tusks),* was published in a bilingual edition in Germany in 1956 under the name Paul Vesey. Allen's poems have been anthologized in over 200 collections, including *American Negro Poetry, New Negro Poets: U.S.A.,* and *I Am the Darker Brother.* He considers African American oral tradition and the southern African American church to be major influences on his poetry.

In addition to writing poetry, Allen writes critical reviews, edits, lectures, and translates literature, including works by Jean-Paul Sartre and Leopold Senghor. He has worked for the United States Information Agency and the Department of Justice and was an attorney until 1968, when he became Avalon Professor of Humanities at Tuskegee Institute in Alabama. He has served as writer-in-residence at Tuskegee and at Rutgers University, and after teaching at several colleges and universities, retired from Boston University in 1981.

About Satchel Paige

The great fastball pitcher Satchel Paige lived from about 1906 to 1982. Although he played from an early age, Paige was not admitted into the major leagues until 1948 because of the color bar. In 1971 he was voted into the Baseball Hall of Fame.

To Satch

— Samuel Allen

Sometimes I feel like I will *never* stop
Just go on forever
Till one fine mornin
I'm gonna reach up and grab me a handfulla stars
Swing out my long lean leg
And whip three hot strikes burnin down the heavens
And look over at God and say
How about that!

❖

Responding to the Selection

Questions for Discussion

1. Part of Satchel Paige's legacy was his phenomenal strength and endurance. How does the poem reflect these qualities of the man?

2. **Alliteration** is the repetition of consonant sounds, usually at the beginnings of words. Find an example of alliteration in Allen's poem. How does it add meaning to the poem?

3. In what way is the poem a celebration of Paige's life?

Activity

Reporting on Negro League Baseball

Find out more about Satchel Paige and the impact of the Negro leagues on baseball in the United States. Prepare a **report** that describes the league, its stars, its popularity, and its eventual demise.

Web Page

Negro League baseball thrived briefly in segregated America. Many African Americans put aside bitterness for a few hours of magic and athletic prowess.

Negro League Baseball: The People's Game

Staff Writer—negroleaguebaseball.com, September 30, 1999

While box scores, standings and statistics fill the literature of baseball, it is the fans that fill the grandstands who give life to the game and generate its history. The story of baseball is nothing less than the story of the American people, a story that now transcends issues of race and creed. But it was not always so.

In a racially segregated America that dictated a separate game for white and black fans, there necessarily developed two distinct baseball cultures. Almost fifty years removed from our view, the color, flavor and meaning of pre-integration Negro baseball can now only be evidenced through the eyes of

those fans who now define it in their recollections and reminiscences.

Rural Georgia—1922 Luther's [Mayweather] memories of the minstrel show baseball game are vivid. "There was this small store about a mile from our house. That's where my father would buy what we needed between trips to Americus. The store was sort of a meeting place for everybody who lived around there. I found out about the minstrel show coming to town from a poster that was put up down at the store. I can still remember how excited all us kids were about it. The poster said there were going to be musicians, comedians, magic acts, snake dancers—just

Base Ball Club
Crawford Recreation Center, Pittsburgh, Pa.

about everything. And, on top of that, there was to be a baseball game. Who wouldn't be excited about all that!"

"The players all had on uniforms. Real baseball uniforms. Of course, I knew what a baseball uniform was and what it was supposed to look like. I'd seen pictures, but I hadn't ever seen anyone wearing one before. They had the name of the team sewn onto the front of the shirt. I don't remember what the name of the team was now. All I can remember is how much I liked those uniforms and how much I wanted to own one."

"Watching those players get ready for the game was something else, too. The way they could throw the ball and catch it. I had never seen anybody who could play that good," Luther still seems incredulous thinking back.

Montgomery, Alabama—1938
"The *Pittsburgh Courier* was always available down at the drug store. The druggist would have a few dozen copies of it sent down every week and put it out for sale there in the store," recalls Rowland Porter. I worked just up the street from the drug store at a gas station. The papers came in on Wednesday morning, I believe, and I would pick one up at my lunch hour."

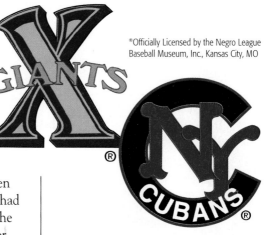

*Officially Licensed by the Negro League Baseball Museum, Inc., Kansas City, MO

"The white man who owned the gasoline station was always wanting to talk baseball with me. He was a St. Louis Cardinals fan. He'd be talking about Dizzy Dean, and I would be talking about Satchel Paige. He'd start in about Joe Medwick, and I'd come back with Buck Leonard. He'd always say to me, 'Do you really think those colored players are as good as the major leaguers?', and I'd tell him they were not only as good, they were better!"

"It was all about bragging, you know. Getting one up on the other guy. My boss was a nice man. Sure, we were talking about black players vs. white players, but it was all in good fun. It wasn't a racial thing between us. It was just two baseball fans, each hoping his favorite team and player would outdo the other guy's favorites."

Questions for Discussion

1. Imagine what it was like to see a Negro League game. Describe your feelings.
2. Do you think the writer is correct to say that "the story of baseball is nothing less than the story of the American people, . . . that now transcends issues of race and creed"? Why did the Negro leagues disappear?

Before You Read

We Alone

Alice Walker
Born *1944*

*"Writing permits me to be
more than I am."*

About Walker

Born into a poor, rural life in Eatonton, Georgia, Alice Walker knew what it meant to be made to feel less than who she was. She knew how it felt to bear the legacy of slavery, racism, and segregation. She recalls that her parents and grandparents worked on what had been a plantation, toiling "all their lives for barely enough food and shelter to sustain them. They were sharecroppers—landless peasants— the product of whose labor was routinely stolen from them."

Awarded a scholarship, Walker entered Spelman College in Atlanta, Georgia, in 1961, at the peak of the Civil Rights movement. She continued her education at Sarah Lawrence College in New York, and after graduation she worked in the New York City welfare department. Returning to the South in 1965, Walker worked for voter registration in Georgia and again the next summer in Mississippi. A year later she married a fellow Civil Rights worker, but she had to do so in the North. She married a white man, and interracial marriage was still illegal in the South.

Walker calls Sojourner Truth her "spiritual ancestor." Walker says it gives her joy to realize that she shares her name with Truth: *walker* and *sojourner* can have roughly the same meaning, and *Alice* means "truth" in ancient Greek. Aside from their names, their common bond, Walker says, is a concern not only for the rights of African Americans but also for the rights of women.

Since the publication of her novel *The Color Purple,* which won both a Pulitzer Prize and an American Book Award, and the subsequent film adaptation of the book, Walker has been a celebrity. In addition to novels, she has written short stories, poems, essays, and children's books.

We Alone

— Alice Walker

We alone can devalue gold
by not caring
if it falls or rises
in the marketplace
5   Wherever there is gold
there is a chain, you know,
and if your chain
is gold
so much the worse
10   for you.

Feathers, shells
and sea-shaped stones
are all as rare.

This could be our revolution:
15   To love what is plentiful
as much as
what's scarce.

Responding to the Selection

1. Does the speaker think it is important to devalue gold? Why? What does gold symbolize in the poem? How can it be devalued?

2. What is the "chain" to which the speaker refers?

3. Who do you think the "we" is in the poem?

4. Describe the revolution the speaker talks about. What makes it revolutionary?

Activities

Reflections on Simplicity

1. What is the value in simplicity? Does contemporary U.S. society teach and respect simplicity? What messages do you find in the media about how to live your life? Write a **reflective essay** in which you discuss the benefits or drawbacks to appreciating what is scarce as much as what is plentiful.

Mining for Gold

2. The love of gold has brought real pain to people throughout history. People have killed and died for gold, and not always in battle. Research current gold-mining practices around the world. Who benefits from these practices? Who suffers? In what ways? Discuss your findings in class.

Before You Read

Geometry

Rita Dove
Born 1952

"Literature gives one a chance to enter into another's world, to understand it intimately, and to not be afraid."

About Dove

"A good poem is like a bouillon cube," says Rita Dove. "It's concentrated, you carry it around with you, and it nourishes you when you need it." Throughout her career, Dove has written poems that nourish her readers by appealing to both their imaginations and their intellects. Her poems emphasize the significance of ordinary people and events, and in doing so, encourage people to look at the world with fresh eyes.

As a child, Dove read constantly, using books to make her imagination come to life. Her love of reading led to a love of writing. "To me, writing was play. It was something you did to entertain yourself, like reading."

In 1973 Dove graduated with highest honors from Miami University in Oxford, Ohio. After graduation she studied in Germany on a Fulbright scholarship, and then she earned a master's degree from the University of Iowa in 1977, the same year her poetry was first published.

In addition to several volumes of poetry, Dove has written a collection of short stories, *Fifth Sunday;* a novel, *Through the Ivory Gate;* and a play, *The Darker Face of the Earth.* In 1987, at the age of thirty-five, she became one of the youngest poets, and only the second African American woman, to win a Pulitzer Prize for Poetry, for her poem cycle, *Thomas and Beulah.* In 1993 Dove became the youngest poet ever named poet laureate of the United States.

Geometry

— Rita Dove

I prove a theorem and the house expands:
the windows jerk free to hover near the ceiling,
the ceiling floats away with a sigh.

As the walls clear themselves of everything
but transparency, the scent of carnations
leaves with them. I am out in the open

and above the windows have hinged into butterflies,
sunlight glinting where they've intersected.
They are going to some point true and unproven.

Responding to the Selection

Questions for Discussion

1. What is a theorem? Why does it need proving? What does proving a theorem symbolize in the poem?

2. How does the house expand? How is this expansion related to what the speaker is feeling?

3. What is the "point true and unproven" the butterflies are drawn to?

4. Explain how you think the title of the poem relates to its meaning.

Activity

Writing About Imagery

Take fifteen minutes or so to **freewrite** about windows and butterflies. Think about the powers windows possess, how butterflies come to be, why butterflies flit from one flower to another. Let your imagination take you wherever it wants to go.

After you've reread what you've written, think about how the images of windows and butterflies enrich the poem. Write an **essay** in which you discuss the importance of these two images to the poem's meaning.

Before You Read

A Swimming Lesson

Jewelle L. Gomez
Born 1948

"What do I hope to achieve by writing? Changing the world!"

About Gomez

Award-winning writer and social activist Jewelle L. Gomez attributes much of her success to her great-grandmother. "My great-grandmother, with whom I lived until I was twenty-two years old, was born on an Indian reservation in Iowa and had been a widow for fifty years. She maintained an intellectual curiosity and graciousness that no amount of education could have created. She formed the basis of much of my intellectual yearnings." Gomez has written poetry, essays, and fiction.

About the Time and Place

This story takes place in the summer of 1957, at Revere Beach in Revere, Massachusetts, five miles north of Boston. Revere, America's first public beach, was established in 1896. It is a city beach that is accessible by public transportation, which places it within reach of people from the entire Boston metropolitan area. Until the late 1980s, the sandy, crescent-shaped beach was flanked by amusement rides, restaurants and food stands, dance pavilions, and arcades. Today, only a few eating establishments remain.

A Swimming Lesson

— Jewelle L. Gomez

At nine years old I didn't realize my grandmother, Lydia, and I were doing an extraordinary thing by packing a picnic lunch and riding the elevated train from Roxbury to Revere Beach. It seemed part of the natural rhythm of summer to me. I didn't notice how the subway cars slowly emptied of most of their Black passengers as the train left Boston's urban center and made its way into the Italian and Irish suburban neighborhoods to the north. It didn't seem odd that all of the Black families stayed in one section of the beach and never ventured onto the boardwalk to the concession stands or the rides except in groups.

I do remember Black women perched cautiously on their blankets, tugging desperately at bathing suits rising too high in the rear and complaining about their hair "going back." Not my grandmother, though. She glowed with unashamed athleticism as she waded out, just inside the reach of the waves, and moved along the riptide parallel to the shore. Once submerged, she would load me onto her back and begin her long, tireless strokes. With the waves partially covering us, I followed her rhythm with my short, chubby arms, taking my cues from the powerful movement of her back muscles. We did this again and again until I'd fall off, and she'd catch me and set me upright in the strong New England surf. I was thrilled by the wildness of the ocean and my grandmother's fearless relationship to it. I loved the way she never consulted her mirror after her swim, but always looked as if she had been born to the sea, a kind of aquatic heiress.

None of the social issues of 1957 had a chance of catching my attention that year. All that existed for me was my grandmother, rising from the surf like a Dahomean queen, shaking her head free of her torturous rubber cap, beaming down at me when I finally took the first strokes on my own. She towered above me in the sun with a benevolence that made simply dwelling in her presence a reward in itself. Under her gaze I felt part of a long line of royalty. I was certain that everyone around us—Black and white—saw and respected her magnificence.

Although I sensed her power, I didn't know the real significance of our summers together as Black females in a white part of town. Unlike winter, when we were protected by the cover of coats, boots and hats, summer left us vulnerable and at odds with the expectations for women's bodies—the narrow hips, straight hair, flat stomachs, small feet—handed down from the mainstream culture and media. But Lydia never noticed. Her long chorus-girl legs ended in size-nine shoes, and she dared to make herself even bigger as she stretched her broad back and became a woman with a purpose: teaching her granddaughter to swim.

My swimming may have seemed a superfluous skill to those who watched our lessons. After all, it was obvious that I wouldn't be doing the backstroke on the Riviera or in the pool of a penthouse spa. Certainly nothing in the popular media at that time made the "great outdoors" seem a hospitable place for Black people. It was a place in which we were meant to feel comfortable at best and hunted at worst. But my prospects for utilizing my skill were irrelevant to me, and when I finally got it right I felt as if I had learned some invaluable life secret.

When I reached college and learned the specifics of slavery and the Middle Passage, the magnitude of that "peculiar institution" was almost beyond my comprehension; it was like nothing I'd learned before about the history of my people. It was difficult making a connection with those Africans who had been set adrift from their own land. My initial reaction was "Why didn't the slaves simply jump from the ships while they were still close to shore, and swim home?" The child in me who had learned to survive in water was crushed to find that my ancestors had not necessarily shared this skill. Years later when I visited West Africa and learned of the poisonous, spiny fish that inhabit most of the coastal waters, I understood why swimming was not the local sport there that it was in New England. And now when I take to the surf, I think of those ancestors and of Lydia.

The sea has been a fearful place for us. It swallowed us whole when there was no escape from the holds of slave ships. For me, to whom the dark fathoms of a tenement hallway were the most unknowable thing so far encountered in my nine years, the ocean was a mystery of terrifying proportions. In teaching me to swim, my grandmother took away my fear. I began to understand something outside myself—the sea—and consequently something about myself as well. I was no longer simply a fat little girl: My body had become a sea vessel—sturdy, enduring, graceful. I had the means to be safe.

Before she died last summer I learned that Lydia herself couldn't really swim that well. As I was splashing, desperately trying to learn the right rhythm—face down, eyes closed, air out, reach, face up, eyes open, air in, reach—Lydia was brushing the ocean's floor with her feet, keeping us both afloat. When she told me, I was stunned. I reached into my memory trying to combine this new information with the Olympic vision I'd always kept of her. At first I'd felt disappointed, tricked, the way I used to feel when I'd learn that a favorite movie star was only five feet tall. But then I quickly realized what an incredible act of bravery it was for her to pass on to me a skill she herself had not quite mastered—a skill that she knew would always bring me a sense of accomplishment. And it was more than just the swimming. It was the ability to stand on any beach anywhere and be proud of my large body, my African hair. It was *not* fearing the strong muscles in my own back; it was gaining control over my own life.

Responding to the Selection ─────────

Questions for Discussion

1. What is Lydia's attitude toward the sea and toward her own body? How does this attitude seem to affect the author's feelings for her grandmother?

2. What historical information has helped Gomez understand her ancestors' attitude toward the sea? Compare her own attitude to that of her ancestors.

3. How does Gomez react when she learns the truth about her swimming lessons? What might the author's reaction suggest about her character?

Activities

Analyze the Author's Purpose

1. "A Swimming Lesson" appears in a collection of autobiographical essays written by Jewelle L. Gomez. Write a **paragraph** explaining why you think Gomez included this piece in the collection. Use evidence from the selection to support your ideas. Share your analysis with several classmates.

Creative Writing

2. Write a **thank-you letter** to a person who helped you master a particular skill. Explain why learning the skill was important to you and why you still enjoy the activity today. Be sure to express your appreciation for the time and effort spent in teaching the skill to you.

Before You Read

Redemption Song

Bob Marley
1945–1981

> *"Bob Marley gave the poor a voice in the international arena of ideas. His message was that the individual has intrinsic dignity and ever shall."*
>
> — Timothy White

About Marley

Robert Nesta Marley was born of two worlds. His father was a white rural overseer in Jamaica, and his mother was the daughter of a black prosperous farmer and bush doctor. He spent his childhood and his teens in both the countryside and the slums of West Kingston, and both cultures shaped his world view and his music.

Like many teenagers around the world, Marley admired American pop and rhythm and blues music. While working as an apprentice welder in the desperately poor West Kingston slum of Trench Town, he began listening to ska, a brew of American R & B and Jamaican mento (folk-calypso) music. Marley formed a vocal group in Trench Town called the Wailers, and in 1963 they recorded "Simmer Down," a cry of anguish that became a huge hit.

The Wailers continued their musical odyssey, adding a rock flavor to the reggae music they recorded. By the early 1970s, they had a global audience, and Marley himself was a superstar. In 1974 the original Wailers disbanded, but Marley continued to compose, producing a series of stellar recordings in the latter half of the 1970s.

In 1980 Marley fell ill and was diagnosed with cancer. Eight months later, just four weeks after being awarded Jamaica's Order of Merit, the Honorable Robert Nesta Marley succumbed to the disease.

Redemption Song

— *Bob Marley*

Old pirates yes they rob I, sold I to the merchant ships
Minutes after they took I from the bottomless pit
But my hand was made strong by the hand of the Almighty
We forward in this generation triumphantly

5   Won't you help to sing these songs of freedom
Cause all I ever had, redemption songs, redemption songs

Emancipate yourselves from mental slavery, none but ourselves can
    free our minds
Have no fear for atomic energy, 'cause none of them can stop
    the time
How long shall they kill our prophets while we stand aside and look
10   Some say it's just a part of it, we've got to fulfill the book

Won't you help to sing these songs of freedom
Cause all I ever had, redemption songs, redemption songs,
    redemption songs

Emancipate yourselves from mental slavery, none but ourselves can
    free our minds
Have no fear of atomic energy, 'cause none of them can stop
    the time

15   How long shall they kill our prophets while we stand aside and look
      Yes some say it's just part of it, we've got to fulfill the book

      Won't you help to sing, these songs of freedom
      Cause all I ever had, redemption songs
      All I ever had, redemption songs
20   These songs of freedom, songs of freedom

Responding to the Selection

Questions for Discussion

1. Identify the merchant ships to which the speaker was sold.

2. What does the irregular grammar of the lyrics add to the first stanza?

3. What does the speaker mean when he says, "we've got to fulfill the book"?

4. What are redemption songs? Are they similar to any other songs you've heard or read about?

5. What do you make of the line, "Emancipate yourself from mental slavery"? In what ways is this idea relevant to what the author has learned about her grandmother and herself in "A Swimming Lesson"?

Activities

Exploring Rastafari

1. Bob Marley and his band mates were Rastafarians. Research Rastafarianism and write a **report** detailing what you discover. What are the origins and practices of Rastafarianism? How did Marley's religion influence his music?

Listening to Reggae Music

2. Listen to a recording of "Redemption Song" and other Wailers' songs that speak to the social and economic troubles of Jamaica's underclass. Discuss the distinctive melodies, rhythms, and lyrics of the music.

Before You Read

If You Lose Your Pen

Ruth Forman
Born 1968

She is the recipient of the 1992 Barnard New Women Poets Prize and the grand prize of the 1992 Black History Marathon. Of Forman's writing, poet and playwright Sonia Sanchez has said, "Hers is a commitment to the possibilities of life. Joy. Beauty (though terrible at times on this earth). What an impressive, rich song she sings."

i say
who will name this
*   Renaissance*
i stand knee deep in
who go tug the elbow of
*   Langston Hughes*
tell him we are yesterday again
to McKay and Cullen and
*   Hurston*
Walker and Baldwin
we doin it again

About Forman

Ruth Forman is the author of two collections of poetry: *We Are the Young Magicians* and *Renaissance.* Forman's poems also have been featured in the PBS series *The United States of Poetry.*

If You Lose Your Pen

— *Ruth Forman*

    and all you find is a broken pencil on the floor
    and the pencil has no sharpener
    and the sharpener is in the store
    and your pocket has no money

5   and if you look again
    and all you find is a black Bic
    and the Bic you need is green

    and if it appears beneath the mattress of your couch
    but the couch is dirty and you suddenly want to clean
10   beneath the pillows
    but you have no vacuum and the vacuum is in the store
    and your pocket has no money

    it is not your pen you are looking for

    it is your tongue and those who speak with it
15   your grandmothers and doves and ebony spiders
    hovering the corners of your throat

    it is your tongue
    and if you cannot find your tongue
    do not go looking for the cat
20   you know you will not find her
    she is in the neighbor's kitchen eating Friskies
    she is in the neighbor's yard making love

if you cannot find your tongue do not look for it
for you are so busy looking it cannot find you
25   the doves are getting dizzy and your grandmothers annoyed
be still and let them find you
they will come when they are ready

and when they are
it will not matter if your pockets are empty
30   if you write with a green Bic or a black Bic
or the blood of your finger
you will write
you will write

Responding to the Selection

Questions for Discussion

1. What is the central message in Ruth Forman's poem?

2. What is the speaker warning against in the first three stanzas?

3. What does the speaker say you are really looking for when you've lost your pen?

4. Why does the speaker caution against looking for the cat if "you cannot find your tongue"?

5. The speaker repeats, "you will write." When? How?

Activities

Writing an Essay

1. Forman writes, "if you cannot find your tongue do not look for it / for you are so busy looking it cannot find you." What is Forman telling you about the writing process? How do her words apply to other aspects of life? Write an **essay** in which you discuss Forman's words and reflect on times in your life when you had to let things come to you because your searching for them was in vain.

Interpreting Poetry

2. The quotation that precedes the biographical information about Ruth Forman is a poem from her collection *Renaissance*. Write a brief **interpretation** of the poem and discuss it with your classmates.

Index of Titles and Authors

A

Address Delivered at the Opening of the Cotton States' Exposition in Atlanta, Georgia, September, 1895, An, 54
Allen, Samuel, 360
And Ain't I a Woman?, 274
Angelou, Maya, 160
April Fools' Day, 230
aunt rubie goes to market, 199
Autobiography of Malcolm X, The, from, 143

B

Back to Baton Rouge, 267
Baldwin, James, 302
Bambara, Toni Cade, 133
Baraka, Amiri, 299
Battle Report, 350
Being There, 357
Black Arts Movement, The, 290
Black Stone Lying on a White Stone, 234
Blues Ain't No Mockin Bird, 133
Blues Don't Change, The, 325
Bluest Eye, The, from, 277
Bronzeville Mother Loiters in Mississippi. Meanwhile, a Mississippi Mother Burns Bacon, A, 72
Brooks, Gwendolyn, 72, 77
Brown, Sterling A., 113
Bury Me in a Free Land, 13

C

Césaire, Aimé, 80
Childress, Alice, 251
Clifton, Lucille, 285
Connecting to the Civil Rights Movement, 96

Conversation with Haki Madhubuti, 296
Cornish, Sam, 108
Creation, The, 3
Cullen, Countee, 40

D

Danticat, Edwidge, 202
Death of Dr. King, 108
Derricote, Toi, 195
Diop, Birago, 8
Dorsey, Thomas A., 27
Douglass, Frederick, 45
Dove, Rita, 368
DuBois, W. E. B., 60
Dunbar, Paul Laurence, 245

E

Eady, Cornelius, 336
Ellis, Thomas Sayers, 357
Equiano, Olaudah, 33

F

Florence, 251
Follow the Drinking Gourd, 17
Forefathers, 8
Forman, Ruth, 378
Freedom's Children, from, 99
fury, 285

G

Geometry, 368
Giovanni, Nikki, 178
Gomez, Jewelle L., 371
Great Migration, The, 166

H

Harlem Renaissance, The, 330

Harper, Frances E. W., 13

Hayden, Robert, 20

Hemenway Sets Author's Story Straight, 124

Hughes, Langston, 30, 328

Hurston, Zora Neale, 117

I

If You Lose Your Pen, 378

I Know Why the Caged Bird Sings, 160

Importance of Pot Liquor, The, from, 339

Isis, 117

I've Got a Home in That Rock, 140

J

Jack in the Pot, 181

Johnson, Helene, 333

Johnson, Jacqueline, 242

Johnson, James Weldon, 3

Johnson, Robert, 321

Juke Box Love Song, 328

K

Kaufman, Bob, 350

Keep Your Eyes on the Prize, 88

Keep Your Hand on the Plow, 87

Kincaid, Jamaica, 208

King, Martin Luther Jr., 92

Knowing, A, 242

Komunyakaa, Yusef, 230

L

Lament for Brothers, 308

Lansana, Quraysh Ali, 199

Last Quatrain of the Ballad of Emmett Till, The, 77

Leaves, 40

Letter from Foreign, 216

Life of Olaudah Equiano, The, from, 33

Lineage, 271

Living for the City, 169

M

Madgett, Naomi Long, 282

Madhubuti, Haki R., 293

Malcolm X, 143

Man Who Lived Underground, The, from, 172

Marley, Bob, 375

Marshall, Paule, 220

McClaurin, Irma, 288

Morrison, Toni, 277

My Bondage and My Freedom, from, 45

My Dungeon Shook, 302

My Mother, If She Had Won Free Dance Lessons, 336

N

Negro League Baseball: The People's Game, 362

Negro Speaks of Rivers, The, 30

New York Day Women, 202

Nikki-Roasa, 178

November Cotton Flower, 127

O

Of Mr. Booker T. Washington and Others, 60

On Being Brought from Africa to America, 239

Oral Tradition, The, 10

P

Patterson, Raymond, 140

Poem for "Magic," A, 353

Poet: What Ever Happened to Luther?, 293

Power of Names, The, 288

Preaching Blues, 321

Precious Lord Story and Gospel Songs, The, 24

Preface to a Twenty Volume Suicide Note, 299

Preserving, The, 130

Preston, Rohan B., 216

Purchase, 282

R

Redemption Song, 375

Redmond, Glenis, 308

Reed, Ishmael, 314

Runagate Runagate, 20

S

Sanchez, Sonia, 311

Sonnet to a Negro in Harlem, 333

Southern Road, 113

Soyinka, Wole, 248

State of the Union, 80

Stride Toward Freedom, from, 92

Struggle for Civil Rights, The, 84

Swimming Lesson, A, 371

T

Take My Hand, Precious Lord, 27

Telephone Conversation, 248

This Is Not a Small Voice, 311

To Da-duh, in Memoriam, 220

To Satch, 360

Toomer, Jean, 127

Torrence, Jackie, 340

Troupe, Quincy, 353

Truth, Sojourner, 274

V

Vallejo, César, 234

W

Walk to the Jetty, A, 208

Walker, Alice, 364

Walker, Margaret, 271

Warr, Michael, 267

Washington, Booker T., 54

We Alone, 364

We Wear the Mask, 245

Weakness, The, 195

Webb, Sheyann, 99

West, Dorothy, 181

What's American About America?, 314

Wheatley, Phillis, 239

Wonder, Stevie, 169

Wright, Richard, 172

X

X, Malcolm, 143

Y

Young, Al, 325

Young, Kevin, 130

Acknowledgments

❖ *cont. from page ii*

"Keep Your Eyes on the Prize, Hold On" Copyright © 1960 by Alpha Music. Reprinted by permission.

"To Satch" by Samuel Allen. Reprinted by permission of the author.

Excerpt from *I Know Why the Caged Bird Sings* by Maya Angelou. Copyright © 1969 and 1977 by Maya Angelou. Reprinted by permission of Random House, Inc.

"My Dungeon Shook" was originally published in *The Progressive*. Collected in *The Fire Next Time*, copyright © 1962, 1963 by James Baldwin. Copyright renewed. Published by Vintage Books. Reprinted by permission of the James Baldwin Estate.

"Blues Ain't No Mockin Bird" from *Gorilla, My Love* by Toni Cade Bambara. Copyright © 1971 by Toni Cade Bambara. Reprinted by permission of Random House, Inc.

"Preface to a Twenty Volume Suicide Note" from *Transbluesency: The Selected Poems of Amiri Baraka/LeRoi Jones*, Copyright © 1961, 1964, 1969, 1975, 1979, 1981, 1982, 1994, 1995 by Amiri Baraka. Reprinted by permission of Sterling Lord Literistic, Inc.

"Hemenway sets author's story straight" by Jan Biles. Reprinted by permission of the *Lawrence Journal-World*.

"A Bronzeville Mother Loiters in Mississippi. Meanwhile, a Mississippi Mother Burns Bacon" and an excerpt from "The Ballad of Emmett Till" copyright © 1991 by Gwendolyn Brooks, from *Blacks*, by Gwendolyn Brooks, published by Third World Press, Chicago. Reprinted by permission of the author.

"Southern Road" from *The Collected Poems of Sterling A. Brown*, edited by Michael S. Harper. Copyright © 1932 by Harcourt, Brace & Co. Copyright renewed 1960 by Sterling Brown. Originally appeared in Southern Road. Reprinted by permission of HarperCollins Publishers, Inc.

"Florence," copyright © 1950 by Alice Childress. Reprinted by permission of the Flora Roberts Agency.

"fury" by Lucille Clifton, from *The Book of Light*. Copyright © 1993 by Lucille Clifton. Reprinted with the permission of Copper Canyon Press, P.O. Box 271, Port Townsend, WA 98368-0271.

"Death of Dr. King" from *Generations* by Sam Cornish. Copyright © 1968, 1969, 1970, 1971 by Sam Cornish. Reprinted by permission of Beacon Press, Boston.

"Leaves" by Countee Cullen, from *Copper Sun* (© 1927 Harper & Brothers, copyright renewed 1954 by Ida M. Cullen). Reprinted by permission of Thompson & Thompson for the Amistad Research Center.

"New York Day Women" from *Krik? Krak!* by Edwidge Danticat. Reprinted by permission of Soho Press.

"The Weakness" is from *Captivity* by Toi Derricotte, copyright © 1989. Reprinted by permission of the University of Pittsburgh Press.

"Precious Lord, Take My Hand (Take My Hand, Precious Lord)" Words and Music by Thomas A. Dorsey. Copyright © 1938 by Unichappell

Acknowledgments

"April Fools' Day" from *Neon Vernacular*, copyright © 1993 by Yusef Komunyakaa, Wesleyan University Press, reprinted by permission of the University Press of New England.

"aunt rubie goes to market" from *Southside Rain*, copyright © Quaraysh Ali Lansana. Reprinted by permission of the author.

"A Conversation with Haki Madhubuti" from *River Oak Review*, Spring 1999. Reprinted by permission of Quaraysh Ali Lansana.

"Us" by Julius Lester. Reprinted by permission of the Ronald Hobbs Literary Agency.

Excerpt from *Freedom's Children* by Ellen Levine, copyright © 1993 by Ellen Levine. Used by permission of G.P. Putnam's Sons, a division of Penguin Putnam Inc.

"Purchase" by Naomi Long Madgett. Reprinted by permission of the author.

"Poet: What Ever Happened to Luther?" by Haki R. Madhubuti, from *Groundwork: New and Selected Poems of Don L. Lee/Haki R. Madhubuti from 1966–1996* by Haki R. Madhubuti. Copyright © 1996 by Haki R. Madhubuti. Reprinted by permission of Third World Press, Inc. Chicago, Illinois.

Excerpt from *The Autobiography of Malcolm X* by Malcolm X with the assistance of Alex Haley. Copyright © 1964 by Alex Haley and Malcolm X. Copyright © 1965 by Malcolm X and Betty Shabazz. Reprinted by permission of Random House, Inc.

"Redemption Song" words by Bob Marley. Copyright © 1980 Bob Marley Music Uprising. Reprinted by permission of Rykodisc Music. All rights reserved.

"To Da-duh, In Memoriam" reprinted by permission of The Feminist Press at The City University of New York, from *Reena and Other Stories* by Paule Marshall. Copyright © 1983 by Paule Marshall.

"The Power of Names" by Irma McClaurin. Reprinted by permission of the author.

Excerpt from *The Bluest Eye* by Toni Morrison. Reprinted by permission of International Creative Management. Copyright © 1970 by Toni Morrison.

Excerpt from "Negro League Baseball: The People's Game" from negroleaguebaseball.com, September 30, 1999. Reprinted by permission of Moxie Publishing.

"I've Got a Home in That Rock" from *26 Ways of Looking at a Black Man*, copyright © 1969 by Raymond Patterson. Reprinted by permission of the author.

"The Real People Loves One Another" by Rob Penny. Reprinted by permission of the author.

"Letter from Foreign," from *Dreams in Soy Sauce*, copyright © 1992 by Rohan B. Preston. Reprinted by permission.

"Lament for Brothers (for Junebug and Tupac)" from *Backbone* by Glenis Redmond. Reprinted by permission of Underground Epics Publishing.

"What's American About America?" from *Writin' is Fightin'* copyright ©

Acknowledgments

Photography Acknowledgments

Cover: *The Street,* 1957 (detail). Jacob Lawrence (1917–2000). Casein on paper, 30.5 x 22.25 in. The Butler Institute of American Art, Youngstown OH. 0 The Phillips Collection, Washington DC; **1** Gail Meese/Meese Photo Research; **2** Library of Congress/Corbis; **7** From <http://perso.infonie.fr/neveu01/birabura.htm>; **10** Jason Laure; **11** Geoff Butler; **12** CORBIS; **16** Hampton University Museum, Hampton VA; **19** Bettmann/CORBIS; **24** Frank Driggs/Archive Photos; **25** (l)Kathy Tarantola/Index Stock Imagery, (r)CORBIS; **26** The Frank Driggs Collection/Archive Pictures; **29** Art Resource, New York; **32** Bridgeman Art Library, London/New York; **39** Amistad Research Center, Tulane University, New Orleans; **42** Stephen Wirtz Gallery, San Francisco; **43** Courtesy The Edna Manley Foundation, photo by Maria LaYacona; **44** CORBIS; **52** Art Resource, New York; **59** Library of Congress/CORBIS; **70** ©Nancy Crampton; **79** AP/Wide World Photos; **84** Bettmann/CORBIS; **85** (t)Reuters NewMedia/CORBIS, (b)Bettmann/CORBIS; **86** The Harmon and Harriet Kelley Collection of African American Art, San Antonio TX; **91** Ernst Haas/Magnum; **96** CORBIS; **98** file photo; **107** Courtesy Zoland Books; **110** Solomon R. Guggenheim Museum, New York. Gift of Mr. and Mrs. Gus and Judith Lieber; **111** The Harmon and Harriet Kelley Collection of African American Art, San Antonio TX; **112** file photo; **116** National Portrait Gallery, Smithsonian Institution/Art Resource, New York; **124** CORBIS; **125** file photo; **126** UPI-Bettmann/ CORBIS; **129** ©Dot Paul, *Athens Daily News;* **132** ©1998 Bill Gaskins; **139** Lynn Saville; **142** Bettmann/CORBIS; **159** Jim Stratford/Black Star; **166** Bettmann/CORBIS; **167** (l)file photo, (r)Stock Montage/ *New Orleans Times-Picayune;* **168** ©Matthew Mendelsohn/CORBIS; **171** Archive Photos; **177** Michael Evans/New York Times Co./Archive Photos; **180** Vincent Frye; **194** Courtesy Toi Derricotte; **198** Brooke Collins; **201** ©Nancy Crampton; **207** Anthony Barboza/Black Images; **215** ©Angela Shannon; **219** AP/Wide World Photos; **229** ©Miriam Berkley; **233** From <http://alcor.concordia.ca/~dj_chung/splash2.htm>; **236** Collection of Dr. Tritobia Hayes Benjamin, Washington DC; **237** The Harmon and Harriet Kelley Collection of African American Art, San Antonio TX; **238** Bettmann/CORBIS; **241** Courtesy Jacqueline Johnson; **244** Archive Photos; **247** ©Nancy Crampton; **250** Courtesy Flora Roberts, Inc.; **266** Steve Garrett; **270** ©Nancy Crampton; **273** Archive Photos; **276** ©Nancy Crampton; **284** Gerardo Somoza/Outline Press Syndicate; **287** Courtesy Irma McClaurin, photo by Ray Carson; **290** Hampton University Museum, Hampton VA; **291** Alan Copeland/ Woodfin Camp & Associates; **292** David Schulz; **296** Courtesy Haki R. Madhubuti; **297** Courtesy Third World Press; **298** Bettmann/CORBIS; **301** ©Nancy Crampton; **307** Courtesy Glenis Redmond; **310** ©Nancy Crampton; **313** Adam Stoltman/AP/ Wide World Photos; **318** Collection Dr. Meredith F. Sirmans, New York; **319** Collection of the Blue Ridge

Acknowledgments

Institute & Museums/Ferrum College; 320 ©1989 Delta Haze Corporation. All rights reserved. Used by permission; 324 Courtesy Al Young; 327 Photograph Copyright ©The Estate of Carl Van Vechten, Gravure and Compilation Copyright ©Eakins Press Foundation/National Portrait Gallery/ Art Resource, New York; 330 UPI/CORBIS; 331 (tl)Frank & Marie-Therese Wood Print Collections, Alexandria VA, (tr)Bettmann/ CORBIS, (b)Art Resource, New York; 332 Museum of Art, Rhode Island School of Design. Gift of Miss Eleanor B. Green; 335 ©Miriam Berkley; 339 John Ullman; 349 Courtesy Bob Kaufman; 352 Fred Greaves/AP/Wide World Photos; 356 Graywolf Press, photo by Lily King; 359 Susan Rankaitis; 362 (l)from the Collections of the Pennsylvania Department, The Carnegie Library of Pittsburgh; 364 F. Capri/Saga/Archive Photos; 367 Robert Severi/Liaison Agency; 370 Diane Sabin; 374 ©Denis O'Regan/ CORBIS; 377 Courtesy Ruth Forman.